MAKING SENSE OF DEATH
Spiritual, Pastoral, and Personal Aspects of Death, Dying, and Bereavement

Edited by:

Gerry R. Cox
Robert A. Bendiksen
Robert G. Stevenson
University of Wisconsin–La Crosse

Death, Value and Meaning Series
Series Editor: John D. Morgan

Baywood Publishing Company, Inc.
AMITYVILLE, NEW YORK

Baywood Publishing Company, Inc.
26 Austin Avenue
Amityville, NY 11701
(800) 638-7819
E-mail: baywood@baywood.com
Web site: baywood.com

Library of Congress Catalog Number: 2002035602
ISBN: 0-89503-249-X (cloth)

Library of Congress Cataloging-in-Publication Data

Making sense of death : spiritual, pastoral, and personal aspects of death, dying, and bereavement / edited by Gerry R. Cox, Robert A. Bendiksen, Robert G. Stevenson.
    p. cm. -- (Death, value, and meaning series)
  Includes bibliographical references and index.
  ISBN 0-89503-249-X
  1. Bereavement--Religious aspects. 2. Church work with the bereaved. 3.
Death--Religious aspects. I. Cox, Gerry R. II. Bendiksen, Robert. III. Stevenson, Robert G. IV. Series.

BL65.B47 M25 2002
155.9'37--dc21

                                              2002035602

Dedication

I would like to dedicate this book to
my two new grandsons

John Patrick Sullivan
and
Isaac Lee Motes

Table of Contents

Acknowledgments   ix

Preface   xi

Introduction   1
Herman H. van der Kloot Meijburg and Robert A. Bendiksen

SECTION I
Facing the Death of a Loved One

CHAPTER 1
The Role of Spiritual Experience in Adapting to Bereavement   13
Louis A. Gamino, Larry W. Easterling, and Kenneth W. Sewell

CHAPTER 2
The Death of a Spouse: A Spiritual and Psychological Crisis   29
Susan J. Zonnebelt-Smeenge and Robert C. DeVries

CHAPTER 3
For Those Who Stand and Wait   45
Kent Koppelman

SECTION II
Meaning-Making in the Face of Death

CHAPTER 4
A Taste of Heaven Here on Earth: For the Dying and for the
Accompanier   55
Rabbi Daniel A. Roberts

CHAPTER 5

Death, Humor, and Spirituality: Strange Bedfellows?.   73
Ruth Dean

CHAPTER 6

Death and the Postmodern Self: Individualism, Religion, and the
  Transformation of the Modern Self   85
Raymond L. M. Lee

CHAPTER 7

The Healing Touch of Awareness: A Buddhist Perspective on
  Death, Dying, and Pastoral Care 101
Arthur O. Ledoux

SECTION III
Extraordinary Death and Loss

CHAPTER 8

Cyber Cemeteries and Virtual Memorials: Virtual Living Monuments as
  On-line Outlets for Real Life Mourning and a Celebration of Life . . . 113
Hermann Gruenwald and Le Gruenwald

CHAPTER 9

Violence is the Dark Side of Spirituality 127
John D. Morgan

CHAPTER 10

Native American Grief and Loss: Conceptualizations of Disenfranchised
  Grief and Historical Trauma at Individual and Community Levels. . . 137
Steven R. Byers, Theresa T. Erdkamp, and Lisa Byers

CHAPTER 11

In the Aftermath of Columbine: Tragedy as Opportunity for
  Transformation 151
Kevin Ann Oltjenbruns, Steven R. Byers, and Suzanne Tochterman

SECTION IV
Professional Caregivers and Spirituality

CHAPTER 12

When a Patient Dies: Meeting Spiritual Needs of the Bereaved in
  a Health Care Setting 163
Fran Rybarik and Diane Midland

CHAPTER 13
An Exploratory Study of the Spirituality of Clergy as Compared
    with Health Care Professionals 173
David W. Adams and Rick Csiernik

CHAPTER 14
Living, Dying, and Grieving in the Margins 191
Rev. Richard B. Gilbert

SECTION V
Conclusion

CHAPTER 15
Spirituality in Nursing: Being in a Liminal Space 207
Cheryl Laskowski

CHAPTER 16
Spirituality and Loss 221
Gerry R. Cox

Contributors 231
Index 237

Acknowledgments

We would like to thank Stuart Cohen, President of Baywood Publishing Company, and his fine staff, including Bobbi Olszewski, Julie Krempa, and Joi Tamber-Brooks, for their aid in this project; Dr. Morgan for his encouragement and assistance; Dr. Jac Bulk, Mary Clements, and our colleagues at the University of Wisconsin–La Crosse for their help and assistance; and other unnamed, but no less important, individuals for their help and assistance in this project whose aim is to improve the understanding of spirituality and dying, death, and bereavement.

Preface

As editors, we undertook this project at the request of Dr. John Morgan who annually hosts the King's College International Conference on Dying, Death, and Bereavement in London, Ontario, Canada, and who serves as editor of the Baywood series, *Death, Value and Meaning.* The topic of spirituality and making sense of death is of great interest to us as long-term faculty members who teach university courses in dying, death, and bereavement. In this volume, it is our hope that this selection of chapters meets the needs of many professional practitioners and academics, and ultimately, through them, those who must face the issues of spirituality as it relates to dying, death, and bereavement.

Gerry R. Cox
Robert A. Bendiksen
Robert G. Stevenson

Introduction

Herman H. van der Kloot Meijburg
Robert A. Bendiksen

The purpose of this chapter is two-fold. First of all we want to introduce the topic by reflecting on some developments that have attracted our attention over the years hoping to arouse your interest. Second, we want to introduce the contributions various authors have made to this book on making sense of death, leaving you with a choice what you like to read first.

MAKING SENSE OF DEATH

In the back of our minds we are all aware that death is a fact of life. Yet, it remains hard for most of us to personalize this phenomenon. From personal experience, we acknowledge that death may come in many different ways; sometimes death comes as a person's best friend, at other times death comes in more horrible ways than we ever expected. It may take a life-threatening situation before we actually "stop, look and listen" as we attempt to make sense of death.

Recently in the media, there was a striking photograph of the face of a young mother who stood in absolute horror and astonishment as a rescue worker dragged the dead body of her daughter ashore from a canal where hundreds of people had been pushed in by the crowds after an ammunition depot had exploded in the middle of Lagos, the capital of Nigeria. Some 1200 hundred people had met their fate in a similar fashion. Likewise, many of us will still remember the expression on the faces of the victims in New York as they attempted to escape the Twin Tower area on the 11th of September 2001.

On closer reflection, death is sometimes individualized to an extent that a single person may confront death in a personal and dignified manner. In the past, in Spain this even led to the notion of what people called "*ars moriendi,*" meaning that there is a personal art to dying. Death also occurs to many of our fellow human beings in an instant or over a defined period of time. Often there is no art in these deaths. Many die at the same time because of some act of terrorism or in a deliberate attempt

1

to eradicate a group of people; "ethnic cleansing" is a euphemism with which we are all too familiar.

In both circumstances, those who remain behind will attempt to find meaning for themselves in these events. This may include personal meaning-making in anticipation of what is inevitable, and/or calling upon collective frameworks of meaning to understand some aspect of the disaster or atrocity. Every year the citizens of Amsterdam assemble at the Auschwitz monument to commemorate the victims of the concentration camps in the presence of those who survived, a commemoration that has been going on in The Netherlands for over 50 years. Making sense out of death seems to mean making sense out of suffering, making sense out of the loss of life, and making sense out of life.

Why the Sadness?

One might ponder the thought of why it is that when one is born it arouses so much excitement, while we seldom seem to party at the end of one's life. Apparently there is not much to celebrate at the end of our life. Then why do people get so excited at the time of our birth? Perhaps we are so excited about the beginning of one's life because at the time of our birth all options seem to be open.

On the other hand, the sorrow we have and the sadness we show over the death of one of our loved ones doesn't seem to be rooted in that person having failed to meet all those expectations or not having achieved any of the goals one may have set before him during his or her life. Maybe it is because death normally comes with old age, when ones' capacities diminish, at a time when we have to come to terms with the fact we loose touch with the pace of life, when we realize we have to let go of those who we remember from days gone by or of those who we still have around us and whom we love dearly. Perhaps letting go and making sense of letting go is the hardest task ever—something we are well aware of at the end of life and, because of that, we are less inclined to celebrate death like we, at one time, celebrated birth. Both events are interpreted as totally different from each other. What could the reason for this be?

In our modern times, many have over-invested in themselves, turning their lives into something no sensible person would ever consider letting go of. Being a living being is overemphasized. Consequentially, letting go of who we are, and of what we have acquired for ourselves, has become such a difficult enterprise for us to undertake. Letting go and making meaning out of what is left becomes an essential aspect for us to consider in the face of death. Not being able to let go, no doubt adds to our suffering.

The Meaning of Life

We can philosophize about the meaning of life, but to the average individual the meaning of his or her life is associated with the kind of person he or she has become, what one has acquired, and how one experiences these assets. The meaning of our life is the meaning of the life you and I have distilled for ourselves. Making meaning out of my life forces me to look at myself in search of my personal make-up, of what is essentially really "me." And what is essentially "me" is best reflected in the choices I have made and the results these choices have rendered.

There is an immaterial as well as a material side to our personal make-up. In our modern world where the notion of stewardship has dwindled, suffering is implied when we have to leave all we have attained for what it is worth at the end of our life. In The Netherlands one often notices that when people are confronted with their own death, they experience this suffering in their life as a confrontation with a void. All of a sudden we realize we have nothing to hold on to anymore. Consequently meaning can no longer be derived from who I am or what I have attained or acquired. Meaning has to be recreated in a circumstance where, existentially speaking, the old familiar co-ordinates we have developed ourselves, often together with others, are no longer of use.

The confrontation with this void may turn out to be the beginning of a very creative process. When given time, this is like venturing into a *terra incognito,* into a territory yet to be discovered. Consequently we have to find our own way, because there are no maps available, although some say there might be some information we could use to help us out. Here we touch upon the traditional role of religion.

The Part Religion Plays in
Making Sense of Death

Religions claim that there is some information about this void available if only we would listen and put our trust in what religions have to offer. Most religions provide the dying and the relatives of the dying person with a sense of direction; some religions actually pretend to know what you and I are heading for. It seems, however, that it is not the void itself but what lies on the other side that is the focus of concern. Overcoming the void we described above by anticipating what may lay ahead can take amazing forms.

In some areas in The Netherlands those present at the death of a loved one will do nothing else but sit around the bed of their dying relative waiting for the last word uttered. The last words uttered are not only indicative whether or not the family member has found the promised land, but these words are also indicative for what needs to be said about that person during the funeral service, whether it is "thumbs up" or "thumbs down" for that person in his or her life hereafter—whether life hereafter will be a matter of entering divine glory or whether this person will slide into hell. Making sense of death boils down to whether one has found the key of eternal life hereafter. One's death is viewed as settling the bills of life.

Of course one may dismiss the Bible Belt solution as outdated and not anywhere near what religion really has to offer, but in my daily practice as a caregiver I do encounter these assumptions on a fairly regular basis when people talk about their attitudes toward religion. With many it is like sediment left behind in one's mind and thoughts contemplating the meaning of religion in their lives. At the moment of death, many still think that all that happened in one's life will be added up and, finally, the accounts will be settled.

In this line of thought it is almost inevitable that in the period before one's death, feelings of guilt pop up. These feelings of guilt will seriously affect the dying process, making people feel uncomfortable and at a loss what to do or say.

Another line of thought religion offers in the face of death is one of compassion. Religion offers consolation to those who have suffered from hardship and illness. In this instance, life is viewed as temporary and death is perceived as a passage way or the entry hall of something soothing, where the soul, where body and mind can come to rest. Life's circumstances and illness are relativized in the light of what we will experience afterwards. After death we will find ourselves in a state of being that lies beyond our imagination, overriding all our speculations. Dying is closing the door to the troubled life behind us and entering a new sphere of being and awareness. Whatever the circumstances, whatever the suffering, it will not compare to anything we will experience in this new state of being. In this fashion death itself is not regarded as a big issue, death marks only the moment of transition. In a way, death makes sense because it comes as a solution.

There are religions that take life deadly seriously. We only live once. The void we have been talking about is not before, but after death. Making sense of death is that it is a fate we all await. After death we become less than shadows of what we once were as human beings, we will have lost all of our vitality and personal characteristics. It is the loss of life that is lamented.

A fourth line of religious thought we must mention in this context is that there is no escaping life and that death is the mere transition of the soul to another form of existence. And this process of recycling will continue until, ultimately, we have managed to free ourselves from clinging on to it. The void we long for is Nirvana, where we will have detached ourselves from any need that could cause us to be born again.

It is clear that in the face of death religions offer the believer trying to make sense out of death, something to hold onto in a variety of ways. Religions either help bridge the gap or help us to refocus our experience of that void we have been talking about. An interesting development is that for the individual various religious options cohabitate peacefully: one can be a Christian and at the same time accommodate Buddhist patterns of thought. There is a lot of cross religious shopping going on these days! Apparently, in making sense out of death, religions have become a vast resource. So we have to acknowledge that religions still play an important role in making sense of death.

However, we also notice that living in a modern western European country where the impact of religion on our thinking and our attitudes toward death is diminishing, we, personally, have a harder time making sense out of death. This brings us to the role of the pastor.

The Pastor: Representative and Guide

For a proper understanding, we would like to make a distinction between pastoral care and spiritual care. For the purpose of this analysis we define pastoral care more narrow than spiritual care, because we take pastoral care to function within the realm of religion. Pastoral care is dominated with religious connotations while spiritual care could, but it does not necessarily have to be that way. Ultimately, pastoral care sees the source of human well being defined in terms of mans' relationship to God. As such, the word "pastoral" is a beautiful word because it expresses an attitude of support and loving care that springs forth from a religious understanding about the position of the human being regardless of the circumstances this person may find him or herself in.

In comparison, the difference between pastoral care and spiritual care lies in the religious affiliation of pastoral care. The void we have been speaking about has already been filled in. Pastoral care is focused on understanding the needs of the individual in the face of death, explaining death and dying in the light of religious teaching, and providing the believer with a solution or at least a sense of direction. In the face of death it helps the believer and his or her relatives to make sense out of this event. In this respect it should not come as a surprise that caregivers often witness the return of someone to the safe haven of religious experience, who, at first, denied having strong religious ties. Religion helps the individual to make meaning out of the great events of life and death.

Traditionally, the pastor functions as the representative of this vast resource of religious insight and belief. To support what he or she represents, the pastor is usually equipped with the authority to draw from these religious resources and to administer them to the dying. These ceremonies and rituals specific to religion help the dying person to make the transition from life to life hereafter and help the bereaved to make meaning out of the death of that person. To some extent these ceremonies and rituals help the pastor to materialize and visualize the meaning of death and dying to those present. As a representative of religion, the pastor mediates what is helpful and meaningful to say and to do in the face of death.

But one may argue that over time the role of the pastor will change from being the official representative of a certain religion, mediating the specific insights and performing certain rituals and ceremonies, to that of a religious resource person helping people to make sense of death their own way. In a modern, secularized society, however, to many the pastor may even cease to be a mere representative of the religious. In this respect the role of the pastor may already have radically changed! When asked, many regard the pastor more of a guide and less of a representative of his denomination—a person who is able to help open up the spiritual dimensions of one's existence and to help look at these dimensions in a more profound way. The pastor may find him or herself already venturing in a realm where traditional religious thinking and practice can no longer be referred to, because people experience both as irrelevant to their situation, or because existentially they no longer make sense whatsoever or because they are simply associated with days long gone by. If religion can no longer fill this new void, may it be that the spiritual approach can help us to make some sort of meaning out of our life and death?

Secularized Spirituality

No longer is spirituality just another word for a range of religious experiences. To some it may still be the case, and there is nothing wrong about that. But in the mind of many today, spirituality reaches beyond what religion can offer. With religion, spirituality has become secularized too. Yet modern spirituality is full of meaning to those who want to make sense out of their life and death. We use our spiritual capacity as a tool to restore awareness about ourselves and to create a context for our quest for meaning. Spirituality has to do with man's search for the core meaning of his existence. There are a couple of things that can be said about modern secularized spirituality.

First of all, spirituality is clearly related to the identity of the person. Spirituality is foremost a search for one's own personal make up: what is this particular individual all about. What is her or his innate identity? The quest is all about "Who am I and what sense can I make out of my life?"

Our second observation is that one's quest for the spiritual is concrete and directly related to the great themes in one's life and how these themes have affected and shaped that life. Whether the themes are good or bad is not really the issue, what really matters in that there is this inner drive to explore these themes in depth, to revive their significance and to accept them as being part of the kind of person one has become.

In addition, the spiritual exercise is about relating to these great themes in one's life in a respectful way, honoring their impact on one's life and death. A sense of awe is involved as we realize how these themes have turned us into the kind of persons we have become. One may call the sense of awe the transcendent dimension of modern spirituality. Understanding our inner drive and why we have made the decisions we have made in our life is like "coming home" to whom we feel we really are.

The fourth dimension of modern spirituality is one of relatedness. Spirituality is not only finding ways how to relate to the inner self; as a human being we also need a response, we need some form of affirmation from others, whether they be family, friends, or caregivers. Modern spirituality reveals itself in the interaction of the intimates involved in the process. It is what one may call the horizontal dimension of modern, secularized spirituality.

In the care setting, it is always interesting to observe who, in this respect, ends up to be the "spiritual buddy" of the patient. It is not necessarily the pastor who gets involved in the spiritual quest of the patient, although professionally speaking he may be the most likely person. Other caregivers, like nurses, the attending physician, or the social worker, may also be invited by the patient to respond to his or her spiritual questions and needs.

Challenges for the Future

We have argued above that death often leaves people puzzled and bewildered. Consequently, we have this inner drive to make sense out of death and dying because death and dying raises the question what life, what one's own life, is all about. We have argued that in the face of death individuals are confronted with a void; we do not know how to assess the course of events. So much was invested in life that thoughts about death and dying were expelled from our mind. Death and dying triggers a search for meaning we are not really prepared for. Traditionally, religions form a vast resource we can draw from.

But one of the shortcomings of religion is that they reach out for what lies beyond death and thereby they tend to relativize the phase in one's life that leads up to the moment of death. It is exactly this pre-death phase of letting go that troubles us and at the same time stimulates us to use our own spiritual resources to explore the significance of that moment to enhance our understanding of ourselves. Where we have to let go of whatever we thought added meaning to our lives, we have to recreate a new sense of meaning with the help of which we can face and understand our own death. The spiritual in us helps us to identify who we are, helps us to explore whatever the great themes in our lives are, helps us to become more reverent toward ourselves and helps us, in our search for affirmation, to share all we discovered about ourselves with others. We call this the process of homecoming.

The best way for caregivers to facilitate the homecoming of those who are in the phase of making sense of death and dying is by understanding the care they themselves receive from the dying. When, for example, they, who we care for, choose a spiritual buddy, they also care for us. At the end of life, those who give care and those who receive care have this rare opportunity to participate in each other's lives. In our quest for the spiritual, there is not in the practice of care that much difference between care giving and care receiving.

We believe that the human need for this spiritual quest at the end of life to make sense of death needs to be acknowledged and conceptualized in our modern understanding of care. For one thing, more research is needed. Time has come to share whatever experiences we have had so far. This is what this book is all about. Time has also come to develop a practice of care to help people to use their spiritual capacities to recreate meaning in this last phase of life in order to make sense out of death. Coming home is all about spirituality. Spirituality is all about engaging oneself in the creative process of meaning-making.

SPIRITUAL, PASTORAL, AND PERSONAL ASPECTS OF DEATH, DYING, AND BEREAVEMENT

The authors in this book address a number of dimensions of meaning-making in the face of death. In *Section I: Facing the Death of a Loved One,* the impact of the death of loved ones is described and explored in three ways. Gamino, Easterling, and Sewell, in "The Role of Spiritual Experience in Adapting to Bereavement," explore the role of internal and external dimensions of religion and spirituality at times of loss. Their data analysis of 159 mourners supports a pattern in previous studies of the "beneficial effects of intrinsic spirituality on health in general and mental health in particular. . . ." Extrinsic religious behavior, e.g., church attendance, shows ". . . little meaningful association with the bereavement process," which is also consistent with previous studies.

The next two chapters focus on the profound and devastating experience of loss in the death of a spouse and that of a child. Zonnebelt-Smeenge and DeVries, in "The Death of a Spouse: A Spiritual and Psychological Crisis," provide a psychological model of spirituality that includes a sense of intimacy with self, God, and others. Deaths are dealt with in terms of the role of God and the bereaved in the death, the reality of evil, and a sense of after-life. The authors conclude with five task-based guidelines for a meaningful and healthy psychological and spiritual coping with loss through death that is based on the four-stage model of mourning by Worden. Koppelman, in "For Those Who Stand and Wait," brings both of the previous chapters into human focus in telling the moving story of his struggle with meaning and meaninglessness as he and his wife faced the death of their teenage son in an auto accident.

Section II: Meaning-Making in the Face of Death includes four articles from a variety of positions and perspectives. Roberts, a practicing rabbi, unpacks dimensions of spirituality in "A Taste of Heaven Here on Earth: For the Dying and for the Accompanier." Dean's discussion of "Death, Humor, and Spirituality: Strange Bedfellows?" explores humor in client-caregiver relationships, in hospice/palliative care, as a coping strategy, as therapy, and concludes with guidelines for introducing humor in critical care settings.

Lee's essay on "Death and the Postmodern Self: Individualism, Religion, and the Transformation of the Modern Self" begins by noting that continuity of self beyond death is not part of the worldview of modernity. Postmodern assumptions, in contrast, view the self as fragmented because of a revival of interest in death consciousness. His theoretical discussion centers on individualism and death, alienation of religion, death consciousness, the postmodern conundrum, and the irony of death.

"The Healing Touch of Awareness: A Buddhist Perspective on Death, Dying, and Pastoral Care" by Ledoux moves the reader to a Buddhist viewpoint that is not often recognized in Western publications. The story of Siddhartha Gautama, the Buddha, and basic assumptions and principles of Buddhism are presented as a foundation for discussing how to apply this Eastern religious and spiritual approach to pastoral care of the dying, particularly the eight-fold path of ethical principles of right knowledge, aspiration, speech, conduct, livelihood, effort, concentration, and mindedness.

Section III: Extraordinary Death and Loss brings attention to four examples of social problems where death, grief, and bereavement are complicated by circumstances. Gruenwald and Gruenwald, in "Cyber Cemeteries and Virtual Memorials: Virtual Living Monuments as On-line Outlets for Real Life Mourning and a Celebration of Life," discuss meaning-making in the virtual reality of cyberspace. They helpfully define cyber cemetery, provide numerous examples of on-line memorials, discuss who offers on-line memorials, and explain the therapeutic importance of direct expression, language, sharing, activity, aesthetics, self-denial, and suffering. The functions of cyber cemeteries include accessibility anywhere anytime, a place to acknowledge special losses and needs, building communication and a sense of community, and the option of making the memorial a private (limited access) or public space. Examples of religious sites include discussion of Buddhist and Jewish cyber memorials, as well as others. "Violence is the Dark Side of Spirituality" by Morgan reflects on the person as a unique substance, death always wins, spirituality is essential loneliness, violence as cleansing the world of tainted ones, and persons need to be comfortable in their own skin.

Byers, Erdkamp, and Byers, in "Native American Grief and Loss: Conceptualizations of Disenfranchised Grief and Historical Trauma at Individual and

Community Levels," document the historical context of Native Americans, the concept of disenfranchised grief developed by Doka, and its detailed application to Native American experience of grief and loss in individuals and communities.

"In the Aftermath of Columbine: Tragedy as Opportunity for Transformation" by Oltjenbruns, Byers, and Tochterman reports on a qualitative survey of professionals about the impact of the shooting deaths of young students in Fort Collins, Colorado, on April 20, 1999. They provide poignant quotes from respondents based on Worden's four-fold model of the tasks of mourning that include the experience of pain, understanding and transforming the suffering, making a connection/healing relationships, and finding meaning in life.

Section IV: Professional Caregivers and Spirituality includes three chapters based on the experiences of a variety of health care professionals who deal regularly with death, dying, and bereavement. Rybarik and Midland, in "When a Patient Dies: Meeting Spiritual Needs of the Bereaved in a Health Care Setting," describe the team approach developed at Gundersen Lutheran Bereavement Services in La Crosse, Wisconsin, of the primary bereavement team role players of physicians, nursing, social services, and pastoral care. A case study illustrates this model. Guidelines are provided for anticipatory grief support, care at time of death, bereavement follow-up, and stages of team development.

Adams and Csiernik, in "An Exploratory Study of the Spirituality of Clergy as Compared with Health Care Professionals," is a study of 149 health care professionals in a Canadian city hospital. Their analysis compared clergy with other health professionals in terms of the meaning of spirituality, importance of spirituality in personal and work life, personal comfort with spirituality, meeting of spiritual needs, strengthening and changing of spirituality, impediments to meeting one's spiritual needs, and consequences of not meeting one's spiritual needs. While the role and function of pastoral care remains, there appears to be an expansion of spiritual awareness, understanding, and integration by other members of the health care team.

"Living, Dying, and Grieving in the Margins" by Gilbert lays a foundation of marginality for spiritual and pastoral dimensions of care for the dying. His data include several case study interviews with clergy.

Section V: Conclusion offers two chapters. The first, "Spirituality in Nursing: Being in a Liminal Space" by Laskowski, is a qualitative research study of 20 registered nurses in the northeast United States. She reviews the history of nursing and nurses' work with the dying that includes factors such as time limitations, rigid settings, lack of knowledge in end-of-life care, lack of support, and demands of technology. The desire of nurses to be more involved in spiritual care of the dying is frustrated by their larger role on the health care team.

The concluding essay by Cox on "Spirituality and Loss" locates loss and growth in the seasons of life, identifies the importance of response to loss, and sees each loss as an opportunity for healing and growth. He provides suggestions for ways to help others develop styles of healthy grieving and things to do with those who experience loss. It is a fitting conclusion to this anthology on "Making Sense of Death: Spiritual, Pastoral, and Personal Aspects of Death, Dying, and Bereavement."

SECTION I

Facing the Death of a Loved One

CHAPTER 1

The Role of Spiritual Experience in Adapting to Bereavement

Louis A. Gamino, Larry W. Easterling, and Kenneth W. Sewell

Dealing with loss is a universal human hardship. How individuals can best cope with losses such as the death of a loved one, and perhaps even grow from them, is a major focus in the contemporary study of thanatology. Our interest is exploring the potential role of spiritual or religious factors in bereavement adaptation based on empirical evidence gathered from the Scott & White Grief Study (Easterling, Gamino, Sewell, & Stirman, 2000; Gamino, Sewell, & Easterling, 2000). Specifically, we wondered whether one's "internal" spiritual beliefs, attitudes, motivations, and experiences (measured by self-report) or one's "external" religious activities (measured by denominational affiliation or church attendance) might be most beneficial to bereft individuals.

Another salient interest of ours is how to apply the results of empirical studies such as our own to aiding those who turn to professional caregivers (e.g., clinical, pastoral) for assistance in coping with grief and loss. For example, pastoral caregivers have long suspected that those persons who simply perform religious rituals or routinely attend worship services do not necessarily cope better with bereavement or other personal crises. Rather, those individuals who are able to *actualize* their spiritual experience in times of crisis and *apply* their belief system to life difficulties such as bereavement seem to cope more adaptively. We have looked to our research findings both to verify this time-honored assumption in pastoral care and to generate corollaries for how spiritual experience can be accessed and utilized with bereaved persons.

CONCEPTS AND HISTORY

The empirical study of how spiritual and religious factors influence human psychology owes much to Allport and Ross (1967) and their original work on

13

intrinsic versus extrinsic religious orientation. Persons with an intrinsic religious orientation are described as embracing their faith as an end-in-itself.

> Persons with this orientation find their master motive in religion. Other needs, strong as they may be, are regarded as of less ultimate significance, and they are, so far as possible, brought into harmony with the religious beliefs and prescriptions. Having embraced a creed the individual endeavors to internalize it and follow it fully. It is in this sense that he *lives* his religion. (p. 434)

Conversely, individuals with an extrinsic religious orientation are seen as using religion as a means-to-an-end.

> Persons with this orientation are disposed to use religion for their own ends. . . . Extrinsic values are always instrumental and utilitarian. Persons with this orientation may find religion useful in a variety of ways—to provide security and solace, sociability and distraction, status and self-justification. The embraced creed is lightly held or else selectively shaped to fit more primary needs. (p. 434)

Allport and Ross (1967) developed their Religious Orientation Inventory (ROI) to measure these respective typologies. Numerous investigators have been intrigued by this delineation of religious motivations and explored how these concepts relate to a variety of social science variables. Donahue (1985) completed an exhaustive review of studies using the Intrinsic-Extrinsic (I-E) dimension with generally favorable results. Donahue found that "intrinsic religiousness serves as an excellent measure of religious commitment, as distinct from religious belief, church membership, (and) liberal-conservative theological orientation . . ." (p. 415). However, intrinsic religiousness was not found to correlate particularly well with nonreligious variables in the social sciences. He further asserted that "extrinsic religiousness . . . does a good job of measuring the sort of religion that gives religion a bad name . . ." (p. 416) such as prejudice, dogmatism, and even fear of death. Donahue concluded "the findings currently available bode well for the potential of the I-E framework as a powerful explanatory tool" (p. 416) in the scientific study of religion.

Much of the empirical work on the intrinsic versus extrinsic religious orientation has been focused on refining measurement issues associated with the ROI. Hoge (1972) reported success validating his own 10-item Intrinsic Religious Motivation (IRM) Scale targeted to reflect the values of "organized American Christianity" (p. 370). His emphasis was to discern the motivation for performing religious behavior rather than measuring the behavior itself. In doing so, he hoped to identify those individuals with ultimate or end-in-itself (i.e., intrinsic) religious motivation in contrast to those with instrumental or mean-to-an-end (i.e., extrinsic) motivations. Hoge's IRM Scale correlated strongly (® = .86) with the intrinsic subscale of the ROI (from which he borrowed some items).

Koenig, George, and Peterson (1998) studied the effects of religious belief and activity on remission of depression in medically ill hospitalized older persons. Intrinsic religiosity was measured using Hoge's (1972) IRM Scale. Organizational (e.g., church attendance) and non-organizational (e.g., private prayer, meditation, or Bible study) religious activity were assessed as well. Intrinsic religiosity was found to be significantly related to time to remission of depression, with those identified as more intrinsically religious taking less time to recover. Neither frequency of church attendance nor private religious activities (both positively correlated with intrinsic religiosity) were related to time to remission from depression. Their conclusion was that "intrinsic religiosity, while related to church going and frequency of private religious activities, is not the same. Neither of these religious activities measures the extent to which religion is the master, motivating factor in peoples' lives that drives their behavior and decision making" (p. 541).

Gradually, instead of intrinsic religiosity, the field has begun to embrace the omnibus term *spirituality* to refer to this constellation of inner beliefs, attitudes, motivations, and experiences that reflect one's intrinsic faith as the organizing principle, or master motive, in life. Unfortunately for purposes of definition, the term spirituality has been criticized as a "fuzzy" concept that has acquired diverse meanings and connotations (Zinnbauer et al., 1997). Much like P. T. Barnum's big tent, spirituality seems to be an overarching term that implies something a little different to everyone, depending on the perceiver's vantage point.

Some scholars (Miller & Thoresen, 1999; Zinnbauer et al., 1997) have argued that spirituality is most often associated with individual subjective experiences, such as belief in God or a higher power, or having a personal relationship with God or a higher power. This broad concept of spirituality, rooted in inner subjective experience and attitude, is contrasted with a narrower concept of religion. The term religion invokes attributions pertaining to organizational or institutional practices, rituals, and beliefs such as church membership, church attendance, and adherence to the dogmas of a particular denomination or sect which prescribe how one relates to that which is sacred or divine.

Zinnbauer et al. (1997) studied a diverse sample of individuals drawn from different churches, institutions, and age groups to see how they would define the terms spirituality and religiousness. They found spirituality and religiousness to be overlapping constructs in that both included references to belief or faith in a Higher Power of some kind and to the importance of integrating one's values and beliefs with one's behavior in daily life. However, "they diverge in the focus of religiousness definitions on organizational or institutional beliefs and practices, and focus of spirituality definitions on the personal qualities of connection or relationship with a Higher Power" (p. 557).

One solution to the dilemma of how to operationally define a broadband concept like spirituality is to focus on spiritual experiences with which persons from diverse religious traditions, not just the Judeo-Christian tradition, may identify. This is what Jared Kass and his associates (Kass, Friedman, Leserman, Zuttermeister, & Benson, 1991) attempted to do in constructing their Index of Core Spiritual Experiences (INSPIRIT). The INSPIRIT was developed to capture:

> ... two characteristic elements: 1) a distinct event and a cognitive appraisal of that event which resulted in a personal conviction of God's existence (or of some form of Higher Power as defined by the person); and 2) the perception of a highly internalized relationship between God and the person (i.e., God dwells within and a corresponding feeling of closeness to God). (p. 204)

The focus of the INSPIRIT is on experiences, mystical and otherwise, which the person interprets as spiritual—hence, spiritual experiences. Evidence supporting the concurrent validity of the INSPIRIT as a measure of intrinsic spirituality came both from Kass et al. who found that it correlated positively $r = .69$) with the Intrinsic scale of the ROI and from VandeCreek, Ayres, and Bassham (1995) who found a significant correlation $r = .61$) between the INSPIRIT and Hoge's (1972) IRM Scale.

Three key elements emerge from this historical review. First, an individual's intrinsic spirituality, or internal spiritual experience, appears to be the most operative variable in mediating possible salutary health outcomes as a function of faith beliefs. Second, indices more closely associated with the notion of religion such as church attendance or church membership (e.g., external behavioral measures) are less likely to influence health outcomes. Third, although clearly there are multiple ways to measure intrinsic spirituality (i.e., ROI, IRM, INSPIRIT), the INSPIRIT has the apparent advantage of inclusiveness by emphasizing spiritual experiences with which those from diverse religious traditions may identify.

SPIRITUALITY AND BEREAVEMENT

What about the role of intrinsic spirituality, or spiritual experience, in bereavement? There have been attempts to document empirically the effects of spirituality on how people manage their grief. However, differences in how the faith construct has been operationally defined and measured leave some continuing level of ambiguity about the findings. For example, Vachon et al. (1982) studied widows' adjustment and found that those who rated religion as "not very helpful" reported higher psychological distress as early as one month after spousal loss. This finding was still apparent as long as 2 years after their husbands died. Although one could speculate that the widows who found religion not very helpful probably had lower levels of intrinsic spirituality, the type of data collected precluded a definitive conclusion.

Bereaved mothers who were members of the Compassionate Friends organization were the subject of a study by Graham-Pole, Wass, Eyberg, Chu, and Olejnik (1989). When these mothers talked to their dying children (and siblings) about death, the perception that the family's religious faith was a significant source of support appeared to aid these delicate discussions. Also, bereaved mothers' recovery after their child's death was positively correlated with a subjective appraisal of having been helped by their religious faith.

"Spiritual support" (e.g., having a personal relationship with God, faith as a coping aid, and regularly experiencing God's loving care) has been studied in relation to depression and subjective distress after loss. In studies of parental bereavement (Maton, 1989) and conjugal bereavement (Levy, Martinkowski, & Derby, 1994), spiritual support has been shown to be inversely correlated with reported depression levels and subjective distress among survivors.

In perhaps the most direct test of the proposition that intrinsic spirituality can aid bereavement, Rosik (1989) investigated grief and depression levels in a sample of 159 elderly widowed persons. Using Gorsuch and Venable's (1983) "age universal" revision of the ROI, Rosik found that extrinsic religiosity was consistently and significantly associated with more grief and depression. However, the predicted negative relations between intrinsic spirituality and the distress measures were not confirmed.

Thus, empirical verification is still needed for the hypothesis that intrinsic spirituality or internal spiritual experience (rather than external religious behavior such as denominational affiliation and church attendance) is related to better psychological adjustment among the bereaved. Our own research in the Scott & White Grief Study was designed to test these propositions as directly as possible.

GENERAL DESCRIPTION OF SCOTT & WHITE GRIEF STUDY

The Scott & White Grief Study is a multiphase, retrospective investigation of grief phenomenology in a diverse group of 159 mourners. Data pertaining to the role of spiritual experience in adapting to bereavement was collected from 85 participants during Phase 2 of our research and has been reported in detail elsewhere (Easterling et al., 2000; Gamino et al., 2000). Heterogeneity among grievers was sought deliberately in our sampling strategies in order to obtain the most generalizable results with the broadest possible applicability.

The Phase 2 sample consisted of a preponderance of women (77.6 percent) with an average age of 50.9 years ($SD = 13.6$) and an average of 15.1 years of education ($SD = 3.2$). The vast majority of participants were White (89.4 percent) reflecting the demographic composition of central Texas. Of non-White participants, 4.7 percent were Hispanic, 2.4 percent were African American, and 3.6 percent were other races. The sample was mixed with respect to those who were married (43.5 percent), widowed (38.8 percent), separated/divorced (10.6 percent), or never married (7.1 percent). Regarding religious affiliation, 34.1 percent were Mainline Protestant, 34.1 percent were Conservative Protestant, 15.3 percent were Catholic, 5.9 percent were Jewish, 4.7 percent were Pentecostal, and 5.9 percent reported no religious affiliation.

Within this diverse sample, causes of death included illness (75.3 percent), accidents (14.1 percent), suicides (9.4 percent), and homicides (1.2 percent). Decedent types included spouses (42.3 percent), parents (36.5 percent), children (11.8 percent), and others (9.4 percent) such as siblings, grandparents, or friends. Over 88 percent of the participants had lost their loved one within three years of the study; the median time since death was eight months.

Bereaved participants first completed two psychometric measures of grief affects: the Hogan Grief Reaction Checklist (HGRC; Hogan, Greenfield, & Schmidt, 2001), and the Grief Experience Inventory (GEI; Sanders, Mauger, & Strong, 1985). To measure internal spiritual experience, we chose the INSPIRIT (Kass et al., 1991) because of its inclusiveness toward persons of various faith traditions. The INSPIRIT consists of six multiple choice items and 13 Likert-style ratings of various spiritual beliefs and experiences. It yields a single mean score that has shown high reliability

(Cronbach's alpha coefficient = .90) and concurrent validity both with the ROI (Kass et al., 1991) and with the IRM (VandeCreek et al., 1995).

Participants were also interviewed about the particulars of their loss experiences, their perceptions of and reactions to their loved ones' deaths, and their coping strategies during bereavement. A measure of external religious behavior, church attendance, was assessed through participants' self-report of "practicing" their religion—specifically, whether they attended church services "regularly," "occasionally," or "not at all." Church attendance was then operationalized categorically as "high" if the participant attended faith services regularly, and as "low" if the participant attended only occasionally or not at all.

SPIRITUAL EXPERIENCE VERSUS CHURCH ATTENDANCE

In our first analysis of the data, we used a median split procedure to categorize the variable of Spiritual Experience into two groups. Those mourners scoring at or above the median of 3.43 on the INSPIRIT were designated as "high" in spiritual experience ($n = 44$; 51.8 percent) and those scoring below the median were considered "low" ($n = 41$; 48.2 percent). Church attendance was also defined categorically as either "high" ($n = 49$; 58 percent reporting regular attendance) or "low" ($n = 36$; 42 percent reporting occasional or no attendance). Spiritual experience and church attendance were the independent variables whereas grief affect scores on the HGRC and the GEI served as the dependent variables.

Analyses of variance (2 × 2 model) found that those mourners who endorsed a higher level of spiritual experience exhibited significantly lower levels of problematic grief affect on both the HGRC ($p = .03$) and the GEI ($p = .01$). On the other hand, analyses of church attendance showed no such effect on HGRC or GEI scores of grief-related misery. Thus, higher levels of spiritual experience appeared to have a moderating effect on mourners' self-reports of distress. Conversely, whether or not mourners attended church regularly appeared to have no impact on how much distress they experienced in the grieving process. Figure 1 graphically shows the respective levels of grief-related distress on the HGRC and the GEI for the four groups in these statistical analyses. Interestingly, those participants with low spiritual experience/low church attendance had the *highest* levels of grief-related distress, followed by those with low spiritual experience/high church attendance. Less distressed yet were those with high spiritual experience/low church attendance. The *lowest* grief distress scores were registered by participants with high spiritual experience/high church attendance.

As compelling as these findings are, the above analyses admittedly lose some potential sensitivity given that the INSPIRIT score (a continuous variable) was split categorically into high and low scorers. To further explore the strength of the relations among spiritual experience, church attendance, and grief affect, multiple regression analyses were performed to allow the INSPIRIT scores to remain in a continuous metric. In the regression analysis, the HGRC and the GEI still constituted the dependent variables whereas INSPIRIT scores of spiritual experience and self-report

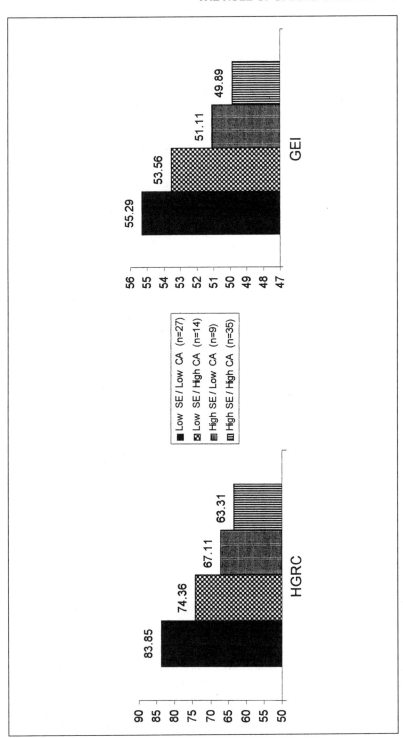

Figure 1. Mean scores on HGRC (left) and GEI (right) for four groups of mourners in 2 × 2 analyses of variance for Spiritual Experience (SE) and Church Attendance (CA).

of church attendance were used as predictor variables. The order of entry of predictors into the equations was varied to investigate the extent to which each predictor could add to the explainable variance over-and-above that accounted for by the initial predictor.

Interestingly, spiritual experience and church attendance were moderately correlated ($r = .52$; $p < .001$) indicating that there was some degree of overlap in what these two factors measured (cf., Koenig et al., 1998). Yet, the multiple regression findings pointed clearly to spiritual experience as the more robust of these two predictors. When spiritual experience was entered into the equation first, it was a significant predictor of scores on both the HGRC ($p < .005$) and the GEI ($p < .005$) and church attendance could add nothing significant to the prediction. When church attendance was forced into the equation first, it showed some predictive value on the grief distress measures (for HGRC and GEI, $p < .05$) but spiritual experience always added additional variance accounted for (for HGRC and GEI, $p < .05$). In each case, the relations were in the expected direction with higher spiritual experience and high church attendance associated with lower levels of grief-related distress. Thus, spiritual experience, in and of itself, was related to a more positive grief response among mourners. External religious behavior, as measured by church attendance, appeared to be related to a more positive grief response mainly when it was coincident with spiritual experience.

SPIRITUAL EXPERIENCE AND PERSONAL GROWTH

Several studies in the past have reported positive indications of personal growth following loss or trauma (Edmonds & Hooker, 1992; Hogan, Morse, & Tason, 1996; Lieberman, 1996; Tedeschi & Calhoun, 1996; Yalom & Lieberman, 1991). Tedeschi and Calhoun (1996) identified three broad dimensions of personal growth: positive changes in self-perception; closer family and interpersonal relationships; and, a changed philosophy of life including an increased appreciation for one's existence, not taking life for granted, and living each day to the fullest. Frantz, Trolley, and Johll (1996) studied 312 bereaved adults from the general (i.e., non-clinical) population approximately one year after the death of their loved one and found 77 percent reported that their religious beliefs were of considerable help in their grief. Those who found their faith beliefs helpful were significantly more optimistic about the future, which is one aspect of post-bereavement growth.

One of the unique features of the Hogan Grief Reaction Checklist is that, in addition to its five scales measuring various types of grief misery, it also has a scale measuring personal growth following bereavement. Examples of items include "I have learned to cope better with life," "I am stronger because of the grief I have experienced," "I care more deeply for others," and "I have a better outlook on life." Use of the HGRC Personal Growth scale was pivotal in enabling us to explore adaptive processes in bereavement in an effort to understand better how some mourners come to fare relatively well despite the presence of complicating factors (Gamino et al., 2000).

Using a stepwise regression analysis to predict HGRC Personal Growth scores as the dependent variable, we sought to identify factors (i.e., predictor variables) that could be linked to higher levels of personal growth in mourners as an outcome of bereavement. Spiritual experience (measured by INSPIRIT scores) was among four behavioral correlates that we identified as characteristic of those mourners who reported greater degrees of personal growth ($p = .036$). (The other three significant predictors were: seeing some good resulting from the death; having a chance to say "goodbye"; and spontaneous positive memories of the decedent.) Thus, internal spiritual experience was not just associated with lower levels of grief-related distress; it appeared also to be an important ingredient in growth-related processes involved with bereavement recovery.

THEORETICAL APPLICATIONS

These findings from the Scott & White Grief Study confirmed the proposition that spiritual experience plays an important role in the course and outcome of bereavement. The influence associated with spiritual experience appears to be two-fold: lowering levels of distressing grief affect during the course of bereavement; and promoting positive personal growth as a bereavement outcome. Our results were consistent with general findings in the field of spirituality and health that spiritual/ religious involvement is inversely related to disorders and positively related to health (Miller & Thoresen, 1999). As such, several aspects of our findings merit some thoughtful reflection.

First, in the Scott & White Grief Study, we used spiritual experience (as measured by the INSPIRIT) to tap the variable of intrinsic spirituality. Intrinsic spirituality refers back to the original concept by Allport and Ross (1967) of religion as the master motive in a person's life, a faith creed that is internalized and *lived* to the greatest extent possible. Later investigators continued to refine this concept. Koenig et al. (1998) echoed that such intrinsic spirituality drives behavior and decision-making. Zinnbauer et al. (1997) showed that, in addition to belief in a Higher Power and integrating one's values with behavior, intrinsic spirituality connotes a personal connection to or relationship with a Higher Power. Based on the evolution of knowledge in the field, assessing spiritual experience via the INSPIRIT appears to be a very worthwhile way to access the phenomenon of intrinsic spirituality in terms that are not limited to any particular faith tradition. Greater use of standard measures such as the INSPIRIT (or the IRM) to identify intrinsic spirituality would reduce the ambiguity proliferated when various research teams operationally define the faith construct in unique ways, as has been the case to date with most studies of spirituality and bereavement. Gorsuch (1984) has called for just such concentration of effort using scales that are already well established.

Second, while spiritual experience was clearly related to better grief adjustment according to the Scott & White Grief Study data, the same did not hold true for church attendance as an external behavioral indicator. This was fascinating to us. Like Koenig et al. (1998), we found church attendance positively correlated with spiritual experience yet they were not the same. In fact, in regression analyses, church attendance had a significant impact on grief adjustment levels mainly when occurring in conjunction with higher spiritual experience. In other words, going regularly to church appears to aid bereavement recovery the most when the mourners' reasons for being in church are a faithful expression of heartfelt intrinsic spirituality. Church attendance does not seem to help the bereaved much when occurring for more perfunctory or utilitarian purposes. As summarized by Gorsuch and Miller (1999) ". . . the frequency of religious attendance is often a less sensitive predictor of health than measures that reflect motivations for participation (e.g., intrinsic vs. extrinsic)" (p. 57). Pastors and clergy have long been convinced of this and now there is empirical support for this widely held assumption. In other words, now we *know* empirically what we *knew* intuitively, that church attendance can occur for multiple motivations but only when it reflects intrinsic spirituality do maximal benefits seem to accrue to the bereaved person.

Third, finding that higher levels of spiritual experience seem to mediate more positive grief adjustment raises speculation about why and how this occurred. Numerous potential explanations come to mind, but it is difficult to know with certainty the pathway that links spiritual experience with reduced levels of grief distress. Do these individuals engage more in prayer, meditation, and spiritual reflection that counteract negative grief affect? In the face of loss, do they draw strength and comfort from their perceived personal relationship with a Higher Power? Do their spiritual experiences convince them of the existence of a cosmic framework (Yalom, 1980) that lends meaning to the death of their loved one by incorporating themes such as salvation, afterlife, and ultimate reunion? Some ongoing analyses from Phase 2 of the Scott & White Grief Study may be helpful in our deliberation of these questions.

Content analyses of Phase 2 participants' written narratives answering the question, "What does the death of your loved one mean to you?" have shown one of the constructs utilized by participants to assign meaning to their loved one's death was "the afterlife." Individuals enumerating this theme included mostly traditional Judeo-Christian notions of God, heaven, and an afterlife. Invoking metaphysical concepts of a life or location beyond earth in which to "place" the deceased loved one and, possibly, anticipate reunion formed a meaning matrix that imparted solace to these grievers who endorsed it. With over 94 percent of our sample comprised of participants from Judeo-Christian traditions, it appears likely that eschatological beliefs about transcendent life after death indeed may be one of the mechanisms by which greater intrinsic spirituality brings greater levels of comfort to the bereaved after the death of a loved one.

Fourth, how does spiritual experience facilitate greater personal growth following bereavement as our results indicate? Our content analysis offers some clues. Among the positive changes mourners reported, there were frequent references to altered priorities. For example, rather than seeking material acquisition or temporal objectives, greater emphasis was placed on the quality of personal relationships and evaluating what was truly meaningful in life. We submit that persons of faith will immediately recognize the similarity between these secular dimensions of personal growth and the spiritual aims of most major world religions. Focusing on ultimate outcomes (i.e., trying to be a good person), emphasizing love in personal relationships, and following the principle of the golden rule are general hallmarks of many organized faith traditions. Accordingly, we posit that the empirical relation between intrinsic spirituality and personal growth following bereavement may come about because of a natural confluence in these two variables (i.e., analogous dimensions undergird both intrinsic spirituality and personal growth). For many, death of a loved one gives pause to reflect on life's highest priorities, and the conclusions resulting from such reflection often lead an individual in the direction of traditional spiritual values of virtue, love, and compassion.

PRACTICAL APPLICATIONS:
THE "REACHABLE MOMENT"

In pondering how clinicians and pastoral caregivers may apply the results of our research findings, we thought about the critical opportunity presented when the death of a loved one occurs among survivors with varying degrees of intrinsic spirituality. We have described elsewhere the value of having an assessment strategy for gauging the extent of a survivor's spiritual experience based on the INSPIRIT itself (Easterling et al., 2000). For example, the caregiver may listen for, "How closely has this person found God (or a Higher Power) to be present in her life?" or "How likely is he to think about God (or a Higher Power) at times like these?" If answers to these questions do not emerge naturally during the conversation, some sensitively posed inquiries along these lines may help assess the person's level of spiritual experience.

Most probably, those grievers high in spiritual experience will be able to engage more readily their theology and faith constructs in how they understand what death means and in how they cope with loss. None of this cancels the emotional pain involved when a loved one dies nor circumvents the need to participate in mourning rituals and formal rites of passage. Rather, meaning attributions grounded in the mourner's faith beliefs can imbue funeral/memorial/burial rituals with important additional meaning and value that ultimately enhances the comfort realized from them (cf., Gamino, Sewell, Easterling, & Stirman, 2000). Likewise, during the subsequent grieving trajectory, those high in spiritual experience can utilize their spiritual beliefs to attain "perspective" on the loved one's death and to accomplish what is thought to be a key task in bereavement recovery: "emotionally relocating the deceased and getting on with life" (Worden, 2002). Such emotion relocation is largely symbolic and may be aided by a sense of continuing bonds between the survivor and the decedent (Klass, Silverman, & Nickman, 1996). In turn, this sense of a continuing bond may be facilitated by a spiritual construction of what death means and what is thought to happen to the loved one after death.

But how should the clinician or pastoral caregiver approach survivors who have lower levels of spiritual experience upon which to draw at the time of death? We encourage practitioners to entertain the notion of the "reachable moment." Most are familiar with the concept of a "teachable moment" when a student is curious about something or needs information to conceptualize a problem, make a decision, or operate on the environment. When the student is "primed," knowledge transmission is optimal. We are convinced that there may be a corresponding "reachable moment" for spiritual experience when a loved one dies.

For the survivor, death often brings to the surface existential concerns about mortality, the meaning of life, ultimate purpose, the possibility of an afterlife, and so forth. In this process of confronting life's greatest mysteries, the mourner may be "primed" to consider (or reconsider) the role of his/her spiritual experiences in how death is understood and how grieving is construed. Thus, a unique "reachable moment" exists when, with the assistance of a well-trained clinical or pastoral caregiver, a mourner may be able to access relatively *dormant* intrinsic spirituality and utilize it to cope with one of life's ubiquitous challenges, the death of a close loved one.

As mentioned regarding assessment strategies, discreet probing could steer the discussion with the bereaved individual toward spiritual experiences as a potential coping tool. A sensitive interrogative may be asking whether the survivor has a background of religious faith that could inform his/her efforts to answer the existential questions evoked by death. Or, the interviewer could inquire whether the mourner is inclined to consider spiritual beliefs or a relationship with God (or a Higher Power) at times like these. Should the mourner successfully "reach" some latent spiritual experiences, he/she would be poised to realize the potential benefits our study has found—namely, reduced levels of negative grief affect and greater personal growth.

Two cautions are in order. First, in describing the possibilities of the "reachable moment," we are not advocating unwelcome, intrusive, or paternalistic proselytizing by caregivers at a time of high emotional vulnerability on the part of the mourner. Our message is not a clarion call to convert or to implant religious conviction where it does not pre-exist. Rather, our recommendation is to help mourners mobilize a potential source of inner strength (i.e., their own intrinsic spirituality) when facing the death of a loved one. We propose that some mourners may be gently encouraged to cultivate or deepen dormant, inactive spiritual beliefs both in how they understand death and in how they manage the emotional and psychological demands of grieving. In short, if the intrinsic spirituality is there, it may need to be awakened or activated. If it is not there (and not desired), the caregiver should refrain from attempting to impose it.

Second, the clinical or pastoral caregiver also needs to listen vigilantly for indications that the mourner's reasons for lower spiritual experience may be based on negative perceptions of God (or a Higher Power). In particular, we found anger at God to be a correlate of maladaptive grieving among Phase 1 participants of the Scott & White Grief Study (Williams, Gamino, Sewell, Easterling, & Stirman, 1998).

Intense anger and negative perceptions of God (or a Higher Power) would appear to be contraindications to promoting consideration of spiritual beliefs by the mourner. Callously pressing forward with suggestions to consider a spiritual perspective would likely serve to make matters worse by further aggravating the mourner and reinforcing his/her rejection of spiritual factors. Respect for the mourner and his/her sensibilities regarding spirituality remains a cardinal rule of competent clinical and pastoral caregiving.

CONCLUSION

Although beneficial effects of intrinsic spirituality on health in general and mental health in particular have been shown, the relation between spiritual experience and bereavement adaptation has been somewhat ambiguous. Data presented from the Scott & White Grief Study clearly indicated that higher levels of spiritual experience among mourners were associated with lower grief-related distress during the course of bereavement and greater personal growth as a bereavement outcome. Conversely, external religious behavior measured by church attendance appeared to have little meaningful association with the bereavement process. Theoretical as well as practical applications of these findings were discussed including the possible pathways by which spiritual experience may influence adaptation to bereavement. Finally, it was argued that the death of a loved one poses an existential challenge to the mourner that may create a "reachable moment" in which those with dormant or inactive spirituality could be encouraged to consider meaningfully the role of spiritual experience in bereavement adaptation. It remains our hope that continuing research will elucidate ways in which psychology and theology can jointly contribute to our understanding of the dynamics of bereavement, and offer directions for sensitive caregiving with the bereaved.

REFERENCES

Allport, G. W., & Ross, J. M. (1967). Personal religious orientation and prejudice. *Journal of Personality and Social Psychology, 5*, 432-443.

Donahue, M. J. (1985). Intrinsic and extrinsic religiousness: Review and meta-analysis. *Journal of Personality and Social Psychology, 48,* 400-419.

Easterling, L. W., Gamino, L. A., Sewell, K. W., & Stirman, L. S. (2000). Spirituality, church attendance and bereavement. *The Journal of Pastoral Care, 54,* 263-275.

Edmonds, S., & Hooker, K. (1992). Perceived changes in life meaning following bereavement. *Omega, 25,* 307-318.

Frantz, T. T., Tolley, B. C., & Johll, M. P. (1996). Religious aspects of bereavement. *Pastoral Psychology, 44,* 151-163.

Gamino, L. A., Sewell, K. W., & Easterling, L. W. (2000). Scott & White Grief Study—Phase 2: Toward an adaptive model of grief. *Death Studies, 24,* 633-660.

Gamino, L. A., Sewell, K. W., Easterling, L. W., & Stirman, L. S. (2000). Grief adjustment as influenced by funeral participation and occurrence of adverse funeral events. *Omega, 41,* 79-92.

Gorsuch, R. L. (1984). Measurement: The boon and bane of investigating religion. *American Psychologist, 39,* 228-236.

Gorsuch, R. L., & Miller, W. R. (1999). Assessing spirituality. In W. R. Miller (Ed.). *Integrating spirituality into treatment: Resources for practitioners.* Washington, DC: American Psychological Association.

Gorsuch, R. L., & Venable, G. D. (1983). Development of an "Age Universal" I-E scale. *Journal for the Scientific Study of Religion, 22,* 181-187.

Graham-Pole, J., Wass, H., Eyberg, S., Chu, L., & Olejnik, S. (1989). Communicating with dying children and their siblings: A retrospective analysis. *Death Studies, 13,* 465-483.

Hogan, N. S., Greenfield, D. B., & Schmidt, L. A. (2001). Development and validation of the Hogan Grief Reaction Checklist. *Death Studies, 25,* 1-32.

Hogan, N. S., Morse, J. M., & Tason, M. C. (1996). Toward an experiential theory of bereavement. *Omega, 33,* 43-65.

Hoge, D. R. (1972). A validated intrinsic religious motivation scale. *Journal for the Scientific Study of Religion, 11,* 369-376.

Kass, J. D., Friedman, R., Leserman, J., Zuttermeister, P. C., & Benson, H. (1991). Health outcomes and a new index of spiritual experience. *Journal for the Scientific Study of Religion, 30,* 203-211.

Klass, D., Silverman, P. R., & Nickman, S. L. (1996). *Continuing bonds: New understandings of grief.* Washington, DC: Taylor & Francis.

Koenig, H. G., George, L. K., & Peterson, B. L. (1998). Religiosity and remission of depression in medically ill older patients. *American Journal of Psychiatry, 155,* 536-542.

Levy, L. H., Martinkowski, K. S., & Derby, J. F. (1994). Differences in patterns of adaptation in conjugal bereavement: Their sources and potential significance. *Omega, 29,* 71-87.

Lieberman, M. (1996). *Doors close, doors open: Widows, grieving and growing.* New York: G. P. Putnam.

Maton, K. I. (1989). The stress-buffering role of spiritual support: Cross-sectional and prospective investigations. *Journal for the Scientific Study of Religion, 28,* 310-323.

Miller, W. R., & Thoresen, C. E. (1999). Spirituality and Health. In W. R. Miller (Ed.), *Integrating spirituality into treatment: Resources for practitioners.* Washington, DC: American Psychological Association.

Rosik, C. H. (1989). The impact of religious orientation in conjugal bereavement among older adults. *International Journal of Aging and Human Development, 28,* 251-260.

Sanders, C. M., Mauger, P. A., & Strong, P. N., Jr. (1985). *A manual for the Grief Experience Inventory.* Palo Alto, CA: Consulting Psychologists Press.

Tedeschi, R. G., & Calhoun, L. G. (1996). The posttraumatic growth inventory: Measuring the positive legacy of trauma. *Journal of Traumatic Stress, 9,* 455-471.

Vachon, M. L. S., Rogers, J., Lyall, W. A., Lancee, W. J., Sheldon, A. R., & Freeman, S. J. J. (1982). Predictors and correlates of adaptation to conjugal bereavement. *American Journal of Psychiatry, 139,* 998-1002.

VandeCreek, L., Ayres, S., & Bassham, M. (1995). Using INSPIRIT to conduct spiritual assessments. *The Journal of Pastoral Care, 49,* 83-89.

Williams, A. M., Gamino, L. A., Sewell, K. W., Easterling, L. W., & Stirman, L. S. (1998). A content and comparative analysis of loss in adaptive and maladaptive grievers. *Journal of Personal and Interpersonal Loss, 3,* 349-368.

Worden, J. W. (2002). *Grief counseling and grief therapy: A handbook for the mental health practitioner* (3rd ed.). New York: Springer.

Yalom, I. D. (1980). *Existential psychotherapy.* New York: Basic.

Yalom, I. D., & Lieberman, M. A. (1991). Bereavement and heightened existential awareness. *Psychiatry, 54,* 334-345.

Zinnbauer, B. J., Pargament, K. I., Cole, B., Rye, M. S., Butter, E. M., Belavich, T. G., Hipp, K. M., Scott, A. B., & Kadar, J. L. (1997). Religion and spirituality: Unfuzzying the fuzzy. *Journal for the Scientific Study of Religion, 36,* 549-564.

CHAPTER 2

The Death of a Spouse: A Spiritual and Psychological Crisis

Susan J. Zonnebelt-Smeenge
and Robert C. DeVries

The death of one's spouse invariably has a profound effect on both a person's spiritual and psychological condition. Regardless of one's religious frame of reference, the death of a spouse triggers questions about the deepest meaning of life. Couples, especially those in a healthy marriage, tend to define a significant portion of their individual lives relative to each other. To some extent their identities seem to blend together. Intricately woven into their marriage relationship is the fundamental question each person must face for him/herself, namely, the question of the "meaning of existence." Shared dreams and visions, similar values and perspectives, and generally consistent religious beliefs often constitute a part of the bond holding their relationship together. When a spouse dies, a person's spiritual and psychological well-being is shaken, eliciting numerous questions which now beg for an answer.

This chapter will examine the spiritual and psychological implications of bereavement following the death of a spouse. First, the important relationship between spirituality and psychology will be considered, especially in the light of a growing integration of these fields. A consideration of what constitutes spirituality will follow, particularly when viewed through the lens of "the soul." The chapter will conclude with a discussion of the psychological and spiritual implications of the tasks of grief applied specifically to spousal loss. These tasks of grief represent what a bereaved spouse can intentionally do in order to move toward a healthy resolution of grief.

This chapter is written from two basic perspectives. As a registered nurse and a licensed clinical psychologist, Susan J. Zonnebelt-Smeenge has engaged in research and clinical practice dealing with grief and loss issues. Robert C. DeVries, as a theologian and pastor, has ministered to the bereaved and reflected pastorally on the issues of death and dying. Together they have conducted workshops and spoken at national and international conferences on issues associated with death and bereavement following the publication of their book *Getting to the Other Side of Grief: Overcoming the Loss of a Spouse* (1998). They have also written *The Empty Chair: Handling Grief on the Holidays and Other Special Occasions* (2001) which deals with managing the holidays in the face of the grief following the death of a loved one—a spouse, parent, child, sibling, or friend. In addition, both authors have personally experienced the death of their first spouses. As a result, they speak from *within* the issue as well as observing the issue of bereavement clinically and pastorally.

PSYCHOLOGY AND RELIGION: MOVING TOWARD EACH OTHER

The disciplines of psychology and religion have historically been intentionally kept separate. This earlier position (in the 1950s–1970s) held that religious values and beliefs should be kept out of psychotherapy (Patterson, 1958). However, in recent years an important movement toward integrating these disciplines has emerged. Psychotherapists and clergy are recognizing the need for a holistic approach to one's physical, emotional, social, and spiritual aspects (Bilich, Bonfiglio, & Carson, 2000; Karasu, 1999; McMinn, Chaddock, Campbell, Edwards, & Lim, 1998). In 1992 the American Psychological Association adopted a statement obligating psychologists to recognize a client's religious values and conflicts in their Ethical Principles of Psychologists and Code of Conduct. Hence, as they consider issues related to spousal loss, a therapist or other caregiver would be remiss in excluding the spiritual perspective and only addressing the client's psychological issues. How widowed people conceptualize values and religious beliefs has a definite impact on their grief journey. The loss experience may alter a bereaved person's spiritual beliefs, values, and behaviors. Who a person was, both psychologically and spiritually, prior to the death of their partner will have a significant impact on the outcome of the grief journey. The grief journey will likely also have a significant impact on that person's psychological and spiritual perspective.

For members of helping professions who deal with widowed people, we believe it is extremely important that they understand the bereaved person's religious beliefs and values and assess the degree to which the client's beliefs might be in conflict with their own. The client's beliefs might also be outside the competence of a caregiver. In these cases an appropriate referral is recommended so that the religious issues can be addressed. If a widowed client has acknowledged religious beliefs, these need to be addressed responsibly in order to proceed effectively with therapy. Mental health workers are increasingly in agreement that they need to integrate a client's spiritual perspective into the therapy process in order to be therapeutically and professionally responsible.

DEFINING SPIRITUALITY

Terms such as "faith," "belief," "religion," and "spirituality" are used almost inter-changeably. Each term, however, has its own distinct point of reference, and the terms need to be clarified to give rightful definition to each.

"Spirituality" refers to a person's basic orientation to a sense of Being, Power, or Existence which is beyond the physical, tangible, or observable. This "power" need not be personal, nor does this "power" necessarily maintain a relationship with humanity. On the other hand, spirituality can refer to a deeply personal relationship with a personal God nurtured through a series of spiritual disciplines. The term "spirituality" will be used in this chapter to refer to the broadest and most inclusive orientation a person maintains toward that (divine) power which is "beyond" us.

"Faith" is the corresponding conscious commitment to the object of one's spiritu-ality. Through "faith" a person attempts to conform his/her cognitions, affections, and behaviors to the perceived expectations of this divine power.

"Religion" consists of the ritual and life-style practice of one's faith. Faith, which can remain largely internal and unobservable, expresses itself ritualistically in the practice of a religion. Within this religious frame of reference, the person (generally in cooperation with like-minded "believers") develops a set of "beliefs" which are conceptual, cognitive expressions of the core values and commitments which arise from one's religion.

Therefore, a certain taxonomy emerges in reference to these terms. Spirituality serves as the foundational concept, followed by faith, religion, and belief—each becoming more observable and specific to a person's socio-cultural setting, per-sonality, and needs.

In this chapter, the focus will be primarily on the deepest issue of spirituality, though occasionally the arenas of faith, religion, and belief will be referenced. A focus on spirituality also serves to cast an ecumenical umbrella over a number of religious expressions. The principles which follow are generally applicable to all religious orientations, be they Christian, Jewish, Muslim, or some other faith.

THE SOUL:
THE CENTER OF SPIRITUALITY

The term "soul" is often used in a variety of settings, especially associated with spirituality. As a single word, "soul" can refer to anything from a genre of music to the deepest and most profound point of identity of a person. Rachael Kessler (2000) presents a helpful analysis by identifying seven primary components of the soul. While her interest is in education—especially educating the "whole person"—Kessler's categories are helpful in this discussion. We have taken her categories and applied them specifically to the grief arena.

The first, and likely the center piece of her theory, is that the soul represents a yearning for *deep connection*. This connection is sought with one's self, others, nature, and/or a higher power. The death of a spouse obviously has an impact on this "soul issue," for most often the spousal relationship is the deepest and most intimate relationship two individuals can have in this world. Death breaks that deep connectedness.

Kessler also characterizes the "soul" as a longing for *silence and solitude*. The Old Testament, which serves as an authoritative word for both Jews and Christians, speaks of sensing one's nearness to God in times of quietness, solitude, and silence (Psalm 23, Psalm 49). Those who are bereaved because of the death of their spouse often need encouragement to seek solitude and silence in order to face their fears, find spiritual peace, and reestablish a center to their spiritual sense. Solitude also provides the bereaved person the necessary context for identifying and reflecting on issues that need to be faced in the grief process.

The search for *meaning and purpose* is also a significant part of the soul. A formulation of a "world-view" is essential to a normal, healthy life. One needs a sense of purpose and direction. The death of a spouse often dislodges or eradicates that sense of purpose and direction while raising fundamental spiritual questions—even pointed questions about the existence of God, God's concern for his people, and why this bereaved person was "selected" by a loving God to suffer this tragedy.

The soul also consists of a hunger for *joy and delight*. Kessler is careful to point out that soul issues do not eliminate the delightful to focus only on the somber and serious. Nearly all religions suggest a form of happiness, Nirvana, blessedness, or joy as an essential part of their belief system. Those thrust into grief following the death of a spouse often grieve not only the death of a partner but all the "good times" they had, and still might have had together, if their spouse had not died. An essential part of the grief process is to help persons begin to find those elements in their lives which they can celebrate and for which they can be grateful.

The soul also is the seat of the *creative drive*. Sometimes referred to as the indomitable human spirit, the soul ultimately does not want to accept defeat. This creative drive urges the person to seek new life. On the other hand, grief can sometimes be so over-powering that this creative drive is diminished or removed. Through healthy mental health practices, the soul can restore its drive and the grieving person can arrive at the point of re-creating a life which is as rich, rewarding, and as fulfilling as before the death.

The soul also represents the *urge for the transcendent*. When under great stress, such as experiencing the death of a spouse, most people still turn to a higher power, or God, for guidance, power, and consolation. They also turn to this sense of the transcendent in order to put their "smaller" life in perspective within the grand picture. They want to make some "meaning" of the death which has occurred, and this meaning often is found only when one considers the death from a cosmological perspective. This, however, is a process and usually takes considerable time as a bereaved person works through the grief journey.

Finally, Kessler indicates that the soul contains the *need for initiation*. While grief may temporarily incapacitate a person, resulting in a somewhat passive orientation to the forces that envelop them, ultimately the need to take control can win out. Control, however, does not always return. Some people get stuck in their grief and are not able to move into an exciting and fulfilling life again. The work of grief is *not* a passive process. A bereaved person needs to find ways at various points in the grief journey to be deliberate and intentional about engaging in grief work.

Hopefully the description of these components of the soul is helpful for understanding a number of issues facing a bereaved spouse. Kessler's approach, however, can be enhanced when layered with the diagram in Figure 1 which highlights the relationship between spirituality and psychology. In this approach, the soul is the nexus of three forms of intimacy: intimacy with self; intimacy with others; and intimacy with God.

Intimacy with Self

The soul is referred to as the essence of what makes each of us a unique human creature distinguishable from each other. This is our private and solitary self. The soul is that part of us that does not die either spiritually (depending on one's religious beliefs) or in the memories of those who have become emotionally and psychologically close to us. Our degree of connectedness, or degree of closeness, with another person while they are alive has a profound impact on us. This is particularly true in the case of a spouse. One of the ways individuals experience growth and development is from meaningful relationships. So it could be said that we are in part an accumulation of our interactions and experiences with others. Healthy spouses typically grow close by sharing their lives together. When a partner dies, the widowed person often feels that a part of them died. They often feel as if they are no longer complete or whole. This, of course, is simply not so. We are still complete individuals in and of ourselves. But this sense of incompleteness is very real for the bereaved. This painful sensation is even more pointed in a marital relationship in which the spouses may have become co-dependent or enmeshed. This enmeshment can disrupt the intimacy with oneself and may create a feeling of being incomplete following a

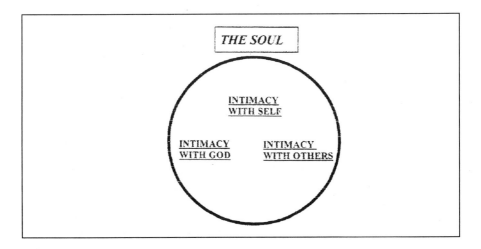

Figure 1. The soul.

partner's death. The amount of time a bereaved person may want to spend in solitude or private reflection depends on several factors, including the type of coupled relationship, the personality structure of each person, and their life-style choices. Our society tends to avoid pain and desires instant cures. Distractions such as busyness or getting back "into the swing of things" may look quite appealing. However, such distractions do not allow enough solitude for the soul and therefore rob time necessary for deeper thought and reflection.

The condition of one's soul prior to experiencing spousal loss is also a significant factor in the grieving process. A person who has at his/her core a healthy soul will be able to eventually see some good in their circumstance as the grieving proceeds, e.g., "it's awful that he had to die, but we did have a happy life together." Being congruent with oneself (i.e., aligning what a person thinks and feels with that person's behavior) will undoubtedly help maintain integrity for those who are grieving which, in turn, will promote self-esteem. When a person does not balance time for solitude with the companionship of others, withdrawal can lead to depression and despair. Some widowed persons seem unable, or disinclined, to be their own companion or to choose to spend time alone, which contributes to a void in the capacity to experience intimacy with self.

Intimacy with Others

Maintaining balance seems to be the critical issue as intimacy with self is joined with intimacy with others. How we as human beings connect with others, and the nature of our relationships, speak to the definition of who we are—to the soul within us. In order to create healthy intimate relationships with family and friends, one needs to be open to higher levels of disclosure and intimacy. Sharing one's thoughts and feelings at a deep level not only creates intimacy but also creates an atmosphere in which the bereaved person can receive the care and support of others. This exchange creates a sense of knowing a person deeply, removing pretense from this exchange. Closeness and intimacy are generated. Within marriage this kind of connectedness is the closest of all human ties. So when a spouse dies, this profound sense of intimacy is gone. Frequently the termination of this deep relationship elicits intense and painful grief which can lead to the dark night of the soul.

Intimacy with God

Intimacy with God is the third element in the soul of a person. As noted earlier, we are created with a yearning to connect to someone outside of ourselves, a power or nature higher than who we are. Hence, people look for a spiritual object with whom they can feel connected, safe, and at peace. This is also woven into a deepened understanding of the purpose and meaning of life, and especially as it comes to expression in the life of the bereaved. People who believe that this higher power or God is ultimately in control of everything and above all wants good for each of us find comfort and security in that belief. The Protestant reformer John Calvin is often quoted in support of the reciprocal relationship between the knowledge of God and the knowledge of self (1953, I.1.i). He asserted that a person cannot truly know God in an intimate way unless he/she knows him/herself, and conversely an individual cannot truly know him/herself without having a true knowledge of God. In following this premise, we find further support for the interconnectedness among all three aspects of one's soul.

"SOUL" ISSUES RELATED TO THE DEATH AND BEREAVEMENT OF A SPOUSE

While it is virtually impossible to identify and address all of the issues associated with spirituality and the soul arising from the death of a spouse, four such issues are fairly common to persons working through their grief. These issues deal with God's role in the death of their spouse, their own role in that death, the reality of evil, and the relationship of this life to a sense of the "after-life."

God's Role in Death

Fundamental spiritual questions seem to arise regarding God's role in the death of a spouse. When their partner dies, a bereaved spouse frequently asks: "why did this happen?" and "where was God?" These questions elicit concern, anger, guilt, and a lack of peace and acceptance for those left behind. Our human nature wants an explanation for things that do not make sense or are unexpected. At the time of their beloved's death, the bereaved spouse asks "why?" If the widowed person believes in a higher power or has a personal relationship with God, they may feel compelled to determine how a God who is supposed to care personally for each individual (as in the biblical tradition of the Good Shepherd) could cause or allow this to happen. The proposed theory goes something like this. If God is all powerful (omnipotent) and all knowing (omniscient), then how could he allow this bad thing to happen?

Theoretically these questions probe the nature of God. Do we see God as a loving being who wants our good, or is God a vindictive ruler who eagerly waits to catch us doing something wrong and zap us with judgment and punishment? If a widowed person holds God directly responsible for "taking" the spouse or causing his/her death, the bereaved might see God as a robber or murderer. He would then either steal loved ones or actually have a hand in their murder. On the other hand, many Christians define God as a loving Father who cares for us. In that perspective God does not *cause* our loved one's death though he may *allow* it to happen. As human beings we must recognize that we all die some time. Death does happen—it is a certainty. Bad things happen to each of us on our life's journey regardless of who we are or how we choose to live our lives. We have very little control over some of the events of our lives, either negative or positive. Our only way to understand and accept the events that are evil is to determine our own perspective on this issue and then assess our options for subsequent behavior.

A widowed person might be helped by assisting him/her in formulating a spiritual explanation for why bad things happen. Answering for themselves the question of God's role in the death of their spouse may be very beneficial. This will allow the bereaved to develop a consistent explanation of the death which will hopefully put these profound questions to rest. In making some sense of why the death occurred, the bereaved can also work through existing anger and attain a sense of peace for the soul. Intimacy with God as a soul issue necessitates that the bereaved spouse eventually work through the question of the role of God in the death of their spouse.

Caregivers are reminded that it is essential for bereaved individuals to experience and express whatever feelings they have (e.g., anger, hurt, frustration) toward their sense of a higher power or God for whatever period of time it takes in order to work toward resolution of these questions for themselves. The caregiver can best assure the bereaved that negative feelings are normal, that God is big enough to see him/her shake their fist at God while asking "why?," and that a sense of closeness with God can be restored.

The Bereaved's Role in Death

A second issue often associated with "the soul" or one's spirituality following the death of a spouse is the role the bereaved may have assumed he/she had in the death of their spouse. Following the death of one's spouse, some bereaved persons have a sense of guilt or regret often fueled by the assumption that they did not do enough, or did not do the right thing, that might have prevented the death. This sense of regret can occur both when the death is sudden ("but I should have seen it coming!") or when the death was the result of an illness with a terminal diagnosis ("if only we had tried the other treatment!"). While this "soul" issue does have implication for one's intimacy with God, this issue tends to focus more on one's sense of intimacy with oneself and with others, especially their deceased spouse. The issue is one of control, of decisions made, or of second-guessing what might have happened. Part of the bereavement process is assisting the bereaved person to come to accept the limits of their control. They may need help in accepting the fact that they did not cause the death and in recognizing that everyone has their own time to die. Some people who are deeply religious may even think that if they (or their friends, congregations, and/or synagogues) had only prayed harder or had more faith, the death may have been prevented. The caregiver can help the bereaved person move these feelings of frustration and/or guilt into a more positive frame of reference, particularly in terms of what they can do now about their own grief. Within their spheres of influence and control, the bereaved person can use that energy, the need for initiation and the creative drive, in addressing their own pain of grief. Coming to a sense of peace with God themselves, and with their deceased spouse in the light of the death, is critical to a satisfying resolution to grief.

The Reality of Evil

It is important to acknowledge that bad things do occur regularly in this world. If we picture life as a journey beginning with birth and finishing with one's death, it would be inconceivable that anyone could complete their life journey without encountering negative, sad, and hurtful experiences along the way. In other words, evil is present. Valued jobs are lost, relationships once cherished are severed, children rebel against caring parents. This is the world we live in. There is disharmony and brokenness. What we hope for often does not happen. What we want to hold on to often slips away. When good times happen, we never want them to end. But in reality these happy moments are intermingled with difficult and agonizing times. Why? In one sense it is a matter of "corollaries." A corollary is a pair of words or concepts which depend on each other for their meaning and cannot exist independent of a reference to the other term. We really don't know or understand what happy is without its corollary of sadness. Opposites give each other meaning. Good and bad are corollaries. They co-exist and every life will experience both. At a deeper spiritual level the quest for understanding resides within us. We have already discussed the premise of God's role in the causation of death. We contend that death and pain are not really what God wants or originally intended in his created order. The Christian tradition confronts the reality of evil with the fall of the human race into sin as outlined in the Bible for it was then, according to the Bible, that humans would know the difference between good and evil. Humankind was given the freedom to choose obedience or experience evil. As a result of this decision, sin and evil entered this world and it now resides as a powerful force. Death is included in this force of evil.

Whether a person chooses the Christian interpretation or another religious philosophy, when an individual experiences the death of a life-partner, the hard question of why bad things happen begs for a response. Obviously, in our human weakness and frailty we can only grasp obscure answers, but somewhere in our grasping we need to factor in belief and faith in order to make some rudimentary sense of it.

The Sense of After-Life

A final issue of the "soul" is the bereaved person's sense of the "after-life" in contrast to "this world." Many religious people firmly believe that their deceased spouse is in a better place, and that place is characterized by perfection, pure joy, bliss, and/or eternal happiness. The down-side of that conviction is often a sense of regret that they are left behind in a situation fraught with imperfection, sadness, anxiety, and struggles. "Why could it not have been me?" is a question a bereaved spouse often asks. Or they at least deeply yearn to escape this world in order to join their deceased spouse in this joyful after-life. From the Christian perspective (as well as many other of the world's religions), the "soul" does live on in some form of immortality. The surviving spouse, however, must recognize that once this transition has occurred, the relationship they maintained with their spouse has ended. There is no indication, for example, in the Christian scripture that a marriage relationship is maintained beyond this world. What is more helpful than attempting to maintain some continuing bond with the deceased is to recognize that, as often vowed at the marriage altar, this marriage has ended with the death of one of the partners. The challenge for the bereaved person is to continue to focus on "this life," to generate the motivation to re-invest in this world and find some way in which life on this earth can be rich and rewarding once again. Because this task often appears overwhelming to the bereaved, we propose framing the grief process around five main tasks, adapted primarily from the research of Worden (1990).

THE TASKS OF GRIEF AND THEIR IMPLICATIONS FOR SPOUSAL DEATH

Elisabeth Kübler-Ross (1969) is rightly credited with raising our initial awareness of the dying process by her development of the stages of dying with their attendant emotional components. Her work initiated continued research not only of the internal and external processes associated with dying, but of death and bereavement as well. Most of the current literature has abandoned reference to "stages" (or later, "phases") in preference for understanding the grief process as consisting of a number of "tasks." The movement has been away from the regimented stage theory of both dying and grief to this more heuristic task modality. The value of referring to the grief process in a task framework is that it fits with the perception that grieving consists of intentional "work" (the term first used by Sigmund Freud (1957) in his writings in 1914) rather than assuming that grief consists of passive endurance ("just give it time"). A bereaved person benefits from being active, intentional, and deliberate in the process of grieving. In other words, there are certain necessary and beneficial reflections, processes, and activities a grieving individual needs to do in order to journey to the other side of grief. These grief tasks become specific expressions of a deeper rhythm that we all face in the changes associated with loss through death.

One benefit in construing the grief process in terms of tasks is that the tasks are not ordered or progressive. Rather, they are bits and pieces of one unified process interspersed, sometimes simultaneously with each other. The grief process is analogous to putting a puzzle together. There are as many ways of accomplishing the task as there are individuals engaged in the activity. Only when the puzzle is complete can the person sit back and appreciate the entire picture for what it is and declare the task to "be done." Hence, there are generally no abrupt changes throughout the grief process, but rather a slow growth or development as these tasks are addressed. C. S. Lewis refers to this in *A Grief Observed* where he writes: "There was no sudden, striking, and emotional transition. Like the warming of a room, or the coming of daylight, when you first notice them they have already been going on for some time" (1963, p. 49). Following the death of his wife, Lewis had discovered that "stages" or "steps" of grief did not express adequately his experience. Grief is a journey, a slow journey. Finding out who one is without their loved one takes time and work. There is no one uniform way to grieve, no right or wrong way. Everyone's grief journey is a unique expression of a common experience. As a caregiver you can serve a significant role in sharing your knowledge of the tasks of grief and pointing out how they can benefit a bereaved spouse by working through the issues associated with each task. Working faithfully on these tasks enables a bereaved spouse to reach a sense of resolution of grief and develop a readiness to move on with life.

Task #1: Recognize and Accept the Fact that His/Her Partner has Died and is Unable to Return

From a mental health perspective, it is necessary (but difficult) for a bereaved spouse to initially realize the finality of their spouse's death. This may sound obvious, but the yearning that exists for the beloved one's presence is a powerful force leading frequently to temporary hallucinations, dreams of the deceased, and/or a sense of his/her presence surrounding the bereaved. The widowed person may be able to cognitively comprehend and discuss his/her spouse's death, but the emotional longing may express itself in searching for the partner upon returning home, wanting to phone the deceased with a message, or even expecting the spouse to walk into the room. A caregiver can do a number of things to encourage a widowed person to accept that their partner is not returning and that the marriage is over. For example, encourage the widowed spouse to use the words "dead" and "died" rather than euphemisms like "gone," "passed away," or "in another place" when talking about his/her deceased partner. Encourage the bereaved to return to his/her home alone as soon as the bereaved person feels even somewhat comfortable. A desensitization period with appropriate support may be useful, but often family and friends do not recognize that acceptance and growth comes by facing the pain rather than avoiding it. The bereaved person might also be encouraged to go out alone with couples with whom the bereaved spouse and deceased partner had socialized. In doing this, the bereaved spouse will face the reality that there is an empty place in the car or at the table as the group gathers. Eventually this can encourage the bereaved spouse in adjusting to the odd number (vs. even) in a group setting. This may also encourage the energy to develop new relationships with others who are single. Differentiating between being alone and being lonely takes some effort. Loneliness is one of the most challenging struggles in spousal loss. The separation process is painful and takes time coupled with a number of personal experiences which eventually demonstrate that one is a whole number. He/she can be adequate in and with her/himself.

This task also has implications for the bereaved person's sense of spirituality. As noted above, many religious practices are notorious in obfuscating or confusing the bereaved on the issue of death. The fascination with immortality, the after-life, and/or heaven can be used to avoid facing the reality and finality of death. While the soul does seek deeper connections with a sense of the transcendent, we encourage the bereaved to transfer their need for affiliation and belonging from the deceased to other important connections that remain in this world. In addition, the bereaved should be encouraged to see their sense of the Divine as one of stability and constancy. Even in the face of death, God is present. In most religious orientations, God is a source of power, comfort, and guidance, especially in traumatic situations such as the death of a spouse. The bereaved person ultimately needs to accept that, from a human viewpoint, a person rarely dies "on time." We either die too early or too late, but rarely when the time is just right from our perspective. From God's perspective, however, this person's life has had meaning; the person did fulfill a purpose; and the bereaved person continues to have a reason for his/her existence beyond the relationship he/she had maintained in the marriage.

Task #2: Allow the Bereaved to Experience All the Feelings Associated with the Death of Their Spouse

To know oneself is deemed a healthy goal. From a mental health perspective, self-knowledge is an essential developmental task for adolescents and emerging adults. "Who am I?" is the fervent question of young people. However, the answer is not static. It is fluid and ever changing. And the question is not only for the young. That question arises again and again throughout our lives and begs for redefinition each time we encounter one of life's changes or transitions. The death of a spouse commands that a bereaved spouse revisit the "who am I?" question as a result of the drastic change in his/her life structure. To be aware of what one thinks, feels, wants, and needs is of utmost importance to live life in a fulfilling and satisfying manner. How well an individual is able to identify and express his/her feelings is important throughout all of life. But a knowledge of oneself comes as well in relation to others. Self-knowledge is of major significance in becoming intimate with oneself and also with others. As humans we are much more than our cognitive side using logical reasoning to make sense of things. We also have feelings, our emotional aspect which affects how we perceive ourselves and our surrounding environment.

When a person experiences the death of a partner his/her feelings must be given credibility and freedom of expression. Grief consists of a number of feelings. If these feelings are not acknowledged and become internalized, they can contribute to depression or manifest themselves in physical ways.

Caregivers, therefore, might encourage the recognition and normalization of the feelings associated with the death, such as feelings of anger, guilt, sadness, remorse, and relief. Journaling and letter-writing are excellent emotional outlets which will assist the bereaved in gaining self-awareness and deepening their understanding of their grief. In so doing, they will also be helping in making decisions about what to do with their various feelings. Caregivers can reassure widowed individuals that there is no "right way" to feel or deal with feelings. Support them in behaving congruently with their feelings and resist the pressure to conform to others' expectations. Grief is an individualized journey—a journey through feelings. An essential aspect of that journey is to name and deal with feelings without suppressing them or distracting oneself.

From the spiritual perspective, the bereaved also need to sense the freedom to express their emotions subsequent to the death of their spouse. Our experience within the Christian tradition is that some believers so focus on the pressure to be "happy" and to "rejoice always" that they develop a sense of guilt over feelings of anger (at God, their deceased spouse, others, and/or themselves), regret, frustration, fear, and a myriad of other "negative" emotions. In using religious beliefs and writings, clergy sometimes minimize the pain, avoid full expression of feelings, and subtly encourage the bereaved to "get back to normal" as quickly as possible. This misrepresents the Christian Bible. Especially in the Old Testament, believers are encouraged to "lament." The Jewish believer is given the freedom to wail in God's presence, to question God's righteousness, and to accuse God of injustice *while still* maintaining a solid faith in God. The story is told of a Jewish Rabbi incarcerated in a concentration camp during World War II. Out of frustration for the atrocities that were occurring in the camp, the Rabbi put God on trial. All day long the inmates accused God, weighed in the balance God's role in their circumstance, and at 5:00 P.M. the Rabbi's gavel fell pronouncing God guilty for their incarceration. Immediately following the declaration of guilt, the Rabbi then said, "Now, it is time for prayers." The bereaved must have the freedom to lament and wail in the presence of their God, confident that their omnipotent God will still ultimately redeem them. Hence, the soul often seeks silence in the presence of God, confident that God will work through their efforts to push through their grief into a renewed life.

Task #3: Find a Place for Memories of the Deceased Spouse Which Honors What They Had Together But Also Make Room to Move On

Memories are reminders of the past which live in our hearts and minds. They signify that portion of our life which is now past. At whatever age a person is widowed, he/she has undoubtedly stored many memories from childhood, adolescence, and young adulthood—all periods of time before the deceased partner even became part of his/her life. The lifeline concept is helpful in seeing the progression of our life in which both pleasant and painful memories are intertwined. They now reside in the memory and can be recalled at will. We move on, and we remember. People who have been widowed need to understand the importance of sorting through the various aspects of their marriage by writing a summary of their coupled time together, making a picture album or scrapbook, arranging slides, re-reading cards and love letters, going through souvenirs or mementoes from occasions together, and removing their spouse's clothing and possessions which are no longer usable by the bereaved partner as they remember their loved one.

Sorting through one's memories means that a widowed person does not forget his/her beloved partner. However, he/she also becomes ready to move on in life rather than to cling to the past. In working at this task the widowed person begins to accept at a deeper level the reality of his/her partner's death. But he/she also begins to realize that he/she has a life which has meaning and purpose in this world. A person cannot focus and live in the past and still enjoy the present with eyes set with hope toward the future.

From the spiritual perspective, this task also requires the bereaved person to begin to formulate a basic explanation for the death—an explanation which addresses the deeper issues of life. Finding this deeper explanation for changes in life requires that a person begins to see his/her life as a journey, passing through a number of natural milestones. This also means that life is continual change, for each day begins anew. Obviously the death of a spouse is a major transition, but when one examines the facts objectively, one begins to realize that very few married couples die simultaneously. One of the partners will be widowed. So one way to "make meaning of the loss" is simply to accept the death as part of "nature's way."

On the other end of the continuum, a person can view the death as God's will and, by some form of faith, capitulate to God's decision. The point here is that the bereaved person needs to find some way to explain the fact of death, with particular application to the death of their spouse. The explanation also frees them to continue to move on in their own life. When this is accomplished, the life of their deceased partner takes on a new form in the shape of memories. The period of their marriage becomes a complete volume, as did other periods in their life such as adolescence, years in high school, or a period of time they might have lived in a different locality.

Emotionally and spiritually separating oneself from their deceased spouse is, however, extremely challenging, especially when (at least in the Christian tradition) clergy tend to emphasize the permanency of marriage. In their attempt to counter rising divorce rates and infidelity within marriage, clergy tend to speak about life-long commitments, faithfulness, Christian "covenant," and vows to God. When the death of a spouse occurs, the question then must be faced on how well the clergy (and others) also assist the bereaved person in recognizing that the marriage is over, and that their task is now to begin to separate from that deceased person emotionally and spiritually in order to build a life independent of their former spouse.

Task #4: Adjust to Life as a Single Person by Deciding Who He/She is as an Individual without a Partner

From a mental health perspective, each bereaved person needs to recognize that her/his life is ultimately an individual journey. Persons who have blended and compromised their lives together in complementary ways may find it difficult to also realize that they were their own unique person before they met, remained an individual within their marriage, and now must redefine this individuality after one of them dies. A sense of individuality and separateness is often lost in a marriage because of the inter-weaving of two lives. The "I" gets woven into the "we." This creates a particularly challenging situation for a bereaved spouse for it now means viewing onself alone without a partner, and yet as a whole, complete individual.

Referring to oneself as single subsequent to the death of a partner is frequently the antithesis of what a bereaved spouse desires. Even though the term "widowed" may not be appealing, it is far more palatable at least initially for many who are widowed than the term "single." The widowed person likely feels so very connected to the deceased that the idea of being separated is repulsive. It is often a long process through the grief journey before this sense of being adequate alone becomes acceptable.

In American society the wedding ring is a symbol of one's union and commitment to another. With a spouse's death the marital contract has ended, and so the widowed person is no longer married. Eventually removing one's wedding ring from the fourth finger of the left hand acknowledges that the individual has accepted the reality of one's partner's death and that he/she is now single.

The spiritual issues associated with this task tend to focus around the issue of self-identity and self-esteem. Especially in the Christian tradition, these issues often express themselves in one of two ways: either in the sense that a person is not complete unless in a coupled relationship, or that a person should not "feel good" about themself because he/she is a "sinner." The creation story in the book of Genesis is often used to emphasize that man (Adam) was not meant to be alone so God created woman (Eve) as a companion. While this obviously is the basis for a marriage relationship, the story is often mis-interpreted to mean that we are not whole or complete as an individual. We often overlook the fact that even in the Christian scripture, there are consistent references to individual responsibility and duties independent of married life. The Apostle Paul was not married and even, at one point, urged others to be like him and consulted against marriage unless a person was not able to contain him/herself sexually (I Corinthians 7:7). The bereaved person can benefit from the constant reminder that we did come into this world individually from our mother's womb. We will likely die individually. We each have our own unique personality, characteristics, passions, and weaknesses. Spiritually, God maintains a personal, individual relationship with each of his human creatures.

A sense of sin, the second factor which may be a barrier to developing a sense of appropriate self-esteem, is also a major factor in a number of religious traditions. The sense of being a sinner, and hence "unworthy," is often so pervasive in some traditions that the person dare not accept themself as a whole, complete person. A bereaved spouse can benefit from the clergy giving suggestions to the bereaved person on how he/she might focus on him/herself, learn to understand how they are an individual creation of God, and know that he/she has the full right (even responsibility!) to pursue individual interests and dreams as a new sense of meaning is carved out.

Task #5: Reinvest in Life According to One's Own Desires and Interests

Following on the heels of the task of figuring out who one is independent of the relationship with the deceased spouse is the challenge to fully reinvest in life. Once a widowed person has separated his/her identity from the prior relationship with their spouse, this person must now set the course for their future journey as a single individual. Their life may look very different than before because, with the death of a spouse, the old ways no longer fit. Or the bereaved person may basically continue with adaptations of the same direction, but their life will still look and feel different.

A person truly begins again when she/he can draw on the accumulated wisdom from the past and reinvest that in the future. The marriage may have ended, but she/he have been changed (hopefully in a positive direction) from the experience. In a real sense, reinvestment in life is a hallelujah for a life well spent with the deceased spouse but also a recognition that all is not lost and that a new volume of life can now be written. Hopefully the bereaved will have learned the importance of self-advocacy and congruence during this grief journey expressed through self-care, assertiveness, and boundary setting. These are not only ways to heal but also to prepare for the yet uncharted phase of life which is now beginning.

The spiritual implications of this task often evidence themselves initially in religious practices. Some people may be tempted to encourage the bereaved person to "return to normal" as quickly as possible by assuming, or even stating, that this bereaved person should return to the same worship and religious involvement he/she had maintained prior to the death of their spouse. The fact of the matter is that the bereaved's involvement pattern will probably *not* remain the same. Returning to "normal" is a figment of one's imagination. The old "normal" no longer exists. A new "normal" is being fashioned, but this will be a pattern of behavior which will likely be somewhat (if not highly) different from the former.

In addition to the pattern of behavior, a bereaved spouse may very likely experience some significant shifts in their belief system. Their faith will be affected by this death experience. The clergy can profitably use this as an occasion to assist the bereaved in developing a more finely nuanced faith through integrating the loss into their belief system and developing the freedom to celebrate their refined sense of spirituality in a wide variety of ways.

CONCLUSION

Rahe, Ryman, and Ward (1980) have suggested that the death of a spouse is the highest stress-producing experience one can have in life. Needless to say, such stress creates both psychological and spiritual turmoil. Collaboration between psychologists and clergy is critical in addressing these deep issues. This collaboration, however, must also focus on an intentional and active grief process which can ultimately result in the resolution of the grief and a reentry to a fully satisfying and rich life.

REFERENCES

Bilich, M., Bonfigli, S., & Carlson, S. (2000). *Shared grace: Therapists and clergy working together.* New York, London, Oxford: The Haworth Pastoral Press.

Calvin, J. (1953). *The Institutes of the Christian Religion,* H. Beveridge (trans.), Grand Rapids, MI: William B. Eerdmans.

Freud, S. (1957). Mourning and melancholia. *Collected Papers, Volume 14.* London: Hogarth.

Karasu, T. B. (1999). Spiritual psychotherapy. *American Journal of Psychotherapy, 53*(2), 143-162.

Kessler, R. (2000). *The soul of education.* Alexandria, VA: Association for Supervision and Curriculum Development.

Kübler-Ross, E. (1969). *On death and dying.* New York: Macmillan Company.

Lewis, C. S. (1963). *A grief observed.* Greenwich, CT: Seabury Press.

McMinn, M. R., Chaddock, T. P., Campbell, C. D., Edwards, L. C., & Lim, B. R. K. B. (1998). Psychologists collaborating with clergy. *Professional Psychology: Research and Practice, 29*(6), 564-570.

Patterson, C. H. (1958) The place of values in counseling and psychotherapy. *Journal of Counseling Psychology, 5,* 216-223.

Rahe, R. H., Ryman, D., & Ward, H. (1980). Simplified scaling for life change events. *Journal of Human Stress, 6*(4), 22-26.

Worden, W. J. (1990). *Grief counseling and grief therapy* (2nd ed.). New York: Springer.

Zonnebelt-Smeenge, S. J., & DeVries, R. C. (1998). *Getting to the other side of grief: Overcoming the loss of a spouse.* Grand Rapids, MI: Baker Book House Company.

Zonnebelt-Smeenge, S. J., & DeVries, R. C. (2001). *The empty chair: Handling grief on the holidays and other special occasions.* Grand Rapids, MI: Baker Book House Company.

CHAPTER 3

For Those Who Stand and Wait

Kent Koppelman

Let me tell you something . . . I'm not done grieving yet, and I don't care who knows it!

The tombstone makes no response. Of course, I wasn't really talking to it. I was simply talking out loud and it was simply there, mute as always. It was Sunday. It was a sunny Sunday and I had decided to drive around for a while. I like to do that on the weekend when it's sunny and warm. I drive around and notice what other people are doing. On this particular day, I saw two children playing on the swings at one of the city's parks. Their mothers sat on a bench talking and laughing because it was Sunday and the sun was shining and their kids were playing and it's still too early for mosquitoes.

Before I return home, I like to stop at Oak Grove Cemetery to visit my "family." That's how I think of them, like an extended family. There's Baby Harley with the toy trucks he must have liked to play with nestled next to the stone with his name and dates. There's Katie with three balloons carved on her stone, floating above her forever, each one representing two years of her brief life. I nod my head solemnly for the veterans of wars both foreign and domestic (there are graves from the Civil War). Many of the markers for Moms and Dads say "Parents of . . ." and list the names of their children. I like that. The stones say to me: whatever else we were, whatever else we did, the best thing about our lives was the children we leave behind.

Some markers whisper clues to passing strangers to provoke speculation about their story. A man born in 1949 died in 1982, and the name next to his was a boy born in 1975 who died in 1991—just sixteen, just beginning a life. Is this a father and son lying next to each other? Did the father die in an accident? Did the son share a similar fate or did he take his own life? Whatever the truth of this tale, it is a tragic one. Somewhere a wife and mother lives with a heavy heart. Were there brothers and sisters? The stone doesn't say.

Most of the people buried in this cemetery are white, but such things as race or gender or social class don't matter much here. Death is the great equalizer and the cemetery is the promised paradise, a place of harmony where the Lion lies down with the Lamb. There are a few huge monuments which proclaim the names of Hixon or Hood, attempting to maintain the dignity and status that money provided during one's lifetime, but big or small, the markers have the same message: beneath this stone is the remains of a life where no life remains.

Although there is racial homogeneity, there is some ethnic diversity. Anderson and Johnson and Peterson and Sorenson give proof of Swedish migration, and Lars Hagen's stone states quite unequivocally that he was born in "Norge" but died an American. I cannot guess the origin of Abplanalp until I read beneath one name on this family monument, "Hier ruht unser lieber Bruder." A slate stone with the name Meinert says "Mein Herz," but gives no names or dates. Is this an individual, a family? The grave does not yield its secrets but preserves the mystery desired by its occupants (or occupant).

There are more German names: Rademacher and Strauss and Molzohn . . . and Koppelman. And there is my son among this family of strangers. Jason David Koppelman—born 1970, died 1989. Whenever I want to protest this outrageously short time, there is a family who reminds me that many have had even fewer years. A small stone announces that Mary Ellen was born and died on the same day: January 2, 1933. The same parents gave birth to Elizabeth Ann who lived just three days. There are no graves in the large gap between these small stones. I like to think those plots were for the children who survived, and who survive still.

I am reminded of my own status as a survivor every time I come here. Next to Jason's name is my wife's name and then my name, with birth dates recorded and death dates yet unknown. It is strange to see your name on such a stone, a preview of coming attractions. This is where my body will be someday. Is there something more to me, something like a spirit or a soul that will transcend the death of my body? I can't be certain, and I certainly can't know what it is or what it does. I doubt that I will ever "know" because even if something survives the death of the body there is no guarantee that individual consciousness survives with it.

It is all a mystery. Although we are provided with clues, it is a mystery that cannot be solved. We all speculate, but I do not have enough confidence to be sure of any answer. I keep asking questions. Here is a clue I can contribute.

At Jason's funeral, family members sat to the right of the coffin. My wife and daughter sat on either side of me, an empty chair next to my daughter as if people expected our son to join us. The coffin was the center of attention for the mourners, the family reduced to a sideshow of grief. We sat there waiting for the funeral to begin, wishing it was over, yet not wishing to follow the pallbearers through the side door into the parking lot where the hearse was waiting. Lined up behind the hearse were a dozen cars to take family and close friends to the cemetery. The other mourners would leave by the front door.

The funeral began with music, an anonymous organist playing "In the Garden." It was neither inspirational nor comforting. I twitched in my chair feeling guilty because I was the one who selected the music. I should have listened to the recorded selections before the funeral. I should have made sure. Jason would have hated such passionless music.

Suddenly the door leading out to the parking lot slammed open as if a child had impetuously dashed out of the room. My wife and daughter had the same thought I did, that Jason had just left. We knew he couldn't stand such music when he was alive, so if something of him was still here, that something would have had to escape. My wife would later say that this incident made it possible for her to go to the cemetery. As she stared at the coffin hovering over the open grave, she knew that she could allow it to be lowered into the ground and covered up. Jason's body was there but his spirit had escaped, flinging the door open wide to let us know.

I have had other moments, fleeting seconds where I have had a sense of Jason's presence, but this was the only time there was tangible evidence of something. A closed door had burst open for no reason It was a calm, autumn day. There was no breeze, nothing to explain how the door could have opened even a few inches. Yet that door had slammed against the wall as if a sudden gust of wind had blown it wide open. For the family, the image was of a child rushing outside to play, careless of closing the door. I still don't know what to make of it, but I know it gave comfort to those who saw it, and the memory comforts us still.

Since then I have had to adjust to my fate, going on with this ongoing grief. I often think of the expression, "a fate worse than death." What does that mean? When you die your suffering is done, so any "fate" that keeps you alive makes you vulnerable to pain, loss, heartache. If you lose a child or anyone you love, you are guaranteed a life of suffering. It is measured out for you each day by the teaspoon or by the tablespoon. Is this a fate worse than death?

This is what I was thinking as I stood before my son's grave, quiet now, tired of talking. I noticed a man riding an old bicycle on one of the paved paths winding through the cemetery. *He is large; he dwarfs the bicycle. He has a sleeping bag, rolled up and tightly tied, hanging from the right handlebar. He has a dirty blue duffle bag whose handle he holds in his left hand. He ignores me, but he looks around intently as if he was lost or was looking for something. A place to sleep perhaps? I watch him bike slowly, looking thoughtfully at the tombstones. He will be back. I am sure of it. After all, this is a place of rest. He will be safe here; no cops will come to roust him out. He can sleep with the others, quiet companions who will not bother him. Perhaps he also thinks of them as family.*

I wondered if he knew about the animals. The cemetery is next to some wetlands and I have seen beavers and deer and other creatures in the cemetery. Driving through at dusk I have seen animals hiding among the stones, darting across the road, betrayed briefly in my headlights as they seek the safety of the swamp. In the winter I have seen their tracks near Jason's grave. I don't think they will bother the stranger. They will probably stay away from his sleeping spot, wherever he decides that will be. It is his fate, apparently, to be homeless. Is his a fate worse than death? It would seem not. He continues to live, even if it means sleeping in a graveyard. And so do I, even if it means coming to a graveyard to be "with" the son I cannot be with. Survivors do what we have to do, trying to find reasons to go on.

In *Mother Night,* Kurt Vonnegut invents a double agent who pretends to be a Nazi during World War II so he can spy for the allies, cleverly sending information encoded in the Nazi propaganda he writes. After the war, the CIA tells him they do not want to inform the public about the true nature of his role during the war for fear he will be a target for assassination by those he betrayed. While trying to create a new life for himself, he stumbles into a meeting of militant Zionists who recognize him and attack him. He is rescued by neo-Nazis who have been monitoring the Zionist meeting and intervene to help him escape. They take him out a side door to the sidewalk, then they re-enter the building to rejoin their colleagues who are assaulting the Zionists. At that moment this man's life seems so strange, so surreal, that he cannot think of a reason to leave. There seems no point in going anywhere nor does he have any place to go. He doesn't move. A police officer comes along and asks what he is doing there. He says nothing. He just stands there shaking his head. The officer says, "Move along," and so he does.

Anyone who has struggled with the loss of a loved one knows this feeling. There are days when you simply go on doing what you do out of a sense of habit, just following the routine, just putting one foot in front of the other. Ultimately you must find better reasons to go on, but it is not easy. For a long time I kept wishing that Jason was still alive, wishing and wanting it with such a ferocious desire that I did not know what to do about the frustration and pain it caused me. Sometimes I tried to drown my desire in drink. If I could dull my senses enough I seemed to find some peace, even if it was only the illusion of peace, even if only for a few hours before going to bed. In the morning I would get up and begin another day. I put one foot in front of the other in response to a voice in my own head which said, "Move along."

In the midst of this struggle I remembered something I had read years ago in a book on world religions. It was in the chapter on Buddhism that talked about how to deal with desire. I found the book and reread the chapter. It said that desire actually consisted of two components: the desire for the thing itself, and the desire that this desire be fulfilled. You cannot stop desiring things, it is part of human nature, but you can control the desire that your desire be fulfilled. That made sense to me. I stopped trying to control my desire to want Jason alive, to be able to hug him and tell him how much I loved him. I indulged in that desire whenever I felt like it. I told myself that this desire was a reflection of my love for my son and gave it free rein. At the same time, I kept reminding myself that what I wanted was not going to happen. This seemed to help me. I wanted to feel that emotion because it allowed me to express my love for Jason. I didn't want to bottle my love up and hide it away, but I didn't want to be irrational about my desire being satisfied. This became a part of my healing process, but the most important part of that process was the way it began, with a dream.

The moment I was told my son had died, my mind went numb; thoughts came in slow motion. I felt as if bags of cement had been placed on my shoulders, pushing me down under water where my legs struggled just to move. I was not getting enough sleep because I kept waking up at 5:00 in the morning. After a week of battling such symptoms, I was exhausted. After waking up at 5:00 once again, I desperately prayed for help, for relief. Afterwards, for the first time, I fell back asleep. I dreamed I saw my son. He was in the living room of our home talking with two of his friends. I saw him as I was coming down the stairs and my heart seemed to break the bonds constricting it as an electric charge raced through my body. But wait, this wasn't my living room. This room had a window wide open with long, white lace curtains blowing in the breeze, but we had a picture window framed by dark drapery. There was no piano in our living room. I realized now that I was dreaming, but even if it was just a dream I could hug my son and tell him I loved him. Before I could do that I woke up.

I was upset and angry about not getting to hug Jason, even if it was only a dream. My wife asked me what was wrong and I told her about the dream, and I wept. As the day went on I became aware of how good I felt. The cement bags on my shoulders were gone, and my legs didn't feel like they were walking against the tide. After putting in a full day's work, I worked at the computer for part of the evening. The next morning I slept until the alarm went off. Although I have not experienced the energy I felt the day after the dream, I now have the normal levels of energy I had known before the accident. The dream seemed to have eliminated my symptoms, and now it was up to me to resume my life as best as I could.

After I started writing about my struggle with grief, I sent excerpts to a friend who was a minister in San Antonio. Since I was coming there to attend a conference, he invited me to meet with people from his church who had formed a "grief group" to help others who had lost a loved one. He thought it would be helpful if I talked to them about my grief experience.

We met on a Saturday morning: two men and about a dozen women, most of them Mexican American. When I described my dream to them, I mentioned my doctor's belief that I had been experiencing a clinical depression and that the dream must have triggered a chemical reaction in the brain which purged me of the symptoms. The Mexican American women smiled as if I were a child. Afterwards my friend thanked me for coming and said the group benefitted from what I told them, ". . . except for that explanation for your dream." I asked him to explain. He had worked with Native American and Mexican American communities for the past 14 years, and he knew that they believed in spirits that survived the body's death, and that such a spirit could come to someone, could visit them in dreams. "You needed to see Jason, so his spirit came to you in a dream. They believe his spirit healed you and allowed you to get on with your life."

I want to believe what these women believe. It is far more comforting than the doctor's explanation, but I'm a product of my culture. It's not easy to abandon an insistence on scientific explanations. I don't read horoscopes; I would not phone a psychic. I demand proof, evidence, a rational basis for belief. Yet I know that life is not always rational. There are mysteries that cannot be solved, questions that can never be answered. We have a consciousness we carry with us throughout our lives. Where was this consciousness before we were born? Where is it after we die? These are matters of faith. We choose to believe in certain answers and live our lives as if they were true. I want to have a faith that says I will see my son again. Can I have such a faith? Can I believe in spirits like the Mexican American women? Can I embrace this truth as confidently as they do? Perhaps, but I cannot do this yet, not yet.

I told a friend who works with me at the university about the grief group in San Antonio. Dan is a Native American. Dan agreed with the Mexican American women. He said a belief in spirits is common among Native Americans, and the idea that the spirit of a loved one could visit someone in a dream was more than just a matter of belief for him. He told me this story.

Before Dan had even dated the woman he married, she had a dream where a stout, older Indian woman came to her with a basket saying sternly, "You have work to do," admonishing her to get to it. Laura had no idea what to make of this dream. When she and Dan began dating, he told her about Beverly, his mother, and what an important person she had been in his life. Laura had noticed the many framed pictures of Beverly in Dan's apartment. After they got married, Laura started to tell Dan about her strange dream where an older woman came to her, but Dan interrupted, "It was my mother." The thought came to him the moment she began talking about this dream.

Laura argued that it couldn't have been his mother because the woman in the dream was very stout and in his pictures Beverly was thin and beautiful. Dan said those pictures were taken when she was younger, but his mother had gained a lot of weight before she died. Dan searched for a picture of his mother toward the end of her life, and when he showed one to Laura she said immediately, "That's the woman." Dan believed that the basket in her dream referred to the grandchild his mother wanted, so when they had their first child, a baby girl, they named her Beverly. Dan's story suggests that a soul or spirit may survive death, but there are other explanations. I can draw no conclusions, but such stories reinforce a sense of wonder, a sense of possibility in the mystery that surrounds life and death.

Late one night I received a phone call from my cousin, a Presbyterian minister. He had lost his oldest child, a son, several years ago. He called to tell me about a dream or a vision he had had during a recent back surgery. Before the operation they gave him an anesthetic, and as the drug took effect he began to see shapes which became gradually more distinct. He recognized our grandmother who had died almost 30 years ago. On one side of her was his son, and on the other side was my son. There were many details in this dream and he remembered them clearly and related them to me. Toward the end of the dream, Jason said, "tell my Dad not to worry about me," and to "look at page 875 in the Bible." When my cousin finished his description of the dream, he said that was all he wanted to say for now. Before he hung up I wanted to make sure I had the right page number, so I deliberately gave him the wrong number, asking if it was page 835, but he corrected me. It was 875.

I thought about this curious reference. It is far more common to cite a book of the Bible by the chapter and verse like John 3:16. Of course, Jason wouldn't know that because he did not go to Sunday School or church. I have five Bibles, each of which is a different translation, so I wondered which Bible I should use. It occurred to me that the page number might refer to the passage from Matthew where God is described as concerned even for the fall of a sparrow which was the basis for the title of my book about Jason's death. I grabbed my King James Bible and found the passage in Matthew, but it was on page 10 because the pagination started over where the New Testament began. I wondered if the last page of the Old Testament was 865 which would make the tenth page of Matthew the 875th page, but the last page of the Old Testament in that Bible was 848. There was no page 875.

I wanted to make sense of this. Why was I given a page number? With a chapter and verse reference I could look up the passage in any Bible. Being given a page number suggested that I would need to look in a particular Bible. Which of the several translations should I use? I wasn't sure. Why did this have to be so confusing? Why didn't Jason just show up in one of my dreams and tell me what he wanted me to hear? Why was he in my cousin's dream? I was even feeling a little jealous of my cousin, and then I remembered.

When Jason graduated from high school my cousin sent him a gift that many ministers send on such occasions—a Bible. I knew immediately that this was the Bible I should use to locate page 875. I found the Bible on a shelf in Jason's old room under several other books. It was the "New International Version" which included extensive footnotes. On page 875, two thirds of the page was devoted to footnotes, but on that page Psalm 84 begins:

> How lovely is your dwelling place
>   O Lord Almighty!
> My soul yearns, even faints,
>   for the courts of the Lord;
> my heart and my flesh cry out
>   for the living God.
>
> Even the sparrow has found a home,
>   and the swallow a nest for herself . . .

Had my sparrow found a home, a haven? Was he trying to tell me this, using an indirect means to deliver this message in order to be all the more convincing? There are no answers to these questions. They can only be answered by faith. If I believe my son is trying to reassure me, then that becomes my truth. I can believe in a God who gives each of us a soul which will return to its maker after the body dies. I can choose to believe, knowing that it may not be true.

This is my challenge: to be a man of faith I must choose to believe in the context of doubt, to embrace a possibility as if it were truth. It is not an easy challenge. I have not mastered it yet. Instead, I find myself in the position of the father who brings his sick child to Jesus to be healed in the fourth chapter of Mark. Unlike that father, I do not come with a living child in my arms. I come with the lifeless body of a child flung into a ditch whose shattered skull leaked his life into the ground on the darkest night I have ever known. And when Jesus says to that father, and to all of us, "All things are possible to him who believes," I feel my heart sink as I wrestle with my fears and doubts, as did the father who stood before Jesus. But I take heart in that father's response, and echo his reply:

> Lord I believe, help thou my unbelief.

So here I stand in this journey of grief, with thousands of faithful fathers and mothers who have lost a child and struggle with despair. The questions are hard. There are no easy answers. I search for a faith which will nurture and comfort me. I want to believe that my son knows I still love him and miss him, and that at some time, in some place, he will come to me, knowing how much that will comfort me. I can only believe, placing a welcome mat before the doorway to dreams, keeping the fire of love going in my heart, hoping for that special guest to surprise me with his presence. Waiting.

NOTE

The title refers to John Milton's Sonnet XIX "When I Consider . . ." which ends with the following lines:

> . . . "God doth not need
> Either man's work or his own gifts; who best
> Bear his mild yoke, they serve him best; his State
> Is Kingly. Thousands at his bidding speed
> And post o'er Land and Ocean without rest:
> They also serve who only stand and wait."

SECTION II

Meaning-Making in the Face of Death

CHAPTER 4

A Taste of Heaven Here on Earth: For the Dying and for the Accompanier

Rabbi Daniel A. Roberts

Spirituality. It is the bane of every clergyperson. It is the newest buzzword. It is the fastest growing area of theological discussion, and it is one of the few growing sectors of the publishing industry. Out of nowhere the word seems to have appeared on people's lips about 7–10 years ago. Whenever I think about this word I shudder, for no one is able to define it for me. I can't put my figurative arms around it because I am too practical. Yet, I love where it has lead congregations and individuals. One of my young congregants told me, "Rabbi, spirituality is just like love. You know when it is and you know when it ain't." I agree. Yet, it makes me nervous.

Spirituality makes me nervous because it often leads people to think that there is a split between the material world and the realm of the spirit. It subtly suggests the idea of leaving the everyday world in order to enter a holy domain of awesome silence found in some vast dark retreat. It makes me apprehensive because I fear that some will get the idea that spirituality is some kind of "high" found in the midst of a worship service. When at the next service nothing seems to happen they will be terribly let down.

I also tremble that most people will incorrectly associate religion and spirituality as being one and the same. What most people do not realize is that religion is a group experience, whereas spirituality is individualistic. Religion is the way an individual expresses a relationship to a higher force through either a belief system or communal ritual, while spiritual experiences are usually not reproducible. Religion is the glue that binds communities together with shared symbols, rituals, myths, ethics, and behavioral norms, whereas spirituality is often found in human encounters and sometimes in mystical moments. Writes David Elkins, "Spirituality involves opening our hearts and cultivating our capacity to experience awe, reverence, and gratitude. It is the ability to see the sacred in the ordinary, to feel the poignancy of life, to know the passion of existence and give ourselves over to that which is greater than ourselves" (Elkins, 1999, p. 44). Robert Wuthnow (1998) continues this thought in *After Heaven: Spirituality in America Since 1950*: "Spirituality is an assortment of activities and interpretations that reflect the past, this includes new ways of understanding the past, and that envision on the horizon something distinctly different from the past" (p. 16).

For some, spirituality is experienced at the meeting point between our self and that which is outside of our self. Spirituality, so to speak, is an inner and an outer experience at the same time. Rabbi Abraham Joshua Heschel (cited in Rabbi Braun, 1989) said, "Spirituality is not striving to be godly, but trying to be deeply human." For some, spirituality is found in the act of seeking forgiveness (Mahoney & Graci, 1999); for others, it refers to the human quest to understand life's meaning in a world that does not at times seem to make sense nor be intrinsically reasonable, particularly at the time when one is dying, or when one has just experienced the death of a loved one. Spirituality often comes in the darkness of life when experiencing the painful thought of life ending, or doing a life review (see below). For some of us, spirituality comes in the sacred moments of doing an act of kindness such as accompanying another human being during their final days.

SPIRITUALITY AS THE BREATH OF LIFE

The word "spirituality" comes from the Latin root *spiritus,* which means "breath," referring to the breath of life. So one might ask, "From whence does this 'breath of life' come?" Some attribute this gift to a higher source identified by many names. Still others credit this to happenstance. However, most people who have been raised in some religious tradition connect the "breath of life" to that divine presence identified in English by the word "God."

To this end there is a wonderful story in Jewish tradition that indicates that man, woman, and God are partners in the creation of a human being. Our Sages taught: "There are three partners in the creation of a human person—God, the father, and the mother. The father inseminates the white substance, out of which are formed the newly born bones, sinews, and nails, the brain in the head, and the white of the baby's eye. The mother inseminates the red substance, out of which are formed the baby's skin, flesh, and hair, and the black of the baby's eye. In the newly born baby, God implants spirit, soul, beauty of countenance, eyesight, the capacity to hear, the capacity to speak, and the capacity to walk, as well as knowledge, understanding, and intelligence. When it is time for a person to depart from the world, God takes away the Divine part, and leaves to the father and mother the parts contributed by them" (Talmud Bavli, Nida 31a). This story reminds us that we have a partnership with God: every breath is a continual gift from God. In recognizing that at any moment this breath of life can be taken from me, I am moved daily to discover my God-given role in this universe.

For me, spirituality is indeed finding the meaning of life. In Hasidic literature, such as the following quote, we find the belief that it is the responsibility of people to discover their particular role. "Every person born into this world represents something new, something that never existed before, something original and unique. It is the duty of every person . . . to know and consider that he is unique in the world in his particular character and that there has never been anyone like him in the world" (Buber, 1958). Spirituality thus is a cultivating and nourishing of the human soul, a paying attention, and an appreciation for the world, added to the task of finding our special role in life. The person of spirit embraces and celebrates life's possibilities. The "breath of life"—to which some refer as the soul—is not merely a surviving part of the self after death, but the deepest most sacred part of self while one is *alive*. The experience with the soul and spirituality does not necessarily come in a single moment, but it can be encountered over and over again until the day we die. Spirituality is found every day in our loves, our deeds, and our experiences. It is thus as diverse and as unpredictable as the daily adventures and as individuals themselves, a vastly complex quest in which each person must seek his or her own way.

A DIFFERENT KIND OF SPIRITUAL EXPERIENCE

In his book, *Man's Search for Meaning,* Victor Frankl (1969) postulates that when people have a reason and purpose for living, they are able to endure hardships and events that for others with less resolve would overwhelm them and lead to their death. An example of this phenomenon is the story of the Jews in Treblinka, a Polish extermination camp, during the Holocaust. As one can imagine, work in the extermination camp was onerous, and coupled with the depression of having been separated from family, loved ones, and community, lead many inmates to commit suicide. According to some of the inmates, the best friend a person could have at that time was one who was willing to tip over the chair. At night in the barracks, it was not unusual to bump into bodies hanging from the rafters. One night all the suicides stopped. It seems that a group of prisoners began telling the others that if everyone not murdered by the Nazis committed suicide, no one would be around to tell the story of their suffering. With this message in mind, with a new mission and a purpose, the suicides stopped.

Lecturing at Southern Methodist University several years before his death, Victor Frankl wrote on the blackboard, S – M = D. This formula, Suffering minus Meaning equals Despair explains what happened in Treblinka. When one gives up hope and has no meaning, death occurs. If one has a will to live, one finds a way. This theory is demonstrated by the two following stories. My congregant, Julius C.*, had decided that he no longer could bear the pain of his illness. He was tired and felt that he had lived a good life and was ready to die. He called his entire family together and told them of his love and concern for them. He then waited for the weekend when one of his grandchildren could come in from out of town. After speaking with her and reiterating his love, Julius got into bed and three days later he was dead. Another friend of mine was told by his doctor that he should go home and put his affairs in order because he had only a few months to live. He was determined otherwise—that he was still needed by his family and his congregation. Now, some four years later, he is well and functioning fully in his job as a rabbi.

HELPING THE DYING OVERCOME DESPAIR

"Birth is a beginning and death a destination and life is a journey" (*Gates of Repentance*, 1978, p. 283). Each of us is a traveler on the road of life. At times we accompanier to others on their journey and at times they accompany us. As we accompany those who are dying (or in mourning) we might ask how we might capitalize on life being extended through living and/or dying with meaning. Note the use of the word "extended"; I do not want to give the impression that we can offer life unending if only certain things are done. Eventually we must all die. This chapter is not a panacea to avoid death, but rather suggestions of how we as an accompanier of the dying might find a taste of heaven while still here on earth by helping another live his or her final days more meaningfully and spiritually.

We have all heard the theory that depression is anger turned inward. I might offer another hypothesis: depression is a turning inward because the world outside no longer seems charged with value and meaning (Wolpe, 1999, p. 127)—a global collapse of faith that life is meaningful. Thus, the challenge for us as caretakers and accompaniers would be to find a way to help people to find faith and purpose, notwithstanding the fact that one has been given an "end of life" pronouncement.

Dr. Joanne Lynn, director of the Center to Improve Care of the Dying, suggests that we speak to people not of having a "terminal illness" but rather telling them that they are living with a "life-defining, eventually fatal condition" (Webb, 1997, p. 401). This concept allows people to plan along dual tracks: one that they could recover; the other that they may not. One track allows them to make long-term plans for life, the other urges them to make peace with family and friends and get their affairs in order. Instead of talking about the odds of survival, doctors and other medical personnel need to begin discussing the quality of life left. They need to emphasize that one can die healthy by *living the last days of one's life rather than simply existing, a spiritual experience.*

Living with a "life-defining, eventually fatal condition" means that what life in the days ahead will be like can be determined by the *person* and not those around him or her. It is not the doctor, friends, nor even the family who will decide how one fills the hours and moments left, but only the dying person. Our job as accompaniers is to help the person gain perspective on this idea. Putting one's affairs in order also means putting order to one's life and understanding that the dying process is part of life. The challenge is how to help another to make sense of and find meaning in a world that is no longer the same, and which is now perceived to be finite. The mission of those who accompany people with a "life-defining, eventually fatal condition" is to demonstrate that even in this situation there can still be meaning and purpose, order and balance in life, a "touch of Heaven here on earth." I believe that this can help minimize people's suffering and despair, resulting in a sense of dying with a sense of completeness rather than dying with chaos all around (a "touch of Hell here on earth"). In my mind, this is the essence of spirituality.

MEANING-MAKING EVEN IN THE
FACE OF DEATH

In the book of Genesis, after Adam and Eve ate from the Tree of Knowledge, they sewed fig leaves together and made clothes for themselves. At that moment they "heard the voice of the Lord God walking in the garden toward the cool of the day; and the man and woman hid themselves from the presence of the Lord God amongst the trees of the garden. God at that moment called unto the man and woman and said: "*Ayecha*—Where art thou?" (Genesis 3:9). The ancient rabbis ask, "Why would the all knowing, all seeing God need to ask, '*Ayecha*—Where art thou?' Why did God not just walk over to the bush, behind which Adam and Eve were hiding, and say, 'Hi?'" The rabbinic answer is that God periodically asks each person, "Where are you in life? How far have you come and what are your accomplishments?"

Constructing meaning when we are faced with the knowledge that soon our wealth and cherished possessions will be distributed to friends, relatives, strangers, and thrift shops—or put in the garbage—is very difficult. When people comprehend that death will snatch away everything they have prized in life, they begin to realize that the only thing left to work on is the soul. The concept of the soul is not meant only to refer to a surviving part of the self after death, but to the deepest most sacred part of self while one is alive.

Ken Doka and John Morgan note, "The human condition is to find ourselves on the stage of life knowing we have a role to play but not knowing what the role is or even the plot of the story. No other animal has to live this terrible condition. The other animals have instincts by which they run their lives. Jean-Paul Sartre says, 'Man is the only animal that can fail'"(Doka & Morgan, 1993, p. 5). The first conclusion one can draw about spirituality is that to be human is to search for meaning. We are not like animals that are born with instincts. We are the only animal that has to decide from moment to moment: "Who am I? For what reason have I been born?" We are the only animal who has to answer the question: "*Ayecha*—Where are you in life?"

We who accompany one who has a "life-defining, eventually fatal condition" need to help the dying understand that although this could be a time of despair and anguish, this can also be a time of enabling the soul to become more vibrant and alive even as the material body decays. When one comprehends that s/he can work toward a final understanding of purpose, then s/he can die in peace. Jeanne Harper (1993) writes, "I have found that the client who is able to find meaning in his/her life experience is better able to deal with the dying process, be that process a matter of hours, days or weeks until death" (p. 315). A person with a "life-defining" condition can reevaluate time, using it to its fullest. One can also reevaluate priorities and acknowledge them to others. David Wolpe (1999) writes in *Making Loss Matter*, "The blessing we seek in life is not to live without pain. It is to live so that our pain has meaning. The spiritually mindful person seeks to live fully despite fear, because to allow fear to direct our lives adds the suffering of anticipation to the pain of the loss" (p. 12). Norman Cousins (1995) writes, "Death is not the greatest loss in life. The greatest loss is what dies inside us while we live" (p. 316).

Spirituality near the end of life involves a review of life, asking which actions, words, or accomplishments made us proud, and which not. To accomplish this one must do a life summary. Writes Marilyn Webb (1997) in *The Good Death:* "At the end, people have to learn how to make sense of the whole of their lives and of the legacy that they have left that might survive beyond their physical beings." Webb (1997) suggests that memory itself—in the process of a life review—might be an important trigger for biochemical and neurological changes in the brain, changes that might lead at the end of life to ecstatic and mystical experiences (p. 236). In other words, we can help people grow at this time by tapping into their memory banks. We can discuss causes that they can still support, and we can teach people how to die with dignity. Leon Kass (1990) notes, "Death with dignity, in it most sense, would mean a dignified attitude and virtuous conduct in the face of death" (p. 40).

People need to be reminded that they must remain actors on the stage of life and not be swept off of it or allow themselves to be abandoned by the other actors. They can now say things, do things, and see themselves in different ways. At this time there is a real opportunity to seek atonement and to forgive others, two areas which often get in the way of a peaceful death. Deathbeds are also powerful places for spiritual and emotional healing. This is why the moment of death is frequently accompanied by confessional prayers (the *Viddui* prayer in Judaism or last rites in Catholicism) seeking forgiveness from God, others, and self. In *The Tibetan Book of Living and Dying* (1992), we learn that through forgiving and being forgiven, we purify ourselves of the darkness of what we have done, and prepare ourselves most completely for the journey through death (p. 213).

Often during a life review, we realize as accompaniers that it is necessary for the dying person to seek repentance from God or from another. People at the end of life are frequently extremely vulnerable to guilt, regret, and depression. The accompanier must allow the dying person to express these feelings openly and freely without condemning or rationalizing them, and try to help him/her figure out potential solutions. We might explore with them the potential of initiating personal contact with the person(s) with whom they need to work out these feelings. If that is impossible or not desirable, perhaps writing a letter, taping or videotaping words of regret and apology might be an alternative. Sometimes, because many years may have passed or the person may be deceased or not willing to make contact, it might not be possible to rectify a situation. Writing down the words in a letter or journal can be very cathartic. It is most important at this time to create a non-judgmental setting. Often, just listening to the grief of unfinished business is all that is needed.

Perhaps the best thing that an accompanier can do to help the dying is to help him/her reconcile themself by accepting their humanness. One can come to the understanding that God does not require us to be more than human. I often remind people that even Moses did not do everything correctly. Moses yelled at people

(Numbers 20:10), he disobeyed God by striking the rock (Numbers 20:11), and he killed an Egyptian (Exodus 2:12). Yet, one would have to admit that Moses is one of the five greatest human beings that ever lived, and certainly would be worthy of getting into Heaven. Other ways to help the dying would be to have the person read some of the readings at the end of this chapter, particularly "Birth is a Beginning." The accompanier could then question what parts impress him/her or which sentences s/he had trouble with.

The nearness of death creates an opportunity to speak with the Holy. This is a time for prayer. The content of the prayer is not as important as the sense that one is communicating with a Higher Source who is responding to them and caring for them. Perhaps the best way for an accompanier to approach the subject is to suggest that a prayer be offered and measure the person's response. If the person is responsive then one can start the prayer as an address to God, Jesus, Muhammad, etc., and an acknowledgment that God's humble servant lies before God. After asking for healing, allow the dying to finish the words. See the end of this chapter for some alternative suggested prayers.

Another way to create spirituality is to help those with a "life-defining pro-nouncement" look for alternative possibilities and new meanings. For some people the practice of Tonglen in *The Tibetan Book of Living and Dying* is a very spiritual concept. The central thought of Tonglen is that one is taking on another's pain and that one's suffering alleviates theirs. Thus, a person's meaning is obtained by dedicating his/her pain to the hope that it will alleviate someone else's pain. One achieves this state by saying to him/herself: "May I take on the suffering of everyone who has this terrible illness. May they be free from this affliction and from all their suffering" (pp. 219-220).

NEW BEGINNINGS
AND BEING REMEMBERED

We need to help people who are dying understand that spirituality is about continued growth, even up to one's final day. To help others to open up to you as an accompanier, you can begin with words like: "Tell me what is happening to you. I would like to know the story of your life, to know about your journey through life and where you have been, what good you did and if given the opportunity what you would like to do over again." You can ask about pains that they are still experiencing, about forgiveness that needs to be obtained or to be given. You can also discuss letting go of guilt, anger, and shame. Talking dissipates these emotions and ultimately allows a person to find the sense of peace for which s/he longs. I remind you of the old adage that when one shares with another, their joys are doubled and their sorrows are halved.

Accompaniers can help people who are in the "life-defining" stage to realize that they no longer need to stand on ceremony when it comes to family relationships. Perhaps words that have escaped them, like "I love you," now can be spoken with sincerity and conviction, without hesitation or embarrassment. Old habits, such as being reticent about expressing emotions, no longer need to dominate communication. We can help the dying realize that this time can be an opportunity to experiment with new, more open behaviors and free expression of emotions with loved ones. One can also help the person examine the answer to the question, "*Ayecha*—Where am I? Why am I still alive? What job is there left for me?"

Another means of helping the dying get to the source of important values could be through music. Talking about the kinds and pieces of music the person enjoys and which lyrics have touched their soul and why can lead to many insights into what the person holds most important in life. Another avenue would be to ask that if the person were to write lyrics to a piece of music what would they be, what would be included?

All of the aforementioned are simply suggestions to help those in the throes of dealing with a "life-defining pronouncement" get in touch with their spirituality. Our goal as accompaniers is to help them find the ongoing meaning of their life in spite of the fact that time might be short.

One of the great spiritual anguishes many dying people have is that their lives held no particular mission. They fear that shortly after their death they will be forgotten. I recall the words of an English detective who proclaimed in despair: "What a perfect crime! The murderer never left a fingerprint!" Many people are afraid that they will be thought of as having committed the perfect crime against life, that they will have departed the earth without leaving a fingerprint anywhere. They fear that they will have produced no fruit, no trace of generosity, no touch of benevolence, no transforming fingerprints of caring or concern. One usually thinks of this too late, but even at this last moment we as accompaniers can help people imprint their love, wisdom, compassion, and sensitivity. We can help them leave their mark regarding their beliefs and observances with regard to worship, religious practice, morals, and values, particularly if these were significant parts of their life. Helping them to write an ethical will (see below) is a wonderful vehicle in helping one to leave a durable fingerprint on the minds and hearts of loved ones.

What is an ethical will and how does this differ from a legal will or a living will? Let me explain the concept by way of some stories. The first is about a woman named Barbara M*. Barbara was 42 years old and dying of breast cancer when I first met her. She had two adorable little girls who lived with her ex-husband. To add to her anxiety of how they would grow up without her, she and her ex were still feuding over divorce issues and he was punishing her by keeping the girls away from her. Her greatest fear was not the added pain that she was about to endure as the cancer progressed, nor was it a fear of death itself. She was worried that her young daughters would forget her, and she was terrified that it would soon be as though she had never lived, had left no "fingerprint." She feared that her ex-husband would remarry, and that a new woman would become their "mother" and all that she stood for and believed would be forgotten. We spoke for a long time about this concern, discussing various alternatives, and finally I suggested that she could write an ethical will.

I explained that an ethical will is a letter that Barbara would write to her daughters about herself, about the kind of person she was, and the dreams and aspirations she had for them. She loved the idea; however, she reminded me that she was already too weak to write such a letter. I suggested that she tape-record this message and give copies of it to a family member to put away for her daughters until they were older. I recently learned that, some 20 years later, her family did present her daughters with the tape. The girls were so touched and thrilled to receive it, and remarked that they felt as if their mother were still talking with them.

Another woman in my congregation was dying of cancer. For the longest time she refused my overtures to visit. One day I received a phone call from a family member indicating that she wanted to see me. When I arrived at her bedside she was weak but very agitated. We spoke of her successes and failures, her fear and her trepidation. Finally, I suggested to her that she might want to write an ethical will and explained to her what it was. We ended our time together with the *Viddui,* a confessional prayer. Her husband later told me that, after I left, she summoned him into the room and asked him to record the words that she was about to tell him. He told me that as she finished her last words she indicated that she was tired, closed her eyes, and lapsed into a deep sleep. She never woke up. He related to me how much all of them treasured these words which were bequeathed to them.

Rabbi Jack Reimer has preserved many examples of ethical wills in his book, *So That Your Values Live On: Ethical Wills and How to Prepare Them* (1991) which is based on *Hebrew Ethical Wills* by Israel Abraham (1972). For more information regarding ethical wills, go to the Web site www.ethicalwills.com. One outstanding ethical will was written by Sam Levenson to his grandchildren. In it, he writes that everything he has he owes to his ancestors, and that he leaves them a bunch of four letter words, like love and care. A member of my congregation, Roz Brenner, wrote an ethical will to her children, which I found deeply moving. I encourage you to read it at the end of this chapter (see Appendix).

To assist one in writing an ethical will, one might begin with words like: "I write this to you, my children/spouse, etc., to share with you the history of my family, important events that happened to me along my journey of life. I also would like you to know that the following religious principles and rituals that have been most meaningful to me. I also would like you to be aware of the following moral and ethical ideals that have moved me the deepest." The will might also include personal history as to who was most influential in the person's life and which events helped shape their life. In addition, whatever dreams and aspirations regarding the kind of qualities the writer admires in people should also be shared. The salutation could end with, "May the Almighty bless you with. . . ."

A TASTE OF HEAVEN FOR THE
ACCOMPANIERS

We have examined how a dying person might find a sense of spirituality. For us as accompaniers, where is spirituality to be found? Spirituality comes from our sense that we are acting as God would have us act, with kindness and love. In the beginning of Genesis 18, God visits Abraham, who is sitting in the door of his tent. The ancient rabbis asked, "Why did God come and what was Abraham doing sitting at home?" The answer is found in the end of chapter 17 where Abraham had just performed a circumcision on his son and himself. Abraham was ill and God had come to visit him. From this, the rabbis extrapolated that it was our duty, acting in God's image, to care for the sick. Secondly, we can fulfill the commandment of comforting the mourner (*Mishnah, Pa'eh* 1:1). Our taste of heaven comes as we, partners of God, allow the God-like qualities within us to come out in the form of compassion, love, and caring for others.

Our taste of heaven comes as we help people glorify their fingerprints. The best way to do this is by listening at the bedside of the dying, hearing their fears and final aspirations. (Maybe this is why God gave us two ears and only one mouth so that we can listen twice as much as we speak.) A person wants to be heard, to be paid attention, and to feel significant to others. Whereas animals need only to satisfy their basic physical needs, a human being needs to be needed. As long as this emotional need is not satisfied a person will be plagued by anxiety. By listening carefully, without forcing or stepping on the other's privacy, the accompanier can play a significant role in the final months of a person's life. By showing that you, as an accompanier, are open to their life's story—that you are not shocked by anything that is said, that you are not afraid to talk about the dying process—you can help the dying to feel important and meaningful. You might achieve your spirituality by recognizing that this is your life's purpose.

You can be of significant help by talking about views of life after death, and to be encouraging (if that is what they believe) about the peace they will find there. This metaphor of a better, more peaceful world to come is a powerful image to quell fears. One way to discover meaning and spirituality is to turn to traditional religious doctrines, particularly the afterlife, reincarnation, or to the concept of some sort of spiritual order to the universe. Books like *Many Lives, Many Masters* by Brian Weiss (1988) or *Does the Soul Survive?* by Rabbi Elie Kaplan Spitzoffer (2000) offer hope for continued life through reincarnation.

I suggest that you give hope by reminding people that God is always there for them. Share the words from the 23rd Psalm, which show us that God is always there when we turn to Him. Point out the change of pronouns. "*He* maketh me to lie down in green pastures" (a reference to good times), but, "Yea, though I walk through the Valley of Death, I will fear no evil, for *Thou* art with me" (in times of trouble God is very close). I remind you that whenever possible our task is to help people to find hope, and if not hope then comfort in God's presence.

The 23rd Psalm is one example of a reading that encourages one to recognize God's presence in his/her life. Some of the other readings at the end of this chapter might also be of help. I encourage you, the accompanier, to find readings from your faith tradition that speak to you and in which you find meaning, purpose, and spirituality. You might introduce the readings with words like, "Some people have found these readings meaningful. Why don't we read them together and then you can tell me what you find significant and that which resonates with you." You might share a piece of your own philosophy of life and death as well—another touch of spirituality.

This is a scary time for you, the accompanier, as you help another to face his/her mortality, for we also face our own. We fear that talking about these matters may be painful to the dying, and the last thing we want to cause at this point in their life is to bring him/her pain. However, I remind you that "our greatest lessons lie in our greatest pain" (Kübler-Ross & Kessler, 2000, p. 14). As painful as this time might be, even at this dying moment we can help the dying to complete their unfinished business of life and we can find a spiritual moment for ourselves, as well. David Kessler and Elisabeth Kübler-Ross (2000) state in *Life Lessons:*

> The dying have always been teachers of great lessons, for it's when we are pushed to the edge of life that we see life most clearly. In sharing their lessons, the dying teach us about the preciousness of life itself. In them we discover the hero, that part that *transcends all* we have been through and *delivers us to all* we are capable of *doing and being.* To not just be alive, but to feel alive. (p. 14)[1]

This is not a good time for you—or the dying—to search for answers as to *why* God has "punished" them with this suffering and pain. The ways of God are mysterious, and I do not believe in the cause and effect philosophy. We all must die. The manner and the timing selected for us is not a result of past misdeeds. The best answer which leads to alleviating suffering and pain is to focus on what action can be taken in the closing moments of life: writing an ethical will, praying even when questioning God, maintaining social contacts, and finding ways to perpetuate one's memory. When you are accompanying a dying person, dwell on their accomplishments and what they have done well. Help them feel as constructive and as happy as possible about their life. Concentrate on virtues and not failings. Remind the person that pain and suffering are not all that s/he is. Find the most skillful and sensitive ways possible to inspire the person, and to seek forgiveness from others and from oneself. Help those who desire to pray. Most importantly, give those with a life-defining pronouncement a sense of hope that their life is and was meaningful.

HELPING THE SURVIVORS

When the dead are gone, let us as accompaniers not forget that they leave behind mourners who still need our guidance as they make their way along the difficult journey of mourning. What mourners must now endure we cannot take away from them, for mourning is the price one pays for loving. We can only be there for them, to share and listen to their fears, their feelings of weakness and being out of control, to hear of the chaos and loneliness that has descended on their world. We can accompany them on their journey but we lack the power to take it away from them. We can only help them discern the meaning of their loss. Our job is to help the mourner to find the answer to God's question, *"Ayecha*—Where are you?" We must help people rediscover meaning without their loved one. Eventually we will

---

[1]Reprinted with permission of Scribner, a Division of Simon & Schuster from *Life Lessons* by Elisabeth Kübler-Ross and David Kessler. Copyright © 2000 by Elisabeth Kübler-Ross Family Limited Partnership and David Kessler, Inc.

understand that as we walk away from having helped a person die with dignity, or when we have helped someone else grieve a loss, we have come face to face with spirituality. It is in moments like this that we have indeed tasted Heaven while we are still here on earth.

CONCLUSION

Composer and vocalist Craig Taubman (1996) writes in his song, "Where Heaven and Earth Touch":

> I'm not sure where
> I'm not sure how
> Maybe later, maybe now
> But somewhere heaven and earth touch.

For me, heaven and earth touch when those with a "life-defining pronouncement" are able to relate to another who helps them to make order out of chaos in their life. Heaven and earth touch when the dying experience the love and devotion of some other person who helps them complete their unfinished business. Through our help, they find spiritual satisfaction in what they have accomplished with the moments they have lived. Without us, their final days would be filled with agitation and anxiety, the closest image I have to life in the netherworld. For us as accompaniers, heaven and earth touch when, hand in hand with one who is dying, or one who is mourning, we feel the warmth of God's presence. Our sense of spirituality is experienced when we witness their sense of calm, and sense their appreciation for our kindness and love, God's gift to us.

Spirituality. I still hate the word, but I love the feeling in us and in others when it happens. We cannot let the spirit die before its time, and we must help it to live in another until the very bitter end. This I know, through our own actions we can taste Heaven here on Earth.

APPENDIX I

TO MY BOYS
by Roz Brenner

These things which I want to say are not because I feel an urgency because death is close at hand. It may be I want you to understand I'm not worried, I'm not frightened. I would like, if it is written, that I have enough time to expand my inner me but that is not the reason for my urgency.

We have a tendency to feel our loved ones understand what's in our hearts. I believe you do but I want to tell you of my love for you, my concerns, and my hopes in black and white so you don't have to conjecture. It will be there for you to see.

Care for each other. Watch your health, be aware, you are sensitive to one another. The greatest care is the love of each other always. Your faults, your foibles—

remember you both have human frailties. Love each other in spite of them and for them. That's not only all right but good. We're all different—you each have much to contribute on to the other.

Know that I hovered in the background of your lives—aware of every nuance of voice and concern—sometimes not knowing what THE PROBLEM was, but aware there was one. I never wanted to invade your privacy. I waited till you came to me or the time was right. Remember how I've been with you in life—I may not be there physically, but everything you felt and saw through your lives is ingrained and will see you through. Only remember to turn to those strengths that are there and are your natural heritage. I will never leave you because I am you and you are me.

Turn to your religion, listen to the liturgy, examine it and stretch your minds to the expanses these words or wisdom encompass.

Rabbi Alan S. Green once gave a sermon, which spoke to the need for an 11th commandment. "Thou shalt not have joylessness of the heart." It hit somewhere that I live and I think often of that sermon. Hold that as good advice. We all have down times—try not to be joyless. There is so much to be grateful and joyous about.

Remember life's race is not to the trophy but the prize is in the journey. Everyday is a challenge and a reward—do it well. Should you falter, and you will, pick yourselves up, put the shoulder to the wheel and you will overcome.

Be kind and understanding to your fellow man. I have seen you do this over the years. Continue to reach out your hand to the wounded and the needy.

When I was ill and considered not taking chemo and radiation, my thoughts were, my job was done. You boys were grown. I'd done all the damage I could to you already so the need for me to live was no longer important, but I'm glad I did what was necessary to live on because you Michael, needed me. Your brother and I were here for you.

It won't always be so therefore you must guide your lives with the wisdom you've garnered and move on ahead.

Shakespeare said, "The evil that men do lives after them, the good is oft interred within their bones." Obviously Shakespeare didn't know about DNA. The good of all the generations behind you is in your bones.

My love for you will always be there. It is fierce, unconditional, and ever abiding.

REFERENCES

Abraham, I. (1972). *Hebrew ethical wills.* Philadelphia, PA: Jewish Publication Society.

Braun, Rabbi C. (1989). Sermon, in *Rabbinical Assembly Homiletics Service.*

Buber, M. (1958). *Hassidim and modern man.* New York: Horizon Press.

Cousins, N. (1995). In N. ben Shea (Ed.), *The word: Jewish wisdom through time.* New York: Villard.

Doka, K. J., & Morgan, J. (Eds.) (1993). *Death and spirituality.* Amityville, NY: Baywood.

Elkins, D. (1999). Spirituality, *Psychology Today, 32*(i5).

Fine, A. I. (1978). *Gates of Repentance*. New York: Central Conference of American Rabbis.

Frankl, V. (1989). *Mans search for meaning*. New York: Washington Square Press.

Harper, J. (1993). Ethical and spiritual concerns: Sexuality and spirituality: A wholistic approach for the living-dying client and the partner. In K. J. Doka & J. Morgan (Eds.), *Death and spirituality*. Amityville, NY: Baywood.

Kass, L. (1990, March). Death with dignity and the sanctity of life. *Commentary, 89*(3).

Kedar, K. (1999). *God whispers*. Woodstock, VT: Jewish Lights Publishing.

Kübler-Ross, E., & Kessler, D. (2000). *Life lessons*. New York: Scribner.

Mahoney, M., & Graci, G. (1999). *Death Studies, 23*(524).

Rinpoche, S., Gaffney, P., and Harvey, A. (Eds.) (1992). *The Tibetan book of living and dying*. San Francisco: Harper.

Reimer, J. (1991). *So that your values live on: Ethical wills and how to prepare them*. Woodstock, VT: Jewish Lights Publishing.

Spitz, E. K., Rabbi (2000). *Does the soul survive?* Woodstock, VT: Jewish Lights Publishing.

Talmud Bavli Nida 31a., as translated by Rabbi Zvi Yehuda in a private communication.

Voice of the spirit, audio recording, Sweet Louise Music—BMI, 1996.

Webb, M. (1997). *The good death: The new American search to reshape the end of life*. New York: Bantam Books.

Weiss, B. (1998). *Many lives, many masters*. New York: Fireside.

Wolpe, D. (1999). *Making loss matter*. New York: Riverhead Press.

Wuthnow, R. (1998). *After heaven: Spirituality in America since 1950*. London, England: University of California Press.

Spiritual Readings
Compiled by Rabbi Daniel A. Roberts

One might suggest people read and respond to these readings:

1. How does this reading, prayer, thought speak to you?
2. How does it speak to you spiritually?
3. One message from this reading that you would like to tell your loved one(s) is. . . .

A Prayer . . .
God, thank You for helping me see
That each phase of my life is perfect.
That I have arrived,
That I've always been where I need to be
Living perfect moments . . .
For the crimes against myself, I am sorry.
For all my slips and slides, I forgive myself.
Kedar (1999), p. 68

I pray: Dear God, I know that there will be pain in my life, and sadness, and loss. Please give me the strength to create a life, together with those whom I love, where loss will not be empty, where pain will not be purposeless. Help me find the faith to make loss matter. Amen.

Wolpe (1999), p. 22[2]

At every stage in my life I could only be what I knew how to be at that moment. As I look back at past moments in my life with a new perspective, I might have chosen a different path. But, that was a different time and a different place, and now, since I can no longer change that moment, and can only change the future, it is time to forgive myself and to accept my humanness. Now I look to the future with new insight as to how to repair relationships which may have faltered, and revisit opportunities I may have missed. I can seek forgiveness, admit that I am human, and ask to start anew from this moment on. I need not be chained to the past. With the moments of life left to me, I can still leave my mark in the hearts of those I love. I can still seize moments and share my soul. I accept myself for being who I was, and embrace the future free of the guilt that crippled me—a future open to the me I would like to be. Give me the strength (O Lord), to achieve my dreams.

Rabbi Daniel A. Roberts

Life After Death

These things I know:
   How the living go on living.
   And how the dead go on living with them
so that in a forest
   Even a dead tree casts a shadow
   and the leaves fall one by one
and the branches break in the wind
and the bark peels off slowly
and the trunk cracks
   and the rain seeps in through the cracks
and the trunk falls to the ground
and the moss covers it
   and in the spring the rabbits find it
and build their nest
inside the dead tree
so that nothing is wasted in nature
   or in love.

Laura Gilpin (source unknown)

---

[2]Reprinted with permission of Riverhead Press, a Division of Penguin Putnam, Inc., New York from *Making Loss Matter* by D. Wolpe. Copyright 1999 © Riverhead Press.

Life's Journey

Birth is a beginning
And death a destination.
And life is a journey:
From childhood to maturity
And youth to age
From ignorance to knowing;
From foolishness to discretion

And then perhaps to wisdom;
From weakness to strength
Or strength to weakness—
And, often back again;
From health to sickness
And back, we pray, to health again;

From offense to forgiveness,
From loneliness to love,
From joy to gratitude,
From pain to compassion,
And grief to understanding
From fear to faith;

From defeat to defeat to defeat—
Until, looking backward or ahead,
we see that victory lies
Not at some high place along the way,
But in having made the journey, stage by stage,
A sacred pilgrimage.

Birth is a beginning
And death a destination
And life is a journey.
A sacred pilgrimage—
To life everlasting.

Alvin I. Fine (Gates of Repentance) [3]

The Invitation

It doesn't interest me what you do for a living. I want to know what you
ache for, and if you dare to dream of meeting your heart's longing.

[3]Reprinted with permission of Central Conference of American Rabbis, New York, from *Gates of Repentance*, by A. I. Fine. Copyright 1978 © Central Conference of American Rabbis.

It doesn't interest me how old you are. I want to know if you will risk looking like a fool for love, for your dreams, for the adventure of being alive.

It doesn't interest me what planets are squaring your moon. I want to know if you have touched the center of your own sorrow, if you have been opened by life's betrayals or have become shriveled and closed from fear of further pain.

I want to know if you can sit with pain, mine or your own, without moving to hide or fade it or fix it. I want to know if you can be with joy, mine or your own; if you can dance with wildness and let the ecstasy fill you to the tips of your fingers and toes without cautioning us to be careful, be realistic, or to remember the limitations of being a human.

It doesn't interest me if the story you're telling me is true. I want to know if you can disappoint another to be true to yourself; if you can bear the accusation of betrayal and not betray your own soul. I want to know if you can be faithful and therefore be trustworthy. I want to know if you can see the beauty even when it is not pretty everyday, and if you can source your life from ITS presence. I want to know if you can live with failure, yours and mine, and still stand on the edge of a lake and shout to the silver of the full moon, "Yes."

It doesn't interest me to know where you live or how much money you have. I want to know if you can get up after the night of grief and despair, weary and bruised to the bone, and do what needs to be done for the children.

It doesn't interest me who you are, or how you came to be here. I want to know if you will stand in the center of the fire with me and not shrink back.

It doesn't interest me where or what or with whom you have studied. I want to know what sustains you from the inside when all else fall away. I want to know if you can be alone with yourself, and if you truly like the company you keep in the empty moments.

Oriah Mountain Dreamer, Indian Elder (source unknown)

Life is not lost by dying!
Life is lost minute by minute, day by dragging day
In all the thousand, small, uncaring ways we engage in.
Stephen Vincent Benet

CHAPTER 5

Death, Humor, and Spirituality: Strange Bedfellows?

Ruth Dean

Drawing by Alfredo Coreas, 2001 ©. Used with permission.

Humor, spirituality, and death; at first glance these are indeed strange bedfellows. Many are captivated by the incongruity of this image. Some people will find this humorous. Some may find it alarming or of questionable taste. Is it even appropriate to associate humor with topics as serious as death and spirituality? This chapter examines the linkages that can lead to death, humor, and spirituality as bedfellows.

Any examination of humor is complicated by its fragile and fugitive nature. Whenever one attempts to analyze it, it tends to dissipate. Dissection of an episode of spontaneous and shared laugher may lead to the question "What was so funny about that?" Humor is essentially an experience, you need to "be there" to fully appreciate what goes on.

Humor and laughter are ubiquitous. They arise so naturally that people may not be conscious of the frequency with which they punctuate day-to-day communication. As necessary constituents of humanity, they arise in many interactions. They enrich, enliven, and frequently transform social relations. "Anthropological constants," they are found in virtually every culture (Berger, 1997, p. x). Humor is so all-pervasive that situations involving death and dying and spirituality are likely to involve humor, despite the incongruence between the seriousness of these matters and the seeming lightheartedness of humor and laughter.

HUMOR IN CLIENT-CAREGIVER RELATIONSHIPS

Humor and laughter are integral parts of human relationship. They first arise in infancy with early smiles in response to the human face. Soon the smiles become particularized to familiar faces and expand to include baby laughter. Laughter is inherent in children's play and continues as a vital part of social relations throughout the lifespan. Given its universal nature, it is not surprising to find that humor is also present in many client-professional relationships.

Several studies of nurse-patient interactions report the significance of gentle humor as a component of communication. In research designed to identify and describe the comforting work of nurses, Bottorff, Gogag, and Engelberg-Lotzkar (1995) identified gentle humor as a central feature of comforting behavior. In an acute oncology setting, nurses used humor to help patients to relax, to endure distressing procedures, and to heighten their spirits. Humor was expressed through exaggerations, gentle teasing, slang or colloquial expressions, and highlighting incongruities. It generally occurred when the nurse was in close proximity to the patient. This is not the hilarity of high spirits and raucous behavior, but the gentle subtleties that punctuate human relationships.

Similarly, research seeking to understand nursing intimacy found humor to be a central component of nurse-patient interaction (Savage, 1995). Nurses used humorous banter as a means of allowing their personalities to become apparent and "to counter the effects of the uniform" (p. 79). Humor was effective for helping both patients and nurses in relieving stress, for lifting patients' spirits, and for raising staff morale.

Sociologists Yoels and Clair (1995) observed interactions in a university-based outpatient clinic and found that gentle humor played an important role in doctor-patient interactions. Doctors who approached topics of a personal or sensitive nature with light-hearted questions created a sense of safety and normality which protected the patient's self-esteem. Subdued and gentle humor served to forge a bond which helped to neutralize personally invasive topics and procedures. Each of these studies illustrate the subtle pervasiveness of humor in client-caregiver interactions and the benefits humor offers for therapeutic relationships.

HUMOR IN HOSPICE/PALLIATIVE CARE

A feisty elderly lady, given to freely expressing her opinions about life and death, was admitted to a palliative care inpatient unit. Her pain and symptoms were rapidly brought under control and she looked forward to a much needed rest prior to returning to her home. Settling herself early into her bed, her intention for sleep was thwarted by the sounds of laughter in the hall. She appeared at the nursing station, frustrated and annoyed, declaring for all to hear "A person cannot possibly die in peace around here because there is far too much laughing."

The observation that laughter is often present in hospice/palliative care units is not uncommon. Families and patients express surprise at how much laughter and lightheartedness they encounter in the setting. Humor has found a particular place in care of the dying for several reasons, including the importance of human relationships, its usefulness as a coping strategy, and its role in dealing with incongruities.

The importance of humor even in the presence of terminal illness is reinforced by research with hospice patients. Herth (1990) conducted an investigation of attitudes toward humor with 14 hospice clients in the final months of a terminal illness. When asked if humor was a part of life prior to the present diagnosis, 57 percent said that they had considered it important. When asked if humor would be helpful in their present circumstances, 85 percent replied that it would be helpful. However, only 14 percent indicated that there was any humor in their lives at present. They reported that family, friends, and caregivers avoided laugher because of the seriousness of their diagnosis. Comments included: "If I ever needed humor, it is now," "I try to be playful but others won't respond," and "Humor could help me feel like I wasn't sinking." Participants indicated that the one circumstance where humor should be limited was when serious dialogue is initiated and at the height of a crisis.

When patients are admitted to an inpatient hospice/palliative care unit, they are frequently in a symptom crisis which requires an immediate response. This is usually not the time for humor. However, hospice/palliative care is more than just physical symptom management. The emphasis is also on living as fully as possible for the time that remains. Once symptoms are better controlled, the emphasis may shift to psychosocial and existential concerns as they arise and to enhancing quality of life. It is here that relationships are paramount, and humor is likely to become more apparent. Humor will often not take the form of raucous hilarity (although this occasionally does erupt), but may be expressed in warm communication from the quieter end of the humor continuum.

Research in a palliative day care setting, where the patients are terminally ill but stable enough to attend a day program, explored communication processes among the persons enrolled in the program (Langley-Evans & Payne, 1997). Observations indicated that patients frequently engaged in "death talk" concerning their situations. Common themes included illness and symptom management, stories about illness and death, talk about the death of other patients, and acknowledgment of personal mortality. The distinctive feature of death talk was the lighthearted, jovial manner in which it was conducted. Although some of the talk was accompanied with overt jokes or humorous comments, much of it was communicated through innuendo, facial expression, gesture, emphasis, and timing. This typifies the subtleties and gentle nuances through which humor permeates social interactions. The authors conclude that lighthearted talk in a social setting enabled these terminally ill individuals to maintain an optimistic outlook and a fighting spirit. The implication for a hospice/palliative care setting is the importance of opportunities for social talk as an element of therapeutic communication and the importance of not resisting joviality as it arises.

HUMOR AS COPING STRATEGY

Humor and laughter are frequently cited as useful strategies for coping with stressful situations. Intensive care nurses in Thornton and White's research (1999) considered humor to be a stress reliever, a means of "letting off steam." Humor was an asset in improving communication, and in establishing and building relationships. Similarly, participants in Astedt-Kurki and Liukkonen's (1994) study of humor among nurses reported that humor was a major factor in managing job-related stress. "Humor can turn a hard and tedious job into an interesting one and at the same time cheer people up" (p. 187).

Many care teams who deal with death and dying are interdisciplinary, composed of a range of professional and semiprofessional members. An interdisciplinary team provides a diversity of strengths but also creates the potential for conflict. Humor often serves as a status equalizer in team work. It helps to blur status lines and cover uneasiness in power relations (Yoels & Clair, 1995). Shared laughter helps to build trust, deflect any anger or defensiveness, and increase acceptance of imperfections in coworkers.

Black Humor

A consistent theme across humor research in health care settings is the frequency with which black or gallows humor appears. Black humor may be particularly salient in settings where death and dying are common. Gallows humor has been reported throughout history in circumstances of vulnerability. Freud is said to have had a high opinion of black humor, considering it a hallmark of maturity (O'Connell, 1968).

A person who indulged in gallows humor was believed not to repress or deny the thought of his own death. Others (Peschel & Peschel, 1985) identify black humor as a kind of lifeline, a way of protecting one's self. Painful emotions are replaced with more pleasant feelings, fears or terrors replaced by a laugh.

People who work with the dying need a sense of perspective and balance in order to be effective in this setting over a sustained period. Humor can serve as a coping mechanism to deal with the potential vulnerability that accompanies constant exposure to loss and death. Participants in Thornton and White's (1999) research observed that humor in critical care areas seemed to be "sicker" than elsewhere in health care, reflecting the constant exposure to stressful situations. Staff found that using humor helped them to cope and survive and also served as a tension relief. In addition to staff humor, they shared humor with patients and families to help to bring a sense of normality in an otherwise alien environment fraught with the realities of serious illness.

Cartoons are excellent examples of black humor which objectify death as an image one dares to laugh about. The image of the Grim Reaper is a graphic example. Death is depicted as an object, assigning it the status of the mundane and familiar.

While black humor is helpful in dealing with repeated exposure to death, there are potential hazards if it used as a sole means of coping. Leiber (1985), discussing humor in a critical care setting, notes that while black humor can relieve fear and help to preserve the energy needed to respond to a crisis, it is not a sufficient substitute for acknowledging and dealing with the consequences. Persons who work with death and dying should be alert for persons who use humor to excess to avoid dealing with the seriousness of what is happening.

Humor as Release

> During the second week of an exhausting bedside vigil, a patient's husband devised an unusual form of traction to correct the malalignment of his wife's head. Entering the room, the nurse noted his efforts and could not avoid being amused by his unusual use of the drawer of the bedside table for securing the device. Scarcely able to suppress a grin, she commended the husband for his ingenuity and inventiveness. He responded "It seems to work, but do you think it is humane?" Without warning, laughter erupted, spread to include the patient's daughter, and accelerated to the point of tears. Afterward, the husband commented, "It was so good to laugh, I needed that."

This is a classic example of the laughter that relieves tension. With a buildup of exhaustion, sadness, and loss, there must be a release. Release often comes in the form of tears, sometimes in the form of anger and aggression, other times in laughter. Freud referred to laughter as a safe and acceptable outlet for pent-up emotions (Kuschel, 1994). Repressed emotion is released in a way which reduces anxiety without completely removing it.

One of the reasons why laughing provides such a sense of relief is physiological (Fry, 1994). During laughter, there is a temporary increase in pulse and blood pressure which then fall below the prelaughter level. Respirations deepen and oxygen intake increases. In accompaniment, muscle tension is released. The relaxation response is accompanied by increased social and psychological animation. Tension is relieved and well-being increases.

HUMOR AND SPIRITUALITY

In response to the question, "How is it with you?" a gentleman on the palliative care unit replies "At this point in my life, every day above ground is a good day."

Those who work with death and dying will recognize the significance of this comment. Humor is often used to express otherwise taboo topics, things that are too emotionally charged to be shared directly. This individual knows that he is dying and is communicating in the way that is most comfortable for him.

Every person is a spiritual being, with a unique history, personal beliefs, and individual concerns. When faced with the reality of imminent death, existential issues concerning meaning and loss frequently arise. Many will seek to formulate an understanding or belief concerning what follows life. Some will explore these issues within a particular religious framework, others will not. When exploring spiritual issues, humor may be particularly valuable. In the case of the vignette, humor was a means of communication, a way of approaching an otherwise taboo subject. Persons who joke around with expressions like "the Man upstairs" or the "pearly gates" (a common theme in jokes about death and dying) may be demonstrating spiritual or existential concerns (see Figure 1).

In a book on the merits of humor in the face of death and dying, Allen Klein (1998) tells a story about W. C. Fields, a self-proclaimed non-believer. A few days before his death his friend found him in bed reading the Bible. "Bill," said his friend, "You don't believe in God. What are you doing reading the Bible?" Replied W. C. Fields, "Looking for loopholes."

Some religious scholars have suggested that there are similarities between spirituality, religion, and humor. Both humor and religion are expressions of freedom of the human spirit, and of the capacity of that spirit to stand outside itself and to view the scene from a point of distance (Niebuhr, 1969). Humor does not provide an escape from the reality of dealing with death, nor does it offer any solutions. What is does do is present a moment's reprieve from the heaviness of the situation. In the words of Eberhart (1993), humor reinterprets "life's demoralizing aspects in ways that strengthen one's morale for living" (p. 98). From this vantage point, humor is elevated to the level of a transcendent experience. Berger (1997) suggests that humor serves transcendent functions both in a "lower and a higher key" (p. 205). In the lower key, humor results in a moment of transcending the ordinary into a different reality where everyday life is briefly suspended. In a higher key, humor may serve a redemptive function. In this case, humor creates a moment where the world is temporarily made whole, and the miseries of the human condition are abolished.

Figure 1. "The good news is you get to stay here, the bad news is
your luggage went to hell."
Drawing by William Canty ©. Used with permission.

When confronting death and dying, one is inevitably faced with making sense of incongruities. Some people simultaneously hope for cure and pray for release from suffering. Exhausted loved ones find themselves overwhelmed with the burden of caregiving, and are often afraid to ask "When will this be over?" Spiritual questions about why the suffering has occurred and why to this particular person are common. While humor cannot offer answers, it is often a means of dealing with the incongruities. Hospice patients in Herth's research (1990) reported benefits from humor that could be interpreted as spiritual functions. Humor helped them to maintain a sense of connectedness with themselves and with others. It served to engender hope and to create a sense of perspective. Connectedness, perspective, hope; each are manifestations of spirituality.

Similar claims about the value of humor in maintaining hope are reflected in a study with adolescent oncology patients (Hinds, Martin, & Vogel, 1987). Participants indicated that when nurses initiated or responded to teasing or other playful interaction, they were perceived as lighthearted and creating a sense of hope. Humor allowed a temporary escape from the burdens of cancer. Participants reported that humor did not distort the reality of the illness but emphasized the nurses' belief in their ability to cope with the illness.

Humor does not provide answers for the big questions regarding meaning and purpose, nor is it a substitute for spirituality. The solemn moments of spiritual anguish are unlikely to include humor. Humor, however, has considerable merit in providing a means of access to otherwise inaccessible territory. As well, its power to transform the moment is too vital to be ignored.

HUMOR AS THERAPY

In recent years, humor and laughter have been increasingly promoted for their healing properties. The popularization of humor as healer largely began with the work of Norman Cousins. In his book *Anatomy of an Illness: As Perceived by the Patient* (1979), Cousins recounts his experiences coping with ankylosing spondylitis. Dissatisfied with conventional approaches, he checked himself out of the hospital and into a hotel where he watched humorous movies including the Marx Brothers and Candid Camera reruns. Cousins claimed that ten minutes of hearty laughter yielded two yearned-for hours of painless sleep. In the wake of widespread interest and demand for Cousins' book, humor began to be acclaimed as a therapy in its own right. The possibility that humor might be viewed as a panacea arose. In a later volume, Cousins (1983) responded to that possibility, stating that he intended that humor be seen as a metaphor for the range of positive emotions, including faith, love, will to live, cheerfulness, creativity, playfulness, confidence, and great expectations. Cousins claims that such positive emotions serve to set the stage for recovery from illness. Persons receiving hospice care are not expected to recover from their illnesses. Humor cannot be offered as a panacea that will overcome the reality of terminal disease. However, the healing effects that humor and positive emotions offer have a rightful place in care of the dying.

GUIDELINES FOR
INTRODUCING HUMOR

Assigned to care for the mother of a stillborn infant, a nurse remarked to her colleagues "I just can't get that woman to talk. I tried my usual humor to break the ice but this time it just didn't work."

Humor appreciation is individual and varies among individuals and also among circumstances. While gentle humor is usually an effective way to establish rapport, there will be times where it may be misunderstood or inappropriate. As hospice/palliative care is an area where crises occur and emotionally-charged moments of loss and death are common, there are moments when humor will not have a place. Participants in humor research consistently report that attempts at humor are not helpful or appreciated at times of crisis (Dunn, 1993; Herth, 1990; Leiber, 1986;

Wallis, 1998). Experienced caregivers will recognize the importance of sensitivity and intuition as guidelines for introducing humor.

When deciding whether or not to introduce humor in a critical care setting, Leiber (1986) identified receptiveness, timing, and content as criteria. Receptivity to humor can be assessed by observing responses to subtle cues such as a wink or a benign playful comment. Attentiveness to family/patient interactions may give a clue as to whether or not humor is a part of their normal communication. Timing is critical in introducing humor. ICU nurses in one study stressed the importance of using care when introducing humor. Humor was "nice to break down barriers, but be careful how you do it" (Thornton & White, 1995, p. 272). As discussed earlier, periods of crises and sadness where sensitivity and compassion are needed will usually not be the time to introject humor. There is some evidence that humor is particularly problematic when anxiety is the predominant feature in a situation (Nezu, Nezu, & Blissett, 1988; Pasquali, 1990). While humor may be effective in modifying stressful situations, persons struggling with acute anxiety are unlikely to be receptive. As well as receptivity and appropriate timing, content is always important. Humor may spontaneously arise around circumstances which are not normally funny and that should certainly not be suppressed. On the other hand, humor of a sexist, racist, or ridiculing nature will always be inappropriate.

Sensitivity and intuition are important factors in knowing when to introduce humor (Astedt-Kurki & Liukkonen, 1994). Nurses in Thornton and White's research (1999) reported that they most often used humor intuitively and not as a conscious act. While humor often arises spontaneously, the caregiver who is sensitive and caring will nevertheless be guided by an inner intuition which will direct when or when not to introduce humor. Similarly, patients in a coronary care unit reported that humor became a part of interactions most effectively after a caring relationship had been established (Wallis, 1998).

> An elderly lady was dying a slow but not painful death. The daughters were holding a patient vigil at her bedside day and night. After several days, one of the sisters poked the other one and said "How much longer do you think this is going to take?" At that point, Mom opened her eyes, looked at her daughters, and proclaimed "A watched pot never boils." (Klein, 1998, p. 29)

Vigils at the bedside as a loved one passes their final days are exhausting and emotionally difficult times. Caregivers may help to ease the situation by encouraging families to share memories about the one who is dying. Humorous anecdotes frequently surface as memories are shared. The laughter that ensues often relieves the tension and warms the atmosphere. Families sometimes will be alarmed that they have dared to laugh in such grave circumstances. Caregivers can offer a gift in reassurance that they are not violating any sense of propriety and that it is alright to laugh in the situation. As in countless other interactions, humor and laughter transform the sadness of impending death into a moment of redemption, a moment when the world temporarily becomes whole.

CONCLUSION

Humor, spirituality, and death: strange bedfellows? At first glance, certainly yes. Upon reflection, certainly not. By virtue of its capacity to transform, increase coping abilities, relieve tension, and foster relationships, humor becomes a welcome bedfellow in the company of death and spirituality.

REFERENCES

Astedt-Kurki, P., & Liukkonen, A. (1994). Humour in nursing care. *Journal of Advanced Nursing, 20,* 183-188.
Berger, P. L. (1997). *Redeeming laughter: The comic dimension of human experience.* New York: De Gruyter.
Bottorff, J. L., Gogag, M., & Engelberg-Lotzkar, M. (1995). Comforting: Exploring the work of cancer nurses. *Journal of Advanced Nursing, 22,* 1077-1084.
Cousins, N. (1979). *Anatomy of an illness.* New York: Norton.
Cousins, N. (1983). *The healing heart.* New York: Norton.
Dunn, B. (1993). Use of therapeutic humour by psychiatric nurses. *British Journal of Nursing,* 468-473.
Eberhart, E. (1993). Humor as a religious experience. In W. F. Fry & W. A. Salameh (Eds.), *Advances in humor and psychotherapy* (pp. 105-118). Sarasota, FL.: Professional Resource Press.
Fry, W. F. (1994). The biology of humor. *Humor, 7*(2), 111-126.
Herth, K. (1990). Contributions of humor as perceived by the terminally ill. *American Journal of Hospice Care, 7*(1), 36-40.
Hinds, P. S., Martin, J., & Vogel, R. J. (1987). Nursing strategies to influence hopefulness during oncologic illness. *Journal of the Association of Pediatric Oncology Nurses, 4,* 14-22.
Kuschel, K.-J. (1994). *Laughter: A theological reflection.* London: SCM Press.
Klein, A. (1998). *The courage to laugh: Humor, hope, and healing in the face of death and dying.* New York: Penguin Putnam.
Langley-Evans, A., & Payne, S. (1997). Light-hearted talk in a palliative day care context. *Journal of Advanced Nursing, 26,* 1091-1097.
Leiber, D. B. (1986). Laughter and humor in critical care. *Dimensions of Critical Care Nursing, 5,* 162-170.
Nezu, A. M., Nezu, C. M., & Blissett, S. E. (1988). Sense of humor as a moderator of the relation between stressful events and psychological distress: A prospective analysis. *Journal of Personality and Social Psychology, 54*(3), 520-525.
Niebuhr, R. (1969). Humour and faith. In M. C. Hyers (Ed.), *Holy laughter* (pp. 134-149). New York: Seabury.
O'Connell, W. E. (1968). Humor and death. *Psychological Reports, 22,* 391-402.
Peschel, R. E., & Peschel, E. R. (1985). Aberrant medical humor: Case studies, literary histories. *Pharos, 48*(1), 17-22.
Pasquali, E. A. (1990). Learning to laugh: Humor as therapy. *Journal of Psychosocial Nursing, 28*(3), 31-35.
Savage, J. (1995). *Nursing intimacy. An ethnographic approach to nurse-patient interaction.* London: Scutari Press.

Thornton, J., & White, A. (1999). A Heideggerian investigation into the lived experience of humour by nurses in an intensive care unit. *Intensive and Critical Care Nursing, 15*(5), 266-278.

Wallis, M. C. (1998). Responding to suffering—The experience of professional nurse caring in the coronary care unit. *International Journal for Human Caring, 2*(2), 35-44.

Yoels, W. C., & Clair, J. M. (1995). Laughter in the clinic: Humor as social organization. *Symbolic Interaction, 18*(1), 39-58.

CHAPTER 6

Death and the Postmodern Self: Individualism, Religion, and the Transformation of the Modern Self

Raymond L. M. Lee

Death in modernity makes no provisions for the continuity of the self. To die a modern death is synonymous with self-effacement. But in postmodernity, the fragmentation of the self suggests that death may not be the same as self-termination. The revival of death-consciousness brings into relief the boundary between modern consciousness of the world and postmodern inquiry into that consciousness. It addresses the meaning of the modern self in an era that can no longer maintain an unequivocal belief in the firmness of being. Death in postmodernity restructures our thinking on the meaning of the self.

The fear of dying is universal. Major and minor religions have evolved from attempts to conquer that fear. Yet as human beings become more determined to master the world, the dread of death is kept increasingly at arm's length. In the end, the realization that the goals of world-mastery cannot but intensify the meaning of human mortality produces more angst in the modern world. But the mysteries of death continue to elude modern understanding of life's end. Death is thus reduced to a passive acceptance of one's fate, a function of actuarial calculations, a clinical pronouncement of organic failure, a demographic assessment of population changes, or simply an existential puzzle that will not go away.

Modern Western philosophy assiduously avoids confrontation with the question of death because it attributes more value to the living. It identifies all manner of being with all manner of life. Death is seen as reflecting the helplessness of humans in the face of the apparent termination of purpose. Philosophy as a discourse on purpose, therefore, cannot address the meaning of death without subverting itself. Consequently, death has to be reinvented as nihilism, the belief that nothing truly exists and that meaninglessness is the only outcome of all experiences in the world. Under this label nihilism makes death, like other phenomena in the world, seem unreal. However, nihilism has not effectively stood up to the intensification of individualism in the 20th century. It is because of individualism that the death knell for death consciousness has been postponed. As Walter (1994) puts it, "[a]n emotionally satisfying, rather than a spiritually efficacious, death is actually a twentieth-century ideal" (p. 22). Hence at the end of the 20th century, we find an increasing social concern with the death experience.

The aim of this chapter is to explore the growing preoccupation with death as a product of the ethical conflict between individualism and technological innovation. This is a conflict that involves the meaning of the modern self. Self-autonomy in modernity implies the right to choose life or death without interference from outside bodies. Even religion, as a sacred realm associated with the meaning of death, has no direct influence on individual decisions and actions stemming from the sense of self-autonomy. The modern celebration of the self, however, has undergone dramatic changes in recent years. Modern reflexivity problematized self-consciousness by intensifying doubt on the essence of self-identity. This doubt has induced a sense of self-fragmentation that challenges the notion of self-autonomy. Emerging from these conditions of reflexive doubt, the postmodern self ponders the meaning of death in an entirely different way. The postmodern approach to death breaks down individualism to suggest new meanings of the self in death.

INDIVIDUALISM IN DEATH

> For the human person, unlike the horse, knows that he is going to die, knows that death can be a friend, and knows how to bring on death at a time when he can suffer no more. He has the capacity for death by choice; the horse does not. (Maguire, 1974, p. 153)

The implication of the above quotation is that human individuals, unlike other living beings, are naturally empowered to determine the time and place of their own deaths in circumstances that seem to warrant it. Except for wars, executions, accidents, natural catastrophes, and events beyond one's control, the determination of one's own death looms as an issue of individual freedom. Naturally, this is not an issue that is unique to modernity. But what is definitively modern about this issue concerns the individual's freedom to choose death in the context of medical and technological developments that can sustain life indefinitely. The modernity of this choice is not just about personal meanings but about one's confrontation with death in an environment that is both psychologically alienating and technologically innovative. In the words of Ahronheim and Weber (1992),

> As with other aspects of modern life, modern death is infinitely more complex, technological, and impersonal than it used to be. Hard choices must be made— medical, ethical, legal, financial, and emotional choices—and many of us are not adequately prepared to confront them. (p. 9)

The fact that Ahronheim and Weber (1992) referred to our inexperience in dealing with these choices suggests an emerging problem of individualism in the context of technological changes. It implies that modernity has increased our range of choices in relation to the growth of new knowledge, but these choices are hampered by rules, laws, and questions of morality that create dilemmas over the meaning of the right to die. In short, the modern self in being surrounded by life-enhancing technologies does not discount death as a fundamental right, but is still embroiled in a moral struggle to make that right acceptable.

The right to die is, perhaps, one of the more profound developments in individualistic thought in the modern era. In the United States, voluntary organizations attempting to promote this right emerged in the middle to late 1930s. But it was not until 1967 that the Euthanasia Educational Council decided to promote the living will as a document of advanced directive to assert the meaning of the right to die (Fulton & Metress, 1995, p. 119). The living will is a peculiar development of death anticipation by the individual. It is a future-oriented statement made by the conscious self in determining his or her right to die at another time when he or she may have possibly lost conscious control (as when a person falls into a coma or persistent vegetative state). Because of the highly publicized cases of Karen Ann Quinlan (1975) and Nancy Cruzan (1987), the legal significance of living wills in the United States has increased to the extent that now every state has passed laws empowering the enactment of living wills and/or durable powers of attorney for health care (that is, the appointment of an agent or proxy to make health care decisions) (see Fulton & Metress, 1995, pp. 72-77, 84-91, 119-127; Corr, Nabe, & Corr, 1994, pp. 337-343, 364-365, 377). In 1991, the U.S. Congress passed the Patient Self-Determination Act that requires all health care providers receiving funding under Medicare or Medicaid to inform patients of their right to accept or refuse treatment and to complete living wills (Fulton & Metress, 1995, pp. 133-135).

These developments in the United States suggest that in a highly modern society, the sanctity of the self in charting its destiny is highlighted as legal directives in death preparation. The self as a symbol of ontological control refuses to relinquish its sense of autonomy even in the final stages of life. In the eyes of Ahronheim and Weber (1992),

> living wills and [durable powers of attorney for health care] simplify the process of getting the law to work for us and *strengthen* our position at the end of our lives. They give us back *control* over our bodies—over what can and can't be done to us. And they enlist everyone else around us—from the health care institution to the doctor, nurse, social worker, friend, or family member—as part of the support team responsible for making sure our wishes are carried out. (p. 225)

This is certainly a statement that emphasizes the reality of the self in struggling to maintain its sense of dignity in the face of bodily disintegration. It reflects the Cartesian dualism inherent in the modernist separation of self and body—the triumph of the self over the perishable nature of the body.

But contradictions have emerged from this dualism that pits the morality of self-preservation against the voluntary destruction of the body. The distinction of the self from the body tends to increase the sense of moral responsibility on the part of individual consciousness toward the healthy maintenance of the body. This is a type of bodily individualism that construes the significance of the body as a special vessel of the self. Hence, the decision of the self to destroy its own body (in cases of suicide) raises the problem of guilt by dualism in which remorse is triggered by the assumption that the self has failed the body. This problem is intensified in cases of euthanasia where other selves are implicated in consensual bodily destruction. Although euthanasia is considered by some people as a moral effort to assist actively or passively in the bodily destruction of someone in deep pain, the controversies raised by such action often bring into relief the difficulties in reconciling the moral actions of the self with the impulse for physical survival.

In the United States, the case of Dr. Jack Kervokian, a retired pathologist who had assisted in the suicides of several people suffering from various terminal illnesses, illustrates the paradox of dualistic individualism in modernity (Fulton & Metress, 1995, pp. 187-198). This is a paradox that juxtaposes freedom with responsibility. On the one hand, the notion of personal choice in modernity symbolizes individual freedom. If a person chooses to die, it is his or her right not to do otherwise since it is assumed that the sovereignty of the self precedes everything else. Thus, an uncoerced decision made by the self to end bodily existence simply means the right to die without external interference. But on the other hand, the moral responsibility of the self toward the body has inculcated a sense of duty in maintaining physical survival. The development of new medical technologies that can prolong life has enhanced this sense of duty. Hence, the role of Dr. Kervokian in providing the apparatus by which terminally ill selves could voluntarily end their bodily existence invariably exposed the underlying tension between freedom of choice and moral duty.

Although the modern self has realized new found freedom not experienced in the past, it is still not free of moral obligations to the preservation of the body. This is a contradiction emerging from the tensions between individual choice and professional authority. But through the newly released authority of the individual self, people are attempting to determine their own end rather than placing such decision in the hands of doctors and administrators (Walter, 1994, pp. 28-31). In other words, there is an attempt to expunge the guilt stemming from body-self dualism. Reducing this guilt is a way of attributing less importance to the rigid separation between body and self.

This reduction of guilt favors an alternative perception of death as more than a physical process. It opens the self to addressing the death process as a state of mind. By rationalizing death as stages in mind transformation, the fear of dying as solely a physical experience is mitigated. Walter (1994, p. 30) treats the work and writings of Elisabeth Kübler-Ross (1973) on death and dying as pioneering this change in death consciousness. He even refers to her as "the prophetess of the new religion of the self, the revivalist *par excellence*." Nevertheless, the focus on the individual in the final stages of life is still confined to the here-and-now. The contemporary revival of death consciousness is very much a secular affair.

THE ALIENATION OF RELIGION

Secularization is the process that gradually reduces the authority of religious institutions and their influence over the personal decisions of the general public. It is a process that goes hand in hand with modernity. In the separation of social and cultural realms, so characteristic of the modern transformation of traditional societies, each realm comes to manifest its own values, norms, and boundaries. Differentiation and specialization typify the maintenance of autonomy that accentuates the unique identity of each social or cultural realm. To the extent that modernity has created diversity and novelty, so secularization has cut into these changes by isolating religion from other social realms to constitute its own domain of practice and knowledge (Chaves, 1994).

Death in modernity is, therefore, an experience embedded in cultural and social differentiation. It is an experience of fragmentation without the sense of religion as an indispensable carrier of ultimate meanings. One can die without being religious or religion can exist without being treated as the resolution to the mysteries of death. In modernity, the symbolic link between religion and death has weakened because religion has been deregulated to serve other purposes that do not necessarily deal with the afterlife (Beckford, 1992, pp. 171-172). This means that religion is no longer addressed as a social or cultural institution inextricably affecting all aspects of an individual's life. On the contrary, religion assumes the role of a voluntary sphere of practice and knowledge that is flexibly connected to other spheres of social and cultural activities. In that sense, religion "can be combined with virtually any other set of values" (Beckford, 1992, pp. 171-172). And these ideas or values may not have anything to do with death.

However, in pre-modern societies we find that religion plays a crucial role in the death process. Religion in pre-modern societies tends not to be independent of other social and cultural activities. The lack of social and cultural differentiation in pre-modern societies implies that religion plays an important part in life-cycle rituals that contribute to the integration of the community. Citing the work of Herbert Spencer, the 19th century evolutionist, who argued for the social cohesion of death, Hill (1973) explained that

> Ecclesiastical institutions thus stand for social continuity and social cohesion, and because they embody the primitive notion of the rule of the dead over the living their function is to preserve the product of earlier experience in the face of the modifying influence of more recent experience. They are above all else bearers of tradition, and agents of social stability. (p. 29)

In other words, the religious function of death is to maintain social cohesion and stability in the face of human loss. The pre-modern notion of death is embedded in religious beliefs and actions that actualize the meaning of existence. Death may unexpectedly strike down members of a community, but certain religious rituals provide the restorative mechanism for realizing cultural continuity and harmony. Some of these rituals may simulate death in order to strengthen the meaning of life in the social order. In Sir James Frazer's (1957) monumental study of magic and religion, his discussion of totemism (the affiliation of clan members' lives with a particular animal or plant) brought him to view the initiatory rites of death and resurrection in many pre-modern societies as critical to the whole notion of social order:

Such rites become intelligible if we suppose that their substance consists in extracting the youth's soul in order to transfer it to his totem. For the extraction of his soul would naturally be supposed to kill the youth or at least to throw him into a death-like trance, which the savage hardly distinguishes from death. His recovery would then be attributed either to the gradual recovery of his system from the violent shock which it had received, or, more probably, to the infusion into him of fresh life drawn from the totem. Thus the essence of these initiatory rites, so far as they consist in a simulation of death and resurrection, would be an exchange of life or souls between the man and his totem. (pp. 905-906)

Frazer was trying to argue that the simulation of death in these rituals was a symbolic act of exchange between human and animal or plant in a broader scheme of things that did not emphasize a separation of phenomenal experiences. Indeed, the sacred nature of life was summarized in the initiatory rites involving the enactment of death. The pre-modern individual did not see the need to distinguish between religion as the sacred interpretation of all experiences and death as a symbolic passage to other experiences.

It was the modern individual who made this distinction an inherent part of life experiences. Religion was institutionalized as the sacred realm of clerics and men of God who provided ideological sustenance for the meaning of salvation. Death took the path of a literal departure from the physical world into the unknown. Religion and death met only at funerals and memorial services, but their symbolic connections to a holistic consciousness were no longer intact. Max Weber, the eminent German sociologist, traced the severance of these symbolic connections to the influences of Calvinism in the 16th and 17th centuries. In his well-known work on the Protestant ethic, he argued that under Calvinism Protestant thought came to regard salvation as attainable without magical means. Hence, death marked the journey of the soul toward salvation but not necessarily the symbolic exchange enacted in religious rituals. This was what Weber (1958) meant when he said,

The genuine Puritan even rejected all signs of religious ceremony at the grave and buried his nearest and dearest without song or ritual in order that no superstition, no trust in the effects of magical and sacramental forces on salvation should creep in. (p. 105)

In modernity, religion has taken on the façade of organized liturgy for the departed but it bears no resemblance to the pre-modern and traditional rites for empowering the symbolic exchange between the living and the dead. Religion is no longer an arena for communication with the dead because, by extension of Weber's thesis, it has been overshadowed by political economy. It is in political economy that the world is created anew by an incessant obsession with production, consumption, and reproduction. In this context of world-affirmation, religion cannot afford to pretend that it is in the business of death and dying, but to establish itself as its own sphere of salvation that is not antithetical to social and economic production. That is why Baudrillard (1993), in his treatise on political economy and death, proclaimed that political economy is only constructed . . . or designed so as to be recognised as immortal by a future civilisation, or as an instance of truth. As for religion, this is unimaginable other than in the Last Judgement, where God recognises his own. (pp. 185-196)

So religion, far from banishing death into the netherworld, recycles death as a preserve of political economy. It means that religion has replaced the symbolic exchange of death with a homiletic display of bereavement. The modern structure of bereavement itself cannot prevent death from occurring, but it is part of what Baudrillard (1993, p. 145) has termed "the political economy of individual salvation." This political economy is not merely about production, accumulation, and consumption but elevates the meaning of value into a deferment of death. More precisely, religion is encompassed by this political economy that in Baudrillard's (1993, p. 146) eyes is driven by "the obsession with death and the will to abolish death through accumulation," and so in the long run it endorses "a productive system no longer familiar with the reversibility of gift-exchange, but instead with the irreversibility of quantitative growth."

The symbolic connection between religion and death that is manifested in premodern societies as an exchange relationship has been distorted in modernity into a desideratum of economic fulfillment or an expenditure of material resources that remakes the centrality of the self. The sacred consciousness attributed to exchange rituals at death cannot be expressed as a holistic experience in modern circumstances because the self-promoting processes of labor differentiation and accumulative accountability have gained priority over the meaning of exchange. Without the sense of sacredness in symbolic exchange, the meaning of consciousness at death becomes superfluous because the question of the afterlife fades out at the borders of modern political economy. What then is the significance of consciousness if death in modernity is constrained by political economy?

THE FATE OF CONSCIOUSNESS

Consciousness is often taken for granted as the *sine qua non* of existence. Without consciousness we would not be in a position to imagine the emergence of world-experiences and their consequences. Yet the consciousness of consciousness makes it imperative for us to question the meaning of existence. By being aware of the presence of knowledge, we are led to inquire into the identity of self, experience, and phenomena.

In modernity, this identity rests upon the construction of concepts that are rooted in the notion of world-mastery. This is not a mere notion of control but of an overarching reality constituted by a commitment to empirical worth. For Berger, Berger, and Kellner (1974, pp. 102-104), this worth is embedded in a symbolic universe arising from technological production and bureaucracy. In this universe, consciousness is guided by various themes related to rationality, differentiation, plurality, creativity, progress, and so on. These are themes of action, movement, and change, thereby suggesting that consciousness in modernity has a restless and irrepressible quality. It is a consciousness that continually seeks to establish new frontiers of experience and meaning in this world without reducing the power of subjectivity. Hence, modern consciousness represents a force of renewal and self-perpetuation in the world.

The tendency toward renewal in modern consciousness is empowered by reflexivity, the unique human ability to cogitate on unfolding experiences and to remake the world based on these cogitations. But reflexivity itself can be destabilizing because whatever is reflected upon becomes the reason for reform and change. Nothing can remain the same under reflexivity since the process of reflecting implies a source of constant dissatisfaction. This was what Giddens (1990, p. 38) meant when he asserted that the "reflexivity of modern social life consists in the fact that social practices are constantly examined and reformed in the light of incoming information about those very practices, thus constitutively altering their character." Reflexivity therefore unmakes and remakes the world without giving consciousness a chance of attaining a state of equanimity. In that sense, consciousness becomes animated by a desire for continuous manifestation. Death is thus construed as a barrier to the fulfillment of that desire.

The reflexive consciousness of the modern self is ultimately weighed down by the symbols of world-affirmation and transformation. The circulation of these symbols anchors consciousness in the struggle to preserve the notion of an empirical self that can only assert itself through the dialectical actions of the world. These are actions that underlie the circular relationship between consciousness and social change: reflexive consciousness compels change, which in turn becomes the condition that imperils quietude of mind. Under these circumstances, it is almost impossible for modern consciousness to apprehend death as a point of transition beyond symbolic circularity. Rather, modern consciousness approaches death as a cessation of the physical self and with it, the termination of symbolic activity. For this reason, symbolic exchange with the dead is not encompassed by that consciousness.

Yet modern consciousness is not totally dismissive of other forms of consciousness, but is unable to fully embrace them within its symbolic universe of production, organization, and change. It attempts to explore other forms of consciousness by labeling them altered states of consciousness, as if to imply that modern consciousness is the center from which other types of consciousness can be identified and evaluated. Altered states of consciousness, therefore, represent mental states and experiences that do not conform to the conventional understanding of consciousness within the modern framework of production and accumulation. Thus Bourguignon's (1973, pp. 4-5) identification of altered states of consciousness with trance and spirit possession (and with psychiatric terms such as dissociation, hysteria, catalepsy, epilepsy, somnambulism, and hallucination) suggests that modern consciousness recognizes other levels of mental experiences. But it places them outside the spectrum of utilitarian meanings. Altered states of consciousness are seen to be non-utilitarian because they fail to contribute to the meaning of political economy. They dispense with the entire notion of work and salvation in favor of non-rationality.

However, altered states of consciousness have not been explicitly associated with death. There is, of course, the metaphorical allusion to trance as temporary death but it is not given the same status as death. Because altered states of consciousness is the "other" of modern consciousness, the former merely reflects what the latter is not. Together both forms of consciousness traverse the territory charted by political economy—one for constituting the dominant identity of self-achievement and system maintenance, the other reflecting the abnegation of self in the non-utilitarian mode. Neither form can transcend political economy because the relationship between self and consciousness is trapped within the rational/non-rational dualism of world construction and production.

Death exceeds political economy but it cannot be embraced by a consciousness devoted to the maintenance of systemic realities and the fulfillment of worldly progress. Hence, this consciousness knows of death but cannot apprehend or comprehend it. Like the various dualistic categories ensconced within political economy, death is conceived as the opposite of life, as an abyss of deep unknowing or unconsciousness. The fear of death in modernity is thus the dread of non-being or the extinction of the self, the end of symbolic action in political economy that endorses the meaning of existence.

Ironically, this fear has contributed to the emergence of death-consciousness. Unlike ordinary and altered states of consciousness, death-consciousness is a peculiar development in modernity that impels the self to re-examine the condition of its inevitable demise. This development represents an increasing awareness of the death process in modern political economy, but it does not seriously probe the possibility of existence beyond life in political economy. The present preoccupation with death is more concerned with the psychological conditions of dying. It orients consciousness toward a personal confrontation with the closing stages of life. To understand the death process in this way, as Elisabeth Kübler-Ross (1973) does with her theory of the stages of dying, is to reflexively collate the final moments of people's lives into a symbolic rapprochement with the termination of self-identity. The dying self, therefore, utilizes death-consciousness as a way to accept the slowing down of symbolic action in political economy. This acceptance allegedly takes the edge off the fear of dying.

In this sense, death-consciousness is a type of panacea for anxiety generated by the anticipation of self-termination. Its emergence can be considered a consequence of realizing the limits of symbolic action in political economy. But this consciousness has yet to engage with the meaning of the conjoined relationship between life and death. In modernity life and death are sharply differentiated, but in postmodernity the self may come to experience the continuity of these two spheres.

THE POSTMODERN CONUNDRUM

The juxtaposition of subjective choice and the insignificance of the subject suggests a condition of fragmentation that is alleged to be characteristic of postmodernity (see Sarup, 1993). This simply means that a dying person simultaneously accepts the imminent demise of his or her physical subjectivity and accentuates the vestiges of his or her self by determining how to die a good death. Walter (1994, p. 47ff) approaches this fragmented condition by calling the new way of dying a neo-modern death rather than a postmodern death. According to him, neo-modern death involves the exercise of choice in the good death and the necessity of accepting professional advice in death preparation. Walter himself does not subscribe to the reality of a postmodern death because he views the negation of the subject in postmodernism as incongruent with the contemporary image of the dying person who hangs on to the notion of self. Moreover, he argues that "[i]t is difficult to see how postmodern culture, a culture that celebrates freedom from natural and physical constraint, can acknowledge the continued reality of death without undermining its own existence" (Walter, 1994, p. 45).

What are we, then, to make of the contemporary revival of death-consciousness under conditions that promote a decentered view of human subjectivity? Walter's notion of neo-modern death offers a benign view of dying without the prospect of losing one's subjectivity. Yet this subjectivity comprises the pivot of death consciousness itself—whether our understanding of death-consciousness can modify subjectivity into accepting a level of existence beyond the mere survival of the self. The postmodern view does not unconditionally reject the reality of death. Neither does it posit an existential level beyond the reality of death. It is in the deconstructive aspects of postmodernism that we find the prospect of redefining the meaning of subjectivity in death. This does not imply the eventual disappearance of subjectivity in death but the disprivileging of the self in death (as in life) in order to suggest a different mode of understanding the significance of impermanence on both sides of the existential divide.

What is the self in postmodernity? Given the large corpus of writings on postmodernity in recent years, it is not unreasonable to assume that there is a changing attitude toward the meaning of the self in the modern conventional sense of the word. The idea of a center, a core of characteristics, or an origin from which a cluster of traits could be clearly identified forms the modern notion of the self. It is the ground on which modern individuals discuss and disseminate their being. Far from treating the self as a source of disillusionment, modern thinkers attribute so much intentionality and autonomy to the self that it stands out like a sore thumb in the universe, to be lavished with attention and nursed repeatedly.

Without the great pacifier that reflexivity has turned out to be, the modern self cannot possibly exist. The belief that reflexive awareness is an unique condition of the self reinforces the dogma of *tabula rasa,* the blank slate on which individual experiences are inscribed and recalled in order that biographical assumptions are made meaningful. Thus reflexivity is the internal dynamic that brings to life the reality continuum in which the modern self is fixated. But the interesting thing about reflexivity is that it is a double-edged sword, one side of which can be used to cut through that reality continuum. In postmodernity, it is that edge which wields the power for eviscerating the innards of self-meanings and self-assumptions.

Postmodernity opens up the discourse on the fragility of the self. In one stroke, reflexivity is turned against itself. The postmodern usage of reflexivity is to garner the sense of irony and parody to immobilize the awareness that gives rise to the centrality of being. It is a subversive reflexivity that fragments as well as denigrates what is often assumed to be stable descriptions and understandings of the self. In postmodernity, as Løvlie (1992, p. 125) expresses it, the "self as the ensemble of stage performance plays up to the idea of a relative self *that knows it is a relative self*." Reflexivity is relativized to produce a peculiar sense of impermanence and transitoriness in order to dislodge the self as a fixture of being. Rather, an awareness of fleeting role performances or shifting subjectivities is attained by relinquishing our focus on the person as an embodiment of infallible identity. It is as though the process of socialization in establishing a reality of the self is being reversed in postmodernity into a kaleidoscope of mish-mash selves.

The idea of a saturated self, proposed by Gergen (1991), suggests a condition of normative multiplicity where it is not possible for an individual to hang on to a fixed identity. In postmodern culture, the vertiginous array of new social experiences and encounters make it imperative for individuals to adopt multiple identities. Thus Gergen (1991) says that

> [a]s we become increasingly conjoined with our social surroundings, we come to reflect those surroundings. There is a population of the self, reflecting the infusion of partial identities through social saturation. And there is the onset of a multiphrenic condition, in which one begins to experience the vertigo of unlimited multiplicity. (p. 49)

Indeed, Gergen and others like him have lost faith in the notion that selfhood is a function of unidimensional socialization. For them, the postmodern age has wiped clean the illusion that we all possess a distinct self—on the contrary, we are witting or unwitting keepers of desultory disguises. How then can we reconcile Gergen's saturated self in postmodernity with the postmodern insistence on the death of the subject?

The death of the subject in postmodernism is not the literal death of a person wearing many masks. It refers to a metaphorical death or a symbolic termination of our valued belief in an essential self, that is a self in which its entire being comes alive in the actualization of meaningful relationships with perceived objects. When this subjective being is denied the privilege of perceiving, defining, and activating relationships but instead relegated to a position of insignificance, the question of a self-directed reality becomes diminished to a point of triviality. The self and its subjective proclivities are overshadowed by an intense bombardment of objects without firm conceptual mediation. In short, the presence of the subject as cognizer and interpreter is replaced by the continuous surfacing of desire in a context of unlimited simulation, a phenomenon often referred to as "the aestheticization of everyday life" (Lash, 1990, pp. 179-180).

In this situation of fleeting images and heightened sensations, the death of the subject cannot be construed as inconsistent with the emergence of a saturated self. A self that is drowning in the abundance of novel experiences and stimuli cannot possibly maintain a centered identity without acknowledging the veritable difficulty of holding together disparate events and relationships. The self is not only saturated with the incessant production of images and experiences but also dwarfed by a hyper-real environment of speed and simulacra (Kroker, 1992). Hence, the death of the subject implies the mitigation of subjective awareness in the face of a recognized instability or relativity of knowledge. It is not as though there is no self behind the masks but that the self knowingly loses all attachments to an illusory center. The self, therefore, attains a new freedom by playfully losing itself in the myriad roles, masks, and sensations without having to carry the burden of an unchanging identity. What then is the relationship between the postmodern death of the subject and physical death?

If physical death simply means the disintegration of the organic form without the possibility of the cessation of consciousness, the death of the subject in postmodernism would suggest a renewed conceptualization of the survival of consciousness that is released from the strictures of a fixed identity. Without the notion that one has to remain unswervingly attached to a single identity in physical reality, the movement of consciousness in the post-physical state would imply an indifferent disassembling of previous roles as a prelude to a new actualization of being. The multiple selves assumed in the physical state do not necessarily disappear upon the termination of the physical body. They could remain in the memories of particular individuals and electronic data banks. However, from a postmodern perspective these selves need not be consciously retained in death but addressed as potentialities for existential transformations. This means that for a dying person the various identities enacted during his or her lifetime are not a constraining factor in attaining new levels of consciousness. On the contrary, the old or fading identities are not anchored to any center and constitute a vehicle for the transformation of consciousness in the post-physical state.

Thus the postmodern decentering of subjectivity and celebration of multiplicity articulate the possibility of interpolated identities in the death state and beyond. These identities correspond to alternative forms of consciousness that may be cultivated during one's lifetime or may arise at the moment of death and be utilized for self-transformation in the post-physical state. It is because of postmodern insistence on the impermanence of identity in the physical state that we can speculate on the activation of other identities beyond the physical state. From this perspective, death is not necessarily the termination of identity but possibly an ironic play on the meaning of identity.

THE IRONY OF DEATH

Why is death ironic? Baudrillard (1990) provides an answer with his anecdote of a soldier who meets Death at a marketplace:

> [The soldier] believes he saw [Death] make a menacing gesture in his direction. He rushes to the king's palace and asks the king for his best horse in order that he might flee during the night far from Death, as far as Samarkand. Upon which the king summons Death to the palace and reproaches him for having frightened one of his best servants. But Death, astonished, replies: "I didn't mean to frighten him. It was just that I was surprised to see this soldier here, when we had a rendez-vous tomorrow in Samarkand. (p. 72)

Baudrillard (1990, p. 73) highlights the theme of his story by asserting that "Death is a rendez-vous, not an objective destiny." In other words, death mirrors our denial of mortality—it is an arrangement as well as an opportunity to deconstruct that denial. Rather than fleeing from death, one should treat death as the occasion for the disentanglement of our confusions, not in the sense of a predestined accomplishment but as a spontaneous realization of our illusory identities.

In postmodernism, irony constitutes a method for accentuating social and cultural absurdities in order to deconstruct what is taken as normal, conventional, and routine (Lemert, 1992). By focusing on the ironic, routine expectations lose their sense of plausibility because we can no longer train our minds on the linear but become jolted by the reversibility of any situation. Irony demolishes the natural progression of events intended as truth or logical order. When applied to the meaning of identity, irony punches a deep hole in the putative foundation of our self-definitions. It reverses all expectations we have of ourselves and of others, thus instilling either a terrible sense of angst or a liberating effect on our personal deliberations. Angst sets in when reversal of identities underscores the fragility of the self: what a person thinks he or she is not is the possibility of what he or she becomes. For example, in the film *American Beauty* (1999) a U.S. Marine colonel expresses to his son his disgust for two gay men who are his neighbors. The colonel defines himself as a normal, straight person. Yet when he mistakenly suspects his drug-dealing son of having a homosexual relationship with another neighbor, he begins to have doubts about his own sexual identity. When he makes a pass at this neighbor, who is actually a straight person, and gets turned down, the wrath of his confusion and embarrassment cannot but end in tragic violence.

When identity is punctured by irony, it becomes a metaphor for transformation. From this perspective, the death of the physical self is not the same as the annihilation of identity. Rather, death drives home the significance of impermanence, freeing us from our commitments to the physical form but at the same time parodying our incessant clinging to the physical roots of social identity. The revival of death consciousness can be thought of as a reawakening of our sense of irony with respect to the way our identities are defined. It comprises not an afterthought on the fate of our identities but a renewed sensitivity to the intricate relationship between identity and consciousness in an era where fragmentation is no longer considered a recondite or anomalous condition. If postmodern irony reflects the ubiquity of fragmentation, then the irony of death addresses the question of being as an illusory play of identities without a center. Death is then construed as the inevitable shedding of physical identities and their transformation into other levels of consciousness that possibly make up various post-physical states. This transformation takes place in a state of irony where flexibility, relativity, and reversibility govern the movement of consciousness.

The introduction of postmodern irony to death-consciousness, therefore, recasts the question of being and mortality in different light. It problematizes the continuity of consciousness and identity beyond the physical form as a state of dynamic interpolations, thus reflecting the broader condition of existential impermanence. From this position, the after-death state is not necessarily considered a nebulous outcome of antediluvian or unscientific thinking, but another way of examining the transformation of being. In this way, the self is treated as a transparent reservoir of consciousness that is not tied down to an indomitable identity. Death is merely a point of transition, a temporal switch from the physical to the non-physical that may be simultaneously experienced as intimidating and liberating.

The irony of death prompts us to reconsider the meaning of the after-death state, not as a descent into nihilism or speculations on uncanny phenomena, but as a continuation of the fragmented self in physically disembodied form. This postmodern approach to death attempts to close the gap between the problem of identity and questions concerning the survival of consciousness. Such an approach does not necessarily emphasize a search for empirical proof of the post-physical state, but adumbrates the relativity of identity that does not necessarily end with the termination of the physical form.

CONCLUSION

For the modern self, the aftermath of physical death lacks credulity because the conjunction of consciousness and identity is only plausible in the embodied state. This is a state of being defined by physical boundaries enclosing an idiosyncratic self differentiated from other selves. However, the postmodern self takes its multiple identities as a parody of social fluidity. The momentum of its interaction is not based on the continuity of relationships, but on the transformability of all identities. For the postmodern self, all identities are decentered and easily dereified. Death is just a phase of dereification. The irony of death is, therefore, the irony of all existing identities.

To study the postmodern self in death is to examine our mutable identities, that is from the way we cling to our self-identity to the way we decenter it. The revival of death-consciousness in postmodernity represents a concern with the changing meaning of self-identity. We are no longer concerned with just the question of physical termination, but with the meaning of self-transformation in the context of plurality and impermanence. For that reason, the postmodern focus on death will not be limited to the structural and symbolic unveiling of life's end, but will encompass the profundity of consciousness in dying and its impact on one's identity in the final stages of life.

REFERENCES

Ahronheim, J., & Weber, D. (1992). *Final passages: Positive choices for the dying and their loved ones.* New York: Simon and Schuster.

Baudrillard, J. (1990). *Seduction.* New York: St. Martin's Press.

Baudrillard, J. (1993). *Symbolic exchange and death.* Thousand Oaks, CA: Sage.

Beckford, J. A. (1992). *Religion and advanced industrial society.* London: Routledge.

Berger, P. L., Berger, B., & Kellner, H. (1974). *The homeless mind: Modernization and consciousness.* Harmondsworth: Penguin.

Bourguignon, E. (1973). Introduction: A framework for the comparative study of altered states of consciousness. In E. Bourguignon (Ed.), *Religion, altered states of consciousness, and social change* (pp. 3-35). Columbus, OH: Ohio State University Press.

Chaves, M. (1994). Secularization as declining religious authority. *Social Forces, 72,* 749-774.

Corr, C. A., Nabe, C. M., & Corr, D. M. (1994). *Death and dying, life and living.* Pacific Grove, CA: Brooks/Cole.

Frazer, J. (1957). *The golden bough: A study in magic and religion.* London: Macmillan.

Fulton, G. B., & Metress, E. K. (1995). *Perspectives on death and dying.* Boston: Jones and Bartlett.

Gergen, K. J. (1991). *The saturated self: Dilemmas of identity in contemporary life.* New York: Basic Books.

Giddens, A. (1990). *The consequences of modernity.* Cambridge: Polity Press.

Hill, M. (1973). *A sociology of religion.* London: Heinemann.

Kroker, A. (1992). *The possessed individual.* London: Macmillan.

Kübler-Ross, E. (1973). *On death and dying.* London: Tavistock.

Lash, S. (1990). *Sociology of postmodernism.* London: Routledge.

Lemert, C. (1992). General social theory, irony, postmodernism. In S. Seidman & D. G. Wagner (Eds.), *Postmodernism and social theory* (pp.19-46). Oxford: Blackwell.

Løvlie, L. (1992). Postmodernism and subjectivity. In S. Kvale (Ed.), *Psychology and postmodernism* (pp. 119-134). Thousand Oaks, CA: Sage.

Maguire, D. C. (1974). *Death by choice.* New York: Doubleday.

Sarup, M. (1993). *An introductory guide to post-structuralism and postmodernism.* Athens, GA: University of Georgia Press.

Walter, T. (1994). *The revival of death.* London: Routledge.

Weber, M. (1958). *The protestant ethic and the spirit of capitalism.* New York: Scribner's.

CHAPTER 7

The Healing Touch of Awareness: A Buddhist Perspective on Death, Dying, and Pastoral Care

Arthur O. Ledoux

THE BUDDHA'S STORY

When Siddartha Gautama, the man who would become the Buddha, was 29, he had a series of experiences that shook him to his core. As common and even universal as these experiences were, they were new to him; he was unprepared for their shock. The son of a king and raised in luxury, he had been shielded from life's harsh realities. But now he was striking out on his own beyond the protective cocoon of his upbringing and he was seeing with his own eyes how things are. He saw someone who was very sick—trembling with fever and nausea, covered with sores; he saw someone who was very old—frail, worn down, and pained by every movement; and he saw someone who was dead—the corpse decaying, the prey of scavenging animals and insects.

Naturally sensitive as he was, Siddartha realized that these were not the sad experiences of isolated unfortunates. No, these were the lot of all people, indeed of all sentient beings and he himself would be no exception. The power of this realization was profound—how could he possibly go back to "life as normal," to a life that tried to keep these truths hidden? How could he possibly unlearn what he now knew and pretend that things were just fine, thank you? It all seemed so empty.

But then Siddartha found a way out, or rather he found a way *through* these experiences. He discovered people who were devoting their lives to spiritual disciplines, monks who didn't run from painful truths but who embraced them in the paradoxical hope that deliberately opening to their pain could help them transcend all pain. Though Siddartha would eventually discover that extreme self-denial was as useless as extreme self-indulgence, he was inspired by these monks to begin a spiritual quest of his own. This quest, tradition tells us, led Siddartha to *nirvana;* he became a Buddha, a fully enlightened being (Dalai Lama, 1982; Thanissaro Bhikku, 1996).

This ancient story of the Four Passing Sights—sickness, old age, death, and spiritual discipline—may feel familiar to those who work with the terminally ill. Every work day you see the ravages of disease and advanced incapacity, and on some days you are actually present for someone's mysterious passage into death. How can you cope with scenes of such power? You know in your own heart of hearts and better than anybody that these things don't just happen to "other people." And so if denial is not an option, how can you maintain your balance and not "burn out" through the intensity of it all?

THE BUDDHA'S TEACHINGS

The teachings of the Buddha may be of interest to you in this regard, for it was in meditating profoundly on issues around death and dying that the Buddha made discoveries that many people over the last 2500 years have found transformative. Buddhism as a major world religion has a rich history and a complicated present, but we will be focusing here on what the many strands and sects of Buddhism have in common. These are the Buddha's first and most basic teachings (Nhat Hanh, 1998; Dalai Lama, 1994).

It is often said that the spirit in which the Buddha proceeds here is like that of a physician whose over-riding concern is to alleviate the suffering of patients (Longaker, 1997). His approach is to: 1) listen in detail to the symptoms; 2) discern a correct diagnosis; 3) determine an effective cure; and 4) prescribe a course of treatment to effect that cure. As a physician of mind and heart, he offers people Four Noble Truths which unfold in just that order: 1) Symptom: suffering pervades our life; 2) Diagnosis: it arises from self-oriented attachment; 3) Cure: it ends when attachment ends; and 4) Prescription: there is a way to end attachment. Let us consider each in turn.

1. Life is filled with suffering (in the Pali language *dukkha*). To begin with, life in this world is filled with experiences of unhappiness ranging from mild annoyance to overwhelming terror. Birth, sickness, old age, death, separation from what we love, and being stuck with what we hate are all forms of suffering.

But the problem is not simply that difficulties keep coming up for us, that bad days are mixed in with the good. The problem is far more pervasive than that. The Buddha claims that our lives are pervaded by a lack of full and dependable satisfaction, and that, in fact, even pleasure is suffering. How can this be? Consider as an example the pleasure of eating a good meal. The pleasure in eating is strongest when we come to the meal hungry, and hunger, of course, is a pain. And if we react to our hunger by eating too much or too fast, we may feel indigestion which is also a pain. But it's not just that this pleasure may be preceded and followed by pain, it's that the very pleasure itself is at some level unsatisfying. Even in the very midst of eating we know the pleasure will not last. The stronger the feeling of pleasure, the more we yearn for it to continue and the more poignant its inevitable loss. All experiences are transitory, and since no experience is truly lasting, no experience can provide lasting satisfaction.

2. The Buddha diagnoses the cause of suffering as self-centered desire or attachment (*tanha*). When we either grasp after things, people, and experiences or push them away, when we seek to impose our will and preferences on the world or avoid facing difficulties, we inevitably meet resistance and frustration. When we yearn for a private satisfaction and insist that things go our way, we find ourselves out of harmony with the way things are and experience suffering.

We can find instructive examples almost everywhere we look from the mundane to the profound. We yearn to go forward while driving in a traffic jam and yet we are blocked; we yearn for health and yet we get sick; we yearn for youth and yet we are aging; and, most poignantly, we yearn for unending bodily life and yet we are dying.

But if we pay close attention to these experiences, we can discover that the problem is not really with the traffic jam or with being sick or with aging or even dying. The problem is with the yearning. And here we come to a fundamental point: though pain is inevitable, suffering is not. By *pain* we mean the actual sensations of physical discomfort (e.g., burning, itching, throbbing, stabbing) and mental discomfort (disappointment, frustration, anger, doubt, fear, sadness, and so on). *Suffering* is the result of a certain response to pain: the response of aversion, hatred, and the spontaneous conviction that "this shouldn't be happening." It is this yearning and craving to escape the way things are that really sours our experience of life; *tanha* always causes *dukkha*. And this flows immediately into the next teaching.

3. Suffering is cured when its cause is removed (*nirodha*—the extinction of craving). When we see craving and attachment for what they are and learn to let them go, then suffering dissipates. Traffic jams cause suffering because we are obsessed with getting somewhere; if we ease up on the obsession, we can accept times of slow pacing and learn to accept things as they come. Sickness causes suffering only if we crave unending health; if we understand sickness to be part of the natural flow of life, then the pains of sickness need not cause the anguish of suffering. Old age causes suffering only if we crave unending youth; once we understand aging to be part of the natural flow of life, we can age gracefully. Death causes suffering only if we crave unending bodily life; once we understand death to be part of the natural flow of life, then dying can be accepted with peace and equanimity.

The great challenge in life, then, is to end craving and attachment. True care and love for self requires cultivating a spirit of non-attachment. The idea of non-attachment can be easily misunderstood and needs to be carefully expressed. Obviously it is not attachment, willfully holding on to things. But then neither is it detachment, willfully pushing things away; striving to be detached and aloof from life is an expression of fear which is itself a form of craving for things to be other than they are. Non-attachment neither clings to nor rejects anything; it is the ability to be fully present to the reality of each moment while yet being able to completely let it go so as to be fully present to the next moment and the next and so on. It is the experience of savoring life to the fullest without becoming enslaved by it. Non-attachment is really another name for freedom: to be free of compulsive clinging and rejection, to feel thoroughly at home with the simple truth of life.

4. The good news offered by the Buddha is that this state of non-attachment is a real possibility for us. There is a path of training the mind and heart that cultivates this peace and freedom. While the First Noble Truth of suffering may have seemed depressing, that impression changes when we find out there is something we can do about it. The bracing yet demanding truth is that the quality of our life is in our own hands. The Fourth Noble Truth is hopeful because it asserts that with the right kind of effort, we can completely overcome suffering. And what is the right kind of effort called for? What the Buddha as physician prescribes is a regimen he calls the Eightfold Path.

Now understanding all the implications of the Eightfold Path would be an enterprise as subtle and complex as life itself. But we can at least indicate the direction in which the Buddha would guide us.

1. *Right Knowledge:* Our efforts need to be guided by an understanding of our real situation; we need to understand the Four Noble Truths.
2. *Right Aspiration:* Our efforts need to be grounded in a strong sense of purpose to reduce the level of suffering in ourselves and in our world.
3. *Right Speech:* Use speech wisely to help and never to injure, avoid lies and gossip, speaking the truth in love and humility when that would help.
4. *Right Conduct:* Observe the Five Precepts—not to kill, not to steal, not to lie, not to misuse sex, and not to use intoxicants.
5. *Right Livelihood:* Make your living in ways that support happiness and decrease suffering; avoid jobs that would lead you or others to break any of the Five Precepts.
6. *Right Effort:* Avoid the extremes of either laziness or panic; make your effort strong, steady, and persevering.
7. *Right Concentration:* Learn to focus your attention on a single object in a steady and stable way.
8. *Right Mindfulness:* Learn to focus your attention on the passing flow of experience in this present moment in a steady and stable way.

The discipline called for here is demanding. Each of the eight parts of this path becomes almost endlessly more refined and subtle as you actively work with it in your life; short of *nirvana* itself, couldn't one always use more knowledge, strengthen ones aspiration, become more skillful in speech, conduct, and livelihood, and improve ones effort, concentration, and mindfulness? And notice too that the eight dimensions of this path are not thought of as steps in a sequence. Each one is intertwined with all the others; change in any one area will have implications for all the others.

It all seems quite overwhelming. But before giving up on the path, consider the supports that are said to be available. Buddhists often speak of the Three Refuges: the Buddha, the Dharma, and the Sangha. Taking refuge in the *Buddha* means recalling that the Buddha, for all his extraordinary achievements, was not a god or an angel but a human being like us; *nirvana* is a real possibility for humans. Taking refuge in the *Dharma* means being impressed enough by what you understand so far of the teachings that you are willing to keep an open mind about teachings that you now find harder to accept; this is especially true for teachings that stress the availability of *nirvana* to human effort. Perhaps of the most immediate help is taking refuge in the *Sangha*, i.e., in the community of people who are undertaking the path; having a support network of like-minded friends to share with and be guided by is invaluable.

WHAT THE BUDDHA'S STORY AND TEACHINGS COULD MEAN FOR PASTORAL CARE OF THE DYING

And so what could all this mean for those who work with the dying and the grieving (Levine, 1982, 1984, 1997)?

First of all you will be able to relate to the story of the Four Passing Sights more directly than virtually anyone else. You see sickness, old age, and death on a daily basis; you know better than most their inevitability as well as the shallowness of any philosophy of life that does not take them fully into account. Likewise you will probably be sensitive to the importance of spiritual discipline in a person's life because you have seen for yourself how those with a spiritual grounding often respond with greater peace and acceptance to a terminal diagnosis than those who do not. And it is likely that you see in yourself the need for spiritual support to sustain you through the intensity of so much loss and grief without either hardening or burning out. With all of this the Buddha showed himself to be thoroughly familiar.

When we advance the Buddha's story to the last scene of his life, we find him summarizing his teaching in a way that challenges all who hear it, including those who work with the dying. His final teaching was: "Be lamps unto yourselves. Be a refuge unto yourselves. Work out your own salvation with diligence" (Thanissaro, 1996). Individual effort is at the core of what the Buddha taught; no one can save you from suffering except you; you are responsible for the quality of your life. The daunting aspect of this teaching is that this supreme effort is necessary. The hopeful and consoling aspect of this teaching is that this supreme effort is possible.

When it comes to the content of the teachings themselves, you will likewise be well poised to understand. As we noted before, you are no stranger to the suffering that is the focus of the First Noble Truth; even if you have reservations about his answers, you will probably be willing to give him credit for asking the right questions. And it is likely that the Second and Third Noble Truths will also make a good deal of sense to you. You have seen people approach their death burdened with unfinished business, pained by remorse over past actions and by regrets for opportunities missed. What is this if not the suffering that comes from attachment, the aching and perhaps turbulent discontent that fuels the yearning for life to have been different? And perhaps you have seen people come to death with a quality of peace and deep acceptance; having worked wholeheartedly with their life, they are now ready to let it go with appreciation. What is this if not the equanimity of non-attachment?

If you find yourself at all sympathetic to the Buddha's analysis of the human situation presented above, then you may feel drawn to explore the implications of what he thought we could do about it. What light might the elements of the Eightfold Path bring to someone like you? Let's touch on each in turn.

1. *Right Knowledge:* Here your work presents you with an extraordinary opportunity. What most people reflexively shun, you open to on a daily basis: you see in detail the ways of suffering and disintegration. There is an ancient meditation practice prized by the Buddha in the *Satipatthana Sutra;* it is the contemplation of the nine stages of the decomposition of a corpse (Nhat Hanh, 1990). Such a meditation is very strong medicine as its intent is to counterbalance the primal attachment we have to our own body. As we contemplate in detail its inevitable decay, our compulsive clinging to this body can soften. But since a corpse is not usually available for viewing, meditators are asked to imagine their own bodies passing through these same stages. The exercise would have more of an impact, though, if it did not have to be imagined but could actually be seen. And just this is what you can prize in your work. Though you are probably not spending much time with bodies that are already dead, you are seeing the stages of decomposition that lead up to death. Don't pass this opportunity by!

2. *Right Aspiration:* Here you could be moved to remember what it was that led you to enter this kind of work to begin with. It is a basic principle of Buddhist ethics that the moral quality of an action is determined by the intention with which it is done (Kornfield, 1993). With what intention did you enter this field? Perhaps it was predominantly noble like that of a Mother Theresa: to relieve the suffering of those coming to the end of their lives, to show mercy and kindness to those most in need. With what intention do you work now? No doubt there are times when you are distracted or worn out where the intention is just to make it through the day. Notice, without giving in to guilt, what the quality of your care for patients is at times like that. It is part of the power of mindfulness that simply noticing and opening to cramped and painful states of mind helps them to soften and break up (Goldstein, 1994; Kornfield, 1993). And as these states weaken, you can move toward reconnecting with the deeper and purer intentions you have known. Refreshed and inspired, you can re-engage work with renewed energy and effectiveness.

3. *Right Speech:* The power of speech in the presence of the dying is incalculable. You have seen how crucially important it is for people to say their good byes and how deep the regret can go when circumstances prevent that kind of speech from happening. Dealing with the agitation of unfinished business is often primarily a matter of finding the right words to ask for and express forgiveness. Indeed, sometimes the greatest service you can perform for the terminally ill and their families is to model for them how to talk at a time like this, how not to hold back out of shyness from sharing what is in one's heart. And this can be one of the greatest challenges: to speak in ways that the patient and family will find helpful, to understand their frame of reference, and to speak effectively in those terms, terms that may not mean that much to you. Sensitive care requires humility.

4. *Right Conduct:* Of the Five Precepts three come immediately to the fore as crucial guides for your work.

    a. "Not to kill" is central to the mission of hospice, for example. Though this can be controversial, the goal of hospice is to make the dying so comfortable that assisted suicide or euthanasia is no longer attractive as an alternative. The wisdom of non-attachment lies neither in desperately evading death by any means possible nor in embracing it prematurely out of panic and fear; rather it lies in opening to each moment fully without grasping, willing to be surprised by moments of happiness and insight right up to the end.

b. "Not to lie" leads one to be honest and clear with patient and family about the course that the illness will likely take. The expectation is that you would respect the dignity of the individual by sharing the truth even if it is unpleasant. And yet there are no rigid absolutes; there may be circumstances where mercy requires you to either soft-peddle or even withhold the full truth. The most sensitive wisdom you can muster is called for.

c. "Not to use intoxicants" aims to preserve the clarity of awareness that is at the core of non-attachment. Intoxicants are a problem to the extent that they cloud the mind and detach you from a wise engagement in your life. And herein lies the art and science of palliative medicine, using analgesic drugs in a skillful way to reduce pain to a minimum while yet leaving the patient as conscious as possible to live the life they have left as fully as possible.

5. *Right Livelihood:* Engaging in the world of work is a major dimension of human life. Though it can at times feel demanding and onerous, work can make us stretch and develop our abilities while being in some way genuinely helpful to others; experiences of personal growth and social service can overlap and enhance each other. Of course for many work is an alienating drudgery endured only for the sake of a paycheck, a tragic sacrifice of a large part of a person's life. How different it can be for those who work with the dying. Given that there is some level of right aspiration moving you, working with the dying is an exquisite example of right livelihood. As for personal growth, have you found yourself stretching in ways you would have found inconceivable before beginning such work? The demands for emotional sensitivity, for wise and patient decision-making, and even for physical endurance can provide occasions for deep inner change. Caring for the dying can be an unusually pure example of unconditional love for others; lavishing care on those who will soon be gone takes a courageous focus on appreciating the present. And as for social service, is there any work more needed by its recipients? The dying become as helpless as newborns. And who can estimate the value of the consolation that may ripple through a society when people realize that their last days can be surrounded by mercy and care?

6. *Right Effort:* One of the great challenges of this work is to persevere through countless experiences of poignant intensity, to go on giving without expectation of return. Once again there is the need to cultivate a wise spirit of non-attachment: if you become strongly attached to your patients, you will burn out on grief; if you are detached from your patients, you will miss the chance to touch others with the mercy they so deeply need. Finding and maintaining that balance is our life's task and the practice of paying mindful attention to your own feelings can be a key to doing it. Simply stay tuned to your emotional responses: notice how attachment leads to the suffering of grief and how detachment leads to the suffering of disconnection and

loneliness. Your own experience will teach you all you need to know if you pay attention.

7. *Right Concentration:* Even though it is simple, the act of paying steady sensitive attention over the long haul is very difficult. Happily, though, there are practices available for working directly with the mind to strengthen that power that is native to us all; I am referring here to practices of meditation (Goldstein, 1994). Now the Buddhist tradition has explored and developed the varieties of meditation with immense sophistication. But in the end all these varieties reduce to the two categories of concentration and mindfulness, and even these are related (Goleman, 1977). Concentration is the ability to focus your attention on a single object in a steady and stable way. Setting aside time every day to pay attention to your breathing is a classic meditation practice; noticing all the many times the mind skips away from the breath and then consciously returning to it builds over time the power to concentrate. This by itself is important to your work: maintaining focus on your patient's needs without being too distracted by sights, sounds, and smells that are repulsive or by irrelevant commotion in the environment or by the press of a busy schedule. Your work takes strength of mind; the faithful practice of meditation develops that strength.

8. *Right Mindfulness:* When we direct concentration to the passing flow of experience in this present moment in a steady and stable way we are practicing mindfulness. The goal is to wake up to the full range of living experience: sensations, feelings, perceptions, thoughts, and the interconnection among all of these (Nhat Hanh, 1990). Mindfulness develops the intuitive ability to sense the appropriate response: what to do, what to say, when to be quiet, and so on. And perhaps in the end, the most precious thing you can bring to others is mindfulness and simple presence. As Dame Cicely Saunders, founder of the modern hospice movement, said, "we are not there to take away or explain, or even to understand, but simply to 'Watch with me,' as Jesus asked of his disciples in the Garden of Gethsemane (Saunders, 1995). Buddhists claim, by the way, that practicing the Eightfold Path is compatible with many different beliefs or lack of belief (Dalai Lama, 1996).

The Buddhist path both invites and requires the highest possible development of your capacities of mind and heart. But don't get discouraged, they would say, because there is support for the journey (the Three Refuges) and the final goal is unutterably wonderful (*nirvana*).

It should not be that hard for those who work with the dying to relate to the refuges. The Buddha is often shown in traditional Asian art as attending to the needs of his own dying monks; someone who fully practices what he preaches can inspire respect for his person and confidence in his teachings—he knows what he is talking about. The *Dharma* originally grew out of profound meditation on the realities of sickness, aging, and death. It has evolved into a highly elaborated teaching that has stood the test of time and is still unfolding today. Some of the most creative works on issues of death and dying in the West have come from those grounded in these teachings (Sogyal, 1994; Halifax, 1997; Levine, 1982, 1984, 1997). The *Sangha* should be especially familiar to those involved with hospice with its strong emphasis on team care giving both coordinated care for patients and mutual support for team members.

And what shall we say of *nirvana*? As little as possible, since it is experienced to be utterly beyond the limitations of word and concept. But perhaps we can get a glimpse. What if the power of concentration and mindfulness became so strong that our normal sense of being an isolated separate self began to melt down? What if one could then completely let go of all desires and actions whose aim was to assert or defend that separate self. Wouldn't this total non-attachment to self beget a profound sense of interconnection with all other beings and feelings of unbounded compassion and love? Wouldn't this be incomparable bliss? As the Buddha says over and over again: try it and see (Thanissaro, 1996).

REFERENCES

H. H. The Dalai Lama (1982). *The path to enlightenment.* Ithaca, NY: Snow Lion.

H. H. The Dalai Lama (1994). *The way of freedom.* San Francisco: HarperCollins.

H. H. The Dalai Lama. (1996). *The good heart: A Buddhist perspective on the teachings of Jesus.* Boston: Wisdom.

Goldstein, J. (1994). *Insight meditation: The practice of freedom.* Boston: Shambala.

Goleman, D. (1977). *The varieties of the meditative experience.* New York: E. P. Dutton.

Halifax, J. (1997). *Being with dying: Contemplative practices and teachings.* Audio Cassette. Sante Fe, NM: Upaya.

Kornfield, J. (1993). *A path with heart: A guide through the perils and promises of spiritual life.* New York: Bantam Books.

Levine, S. (1982). *Who dies?: An investigation of conscious living and conscious dying.* New York: Anchor Press.

Levine, S. (1984). *Meetings at the edge: Dialogues with the grieving and the dying, the healing and the healed.* New York: Anchor Press.

Levine, S. (1997). *A year to live: How to live this year as if it were your last.* New York: Bell Tower.

Longaker, C. (1997). *Facing death and finding hope: A guide to the emotional and spiritual care of the dying.* New York: Doubleday.

Nhat Hanh, T. (1990). *Transformation and healing: Sutra on the four establishments of mindfulness.* Berkeley, CA: Parallax Press.

Nhat Hanh, T. (1998). *The heart of the Buddha's teaching: Transforming suffering into peace, joy, and liberation.* Berkeley, CA: Parallax Press.

Saunders, C. (1995). *Living with dying: A guide to palliative care.* New York: Oxford University Press.

Sogyal, R. (1994). *The Tibetan book of living and dying.* San Francisco: Harper.

Thanissaro, B. (1996). *The wings to awakening.* Barre, MA: Dhamma Dena.

SECTION III

Extraordinary Death and Loss

Cyber Cemeteries and Virtual Memorials: Virtual Living Monuments as On-line Outlets for Real Life Mourning and a Celebration of Life

Hermann Gruenwald and Le Gruenwald

Cyber Cemeteries are being created on-line by individuals and corporations to memorialize loved ones 24/7 worldwide. Virtual memorials offer some of the same features of physical monuments and traditional newspaper obituaries, but they also provide added dimension that can provide help in the grief and bereavement as well as the remembrance and immortalization process. In this chapter, we examine the following dimensions of virtual monuments: Accessibility both from a time and distance standpoint; A special place for losses and bereaved with special needs; Building communications and community on-line; Private and Public Space, Life and Love—Remembrance and Commemoration; Limitations and Control—from VIP to Pets From Obituaries to Monuments; Religion and Culture; Features and Costs; and the Present and the Future.

WHAT IS A CYBER CEMETERY?

One should not mistaken a Cyber Cemetery with the numerous Web sites which exist to find loved ones in physical cemeteries or to document cemeteries. It is not a place to sell monuments on-line either. A virtual monument or virtual memorial may take on various forms. Reaching from an obituary similar or identical to those in the local newspaper, which provides basic information about the deceased and the funeral, to an upright memorial. While some sites try to copy reality by providing two or three-dimensional representations of physical monuments to create the atmosphere of a cemetery, other sites try to find the virtual space by creating on-line memorials with added dimensions such as photographs, epitaphs, eulogy, poems, scripture passage, artwork, music, voice, and video. This may be a collection of memories created by one person or contributed by various people. Most of the sites allow for e-mail submissions of contributions by friends and relatives. Some even offer virtual flower arrangements and candles to be placed on the monuments.

HOW TO FIND ON-LINE MEMORIALS?

The following search words or combinations thereof will help you find what we will call On-line Memorials for the purpose of this book. Search words that contain Cyber, Electronic, On-line Virtual, together with the words such as Cemetery, Grave, Graveyard, Memorial, Mausoleum, Monument, Obituary, Park, Testament, Tribute, result in key words such as Cyber Cemeteries, Virtual Cemeteries, Virtual Monuments, On-line Memorials, On-line Monuments, On-line Obituaries, On-line Memorial Gardens, On-line Graveyards, or On-line Memorial Parks. The following is a range of virtual cemeteries hosted by the same provider under different Internet portals. The combination of possibilities is vast:

Virtual Burial, Virtual Cemetery, Virtual Memorial Plot, Virtual Family Plot, Virtual Resting Place, Virtually Buried, Virtually Laid to Rest, Virtual Grave, St. Michael's Catholic Virtual Cemetery, St. Paul's Evangelical Lutheran Virtual Cemetery, Heaven's Gate Assembly of God Virtual Cemetery, Beth El Conservative Jewish Virtual Cemetery, Fellowship Messianic Jewish Virtual Cemetery, Torah Congregation Orthodox Jewish Virtual Cemetery, Temple David Reform Jewish Virtual Cemetery, St. John the Baptist Virtual Cemetery, Our Savior Church of the Nazarene Virtual Cemetery, Holy Cross Episcopal Virtual Cemetery, The Apostles Church of the Latter Day Saints Virtual Cemetery, Calvary United Presbyterian Virtual Cemetery, Emmanuel Christian Science Virtual Cemetery, Holy Trinity African Methodist Episcopal Virtual Cemetery, Holy Spirit Jehovah's Witness Virtual Cemetery, Mt. Zion Pentecostal Virtual Cemetery, Muhammad Islamic Virtual Cemetery, Admiral Nimitz United States Navy Virtual Cemetery, Commander Yeager United States Air Force Virtual Cemetery, French World War I Veterans Virtual Cemetery, French World War II Veterans Virtual Cemetery, General Patton United States Army Virtual Cemetery, German World War I Veterans Virtual Cemetery, German World War II Veterans Virtual Cemetery, Italian World War I Veterans Virtual Cemetery, Italian World War II Veterans Virtual Cemetery, Japanese World War II Veterans Virtual Cemetery, Polish World War I Veterans Virtual Cemetery, Polish World War II Veterans Virtual Cemetery, Russian World War I Veterans Virtual Cemetery, Russian World War II Veterans Virtual Cemetery, United Kingdom World War I Veterans Virtual Cemetery, United Kingdom World War II Veterans Virtual Cemetery, United States Civil War Veterans Virtual Cemetery, United States Gulf War Veterans Virtual Cemetery, United States Korean War Veterans Virtual Cemetery, United States Vietnam War Veterans Virtual Cemetery, United

States World War I Veterans Virtual Cemetery, United States World War II Veterans Virtual Cemetery, World Wide World War I Veterans Cemetery, World Wide World War II Veterans Cemetery, World Wide Military Veterans Cemetery, American Indian Virtual Cemetery, Asian American Virtual Cemetery, Black American Virtual Cemetery, Hispanic American Virtual Cemetery, Irish American Virtual Cemetery, Italian American Virtual Cemetery, Brazilian National Virtual Cemetery, Canadian National Virtual Cemetery, English National Virtual Cemetery, Estonian National Virtual Cemetery, Finnish National Virtual Cemetery, French National Virtual Cemetery, German National Virtual Cemetery, Greek National Virtual Cemetery, Icelandic National Virtual Cemetery, Indian National Virtual Cemetery, Irish National Virtual Cemetery, Israeli National Virtual Cemetery, Italian National Virtual Cemetery, Japanese National Virtual Cemetery, Korean National Virtual Cemetery, Latvian National Virtual Cemetery, Lithuanian National Virtual Cemetery, Mexican National Virtual Cemetery, Norwegian National Virtual Cemetery, People's Republic of China National Virtual Cemetery, Polish National Virtual Cemetery, Republic of China National Virtual Cemetery, Russian National Virtual Cemetery, Scottish National Virtual Cemetery, Spanish National Virtual Cemetery, Swedish National Virtual Cemetery, Turkish National Virtual Cemetery, Ukrainian National Virtual Cemetery, and United States of America National Virtual Cemetery.

WHO OFFERS ON-LINE MEMORIALS?

Initially, family members of the deceased created memorials for their loved ones and later opened cemeteries as non-profit organizations to the general public. Virtual monuments are provided by six different types of organizations: funeral homes, monument companies, cemeteries, discount casketers, dot.com companies, and non-profit organizations. Each has a different motive to enter this e-commerce arena. The funeral home may start to offer on-line obituaries to compliment a printed obituary in the local newspaper. The same may be true for the discount casket seller who may opt to offer this service for free or as an ad for sale. Monument companies may see it as a natural way for them to offer on-line monuments in addition to physical monuments or as a replacement in the future. The monument companies approach it more from a physical design aspect utilizing their existing monument designs and symbols. Dot.com companies and non-profit organizations, on the other hand, explore the new dimensions that the Internet offers and try to define cyberspace.

WHY ON-LINE MEMORIALS?

There are a number of reasons why on-line memorials, in many ways, have the similar therapeutic values as those found in funerals: 1) The Therapy of Direct

Expression: the virtual monument provides a setting for the direct physical expression by the bereaved of the emotional surcharges generated by death; 2) The Therapy of Language: whether language is considered purely as self-expression, as when a person "talks to himself," or an expression resulting in communication; 3) The Therapy of Sharing: in all cultures the kinship group draws together to give emotional, physical, and frequently financial support to the bereaved when death occurs; 4) The Therapy of Activity: the performance of creating a monument has therapeutic values because it prevents withdrawal from reality and activity, and provides an individually helpful and socially non-objectionable outlet of emotions; 5) The Therapy of Aesthetics: it permits the bereaved to view the loved one on-line and thereby regain and reinforce the sense of reality; and 6) The Therapy of Self-Denial and Suffering: it is an opportunity to say what has been left unsaid to the deceased by leaving an e-mail on the site and relieve the bereaved of the guilt. One can also categorize the benefits as followed: Accessibility from both a time and distance standpoint; A special place for losses and bereaved with special needs; Building communications and community on-line; Private and Public Space, Life and Love— Remembrance and Commemoration; Limitations and Control—from VIP to Pets, from Obituaries to Monuments; Religion and Culture; Features and Costs; and the Present and the Future.

ACCESSIBILITY 24/7/365 WORLD WIDE

An increasing number of people are turning to the Internet to help them cope with the loss of a loved one. The medium enables those in mourning to set up virtual memorials that can have an emotionally healing effect. Cyber cemeteries offer 24-hour access 7-days-a-week all year round.

For many, the memorial sites provide a vital outlet for their grief. For some, virtual memorials mean being able to visit a loved one anytime. Like the man who missed his wife very much but did not know what to do with himself because he could not leave at 2 or 3 in the morning to visit the cemetery. But once he had a memorial on-line, he could just click and spend as much or as little time with her as he wanted to. 24/7 access all year round allows one to visit the memorial at any time without being limited to the hours of the cemetery or daylight. Many may find the time to write a short e-mail to a loved one, or to leave virtual flowers on a memorial. A Web page is accessible from anywhere in the world and allows people to "visit" a memorial even though they could not attend the funeral due to distance and time or were unaware of a death. The World Wide Web, shared globally by more than 30 million people, is an ideal place to announce the loss of someone we cherish and to erect a permanent monument to their memory. It is a way for the international family to meet. Indeed, families spread across the world—or traveling away from home—can "stop in'' to pay their respects any time they want. Be it for political or economic reasons, people may not be able to visit their loved ones in various parts of the world. Families are geographically more dispersed now than ever. In an increasingly mobile society, we are less likely to live close by the graves of our ancestors, and thus even a visit on

Memorial Day may be hard to be accomplished. So what would replace a visit in a snow-covered cemetery with small candle lit Christmas trees on a cold Christmas evening? A live cemetery cam?

A SPECIAL PLACE FOR SPECIAL LOSSES AND THE BEREAVED WITH SPECIAL NEEDS

Grieving the loss of what could have been is one of the most difficult mourning processes, whether it is pregnancy loss or infertility. To a mother, a baby, not a fetus, has died. But for others, the pregnancies were "miscarriages." Mothers suffer with a very personal and intimate relationship to motherhood that is invisible to others. They experience their pregnancies as lost children. Their attachment to motherhood has grown to the point of experiencing the baby and naming him or her. Despite the fact that the pregnancies ended early, they were already bonding, even mothering (Borg & Lasker, 1981). The process of building a Web page allows them to continue this mothering process. It also allows them to create a virtual monument for a person who otherwise may not have had a funeral or a grave. Sudden Tragic deaths such as car accidents, natural disasters, or homicide, lead us to ask the question why? The Web offers through hyper links a way of being buried in a multitude of cemeteries and share experiences with people who went through the same or similar tragedies. The Internet is the perfect place to memorialize a person whose remains were never recovered. Family members who have loved ones missing in action come to the conclusion that the person has deceased, but for legal reasons cannot have a funeral, may find peace by creating a virtual monument. How do we bury a person when there are no remains as in the case of missing people, victims of disasters, or people buried at sea (Baden, 1989)? Web sites are a way for parents to keep their children's memory alive. It means a lot to parents to see this outpouring of love for their child (Bermann, 1973). They are usually touched by e-mails and the fact that people take the time to read about their children. And parents may hear even more about their deceased child from the child's friends, a perspective they never had. Kids feel very comfortable with the Internet, so they type away all these great stories that they probably would not tell the parents about. It is a place for mothers to remember their children. Some miss mothering their son or daughter. They miss being able to do things for them. Actively working on the design and construction of the site allows them to continue the care giving process (Kübler-Ross, 1969). Men, in general, grieve less publicly than women, so the Web offers a perfect venue for their grief as for more introverted people. Although it is natural for husbands and wives to mourn differently, it is critical that spouses turn toward each other, rather than away from each other, in time of crisis (Davidson & Doka, 1999). The creation of a Web site may allow husbands and wives to connect through this period and will strengthen their bond. Another interesting fact is that in the United States, more and more people live in correctional institutions, and the Web offers them the opportunity to visit the memorial through the computer in the prison library. The elderly and handicapped face a similar dilemma and may be able to access the site from their home, hospice, or hospital.

Large families may be divided over the decision of a loved one to be cremated or buried at sea, or they may have supported the idea initially and now find themselves without a place to memorialize the deceased. The Web offers them a venue to create a virtual memorial.

BUILDING COMMUNICATION
AND COMMUNITY

When a person we love or are close to dies, the desire to communicate our loss is both natural and strong (Jackson, 1957). We use the media—all forms of print, as well as radio and television—to notify others of a loved one's passing. The Internet represents humankind's greatest revolution in communication since Gutenberg invented the printing press. People who have created Web memorials for their loved ones say one unexpected advantage over tombstones is that they hear from people who knew the person—when they were a child, in college, or from an earlier job. The Web allows a person to be memorialized next to his/her loved one with simply a link away. A person's memorial can be placed in a multitude of cemeteries, the person can be linked both in accordance to ethnicity, religion, profession, military service, or cause of death. Probably the most important aspect of virtual memorials is that the Web sites remind grieving people that they are not alone. There is a large community out on the Internet and there is an incredible amount of love that comes from people from all walks of life. In terms of grief, any possible way people can communicate with other people will help them heal. Virtual Memorials help the bereaved pay tribute to their deceased, and share this with the global family of the Internet. Perhaps it is inevitable that just as more and more people seem to live on-line, others are dying there. For the dead, cyberspace cemeteries serve as memorials; for the living, they are a place to mourn, to offer condolences, and to recall losses.

PRIVATE–PUBLIC SPACE

Standard Memorials may be Public or Private. Public Memorials are placed in the public park like a cemetery and are available for viewing by all visitors. All of the information in a Public Memorial is placed in the database to facilitate the finding of the Memorial by visitors. Private Memorials are placed in a Private area and can only be viewed by the use of a computer password. None of the information in the Memorial is available to anyone and cannot be seen without a password. Only the owner of the Memorial has access to the password. Some odd connections can be made at on-line memorials. Strangers frequently happen to stumble upon memorials while looking for something else on-line or because, like a pedestrian, they are wandering around the virtual cemetery, as they are searching the net (Murphy, 1995). Your site may get visited by people who are looking for information on a particular deceased or a family name. Some people do not want this kind of attention for their memorials, and try to keep them private. Many others love the global, unplanned interaction that on-line memorials can create. A virtual memorial is really different from a physical monument and takes on another dimension. Monuments in the World Wide Web cemetery allow people to share the lives of their loved ones in ways that traditional printed death announcements or stone inscriptions cannot. Photographs, moving images and even sounds can be included with a monument. People can create hypertext links among family members, and in doing so forge a genealogy of Internet users and their families on-line and in real-time.

LIFE AND LOVE—REMEMBRANCE AND COMMEMORATION

Cyber memorials are really a celebration of life. Our lives are so much more than the little dash between two numbers on a tombstone. This site is not about death. It is about love. Eternal Love. We do not forget our loved ones, we love them eternally and their name engraved in cyber world will live beyond their lives. Here we can open a home page for those we want to commemorate. We, our family, and millions of people all over the world can visit, put a flower, lay a wreath or leave a rock, see a photo album of the deceased, hear an audio recording, or even watch a live video. May all rest in peace in the virtual eternal endless cyber space. Technology offers something very primal: a path to immortality. Almost everyone hopes for some level of immortality and craves his/her 15 minutes of fame (Wilkins, 1996). A virtual monument is a way to get it. You will be famous not only in your local community but people from all over the world will be able to visit you. Today's early cyber memorials attract a lot of attention from both the curious and the media. The desolate cemetery with its indistinguishable rows of tombstones has taken on a different tone in cyberspace, where more and more grievers are turning to memorialize the dead. The cyberspace cemeteries posted on the World Wide Web allow mourners to share their grief and, in return, strangers who stumble onto the site often respond with poignant thoughts about their own losses or just offer condolences. A cyber cemetery is a place of remembrance that is not a cemetery. Some may find it strange that technology is being put to such a sentimental use. Memorializing dead loved ones—whether that is through a pyramid, headstone, poem, or roadside wreath—has always been important to humans (Habenstein & Lamers, 1994). As part of the mourning process, it is important to people that they create something out of that grief. People create things that are important to them. They do it in their own way. Monuments are a public way to share grief with the "tribe" (Arvisio Alvord, 1999). They memorialize the special characteristics of a lost individual. They can even help transform a specific site into a "special-sacred place" for a community. In our virtual communities we also create these sacred places. Putting together a memorial also may help to accept the loss and allows one to see more of what the deceased's life had been. This new, on-line way of memorializing dead loved ones fits today's lifestyle. More and more people are getting cremated now and their ashes are dispersed. There is nothing tangible one can go and look at. The on-line memorial gives relatives some place to visit.

FROM OBITUARIES TO MONUMENTS

Virtual obituaries are very much like obituaries in local newspapers because they provide basic information about the deceased. Nowadays you may find at the bottom of the death notice in a newspaper a URL providing the Web address of the virtual obituary. Over time, on-line obituaries may not only supplement newspaper obituaries but also replace them as fewer families live close together and are separated by distance and the Web allows them to stay informed. A final advantage to on-line memorials, say those who use them, is that they are longer lasting than, say, a newspaper advertisement because a newspaper is only in print for one day. But who needs the on-line obituaries? New services actually offer e-mail notices to friends and family members in case of a death with a link to a Web site for funeral service information. On-line memorials are great for those who want to use them. Internet memorials can show video and sounds in a way that stone monuments cannot. It puts the person's life out there for all to see. Still, most people do not think that cyber monuments can be compared to carving memories in stone. Since cavemen times, people have marked graves with stone (Raether, 1994). They last forever. If it is not going to last forever, they do not want to do it. On-line memorials are more transitory. People delete on-line memorials from a computer's memory after a time. Nobody is going to remove a stone from granny's grave and says, "This has been here long enough." However, this may not be true in some other countries like Germany where graves are leased (Habenstein & Lamers, 1994). Monument companies do not expect on-line memorials to put them out of work any time soon. A foot marker has only enough room for a date, a dash, and a name. The Internet allows people to create something lasting and to fill in everything that happens between the dashes on a tombstone. Many people start to look at a cyber monument as a replacement for a physical monument, and the layout of the Web sites tries to duplicate reality as close as possible. The monuments range from footmarks, upright monuments, private estates, crypts, mausoleums, to private chapels. And virtual monuments, unlike real ones, will not weather with the passage of time and can be visited easily by people from around the world.

LIMITATIONS AND CONTROL—
FROM VIP TO PETS

It is also possible to create on-line personal tributes to others who have touched our life from near or far. Every one of us can create our own tributes to the heroes in our life in our own way. Cyber Cemeteries are adding, at their own expense, information on notable figures in every field and walk of life in world history—from Abbots to Zoologists, from Arts and Entertainment to Sports and Science, from the distant past up to today. By doing this, the cemetery's owners feel they enrich and broaden the significance of each individual memorial. There are also no restrictions or limits to the number of listings any individual can post. Nor are there any time limits, so the bereaved feel free to add memorials for their ancestors, friends, or pay tribute to a famous movie star or historic figure. Tributes to fictional characters and/or pets are allowed by some on-line cemeteries and not by others. The more stringent places review all submissions before being published onto their sites. This is similar to restrictions in traditional cemeteries, where only certain materials or sizes are allowed for the construction of monuments. The baby boomer generation is used to having a choice in products as well as life styles, and is used to asking the question why. Why does it have to be a traditional funeral? Why could I not create a memorial for my loved one on line in addition to or instead of a traditional monument? The one thing that virtual monuments are really tapping into is our desire to have a little bit more control over how we say good-bye to our loved ones. People mourning the death of a loved one do not have to listen to a preacher. They can say: Wait a minute, I knew that person. Personal memorial pages are expected to grow. They provide certain immortality, an afterlife. It gives people the opportunity to mourn privately, yet express it publicly. In an increasingly crowded world; Web pages have the advantage of taking up less space than gravestones and crematory urns. But Web pages will not replace gravestones—not in our lifetime, maybe 100 years from now.

RELIGION AND CULTURE

In Japan it is already possible to be virtually dead. A Buddhist temple in Hiroshima opened a "virtual graveyard" on the Internet. Visitors can choose different types of electronic tombstones and include photos of the deceased and family records on a Web page. They can create their own memorials in advance and leave informal wills for their families. A monk at the Kannonin temple said the idea came from people who live too far away from the temple to visit, but wanted to tend family memorials and pay respects to ancestors. The World Wide Web Cemetery is open to people of all religious faiths, and will allow us all to share the lives of our loved ones with people from all over the world. When you erect a monument to a loved one in the Web cemetery, doing so should provide you with a measure of solace, and, if you walk through the cemetery, that you delight and wonder in the diversity, uniqueness, and accomplishments of its inhabitants. Some bereaved think there is something powerfully spiritual about the Internet, a hard-to-describe feeling that the Net connects them to family members after they have passed away. These individuals think that they can communicate better with the spirit (of dead ancestors) from the Internet, from cyberspace, than through cemeteries, headstones, or other earthly monuments they visit or touch. This may be particularly true for Buddhists, who believe that their forebears' spirits live on after their deaths. The literal translation of *levayah*—funeral "accompanying"—teaches us that the *nature* of a Jewish funeral implies involvement, which can be accomplished through the Internet. A candle, which burns continuously for seven days, is lit upon returning home from the cemetery. The light of the candle symbolizes the soul. "The soul of man is the light of the Lord" (Proverbs 20:27). This can be accomplished through virtual candles (animated gif files) on the virtual memorial. The mitzvah of comforting mourners (*nilhum aveilim*) is fulfilled by a personal visit to the house of mourning. Fulfilling this mitzvah, in Rabbinic tradition, is "one of the things which bring good to the world." The very fact that you have come to the house of mourning is an act of respect and comfort. Distance and time may forbid one to physically visit the house. An e-mail which focuses on the person who died and his or her life may be a substitute. A visit should not be unduly long, and certainly is not the time for general socializing. Upon leaving the site, one may offer a sentence of the Tradition to the mourners: *Hamakom ye-nakhem etkhem b'tokh shear aveilei tzion virushalayim.* "May the Almighty comfort you with all the other mourners of Zion and Jerusalem." It is not proper to visit the grave of the deceased until 30 days have passed since the funeral. This provides the bereaved with time to create an on-line memorial. When speaking of the deceased, a Hebrew phrase is generally added: *alav hashalom* (may he rest in peace) or *aleha hashalom* (may she rest in peace). *Zikhrono livrakhah* (for a male) and *Zikronah livrakhah* (for a female) are also used, meaning "of blessed memory." It is customary to place a tombstone (*matzeivah*) on a grave, dedicating it in a brief ceremony, known as unveiling, which usually takes place within a year after the death. However, it may take place at any time after the 30-day period, no matter if it is a physical or a virtual monument. There is a variety of practices concerning inscriptions, though the tendency emphasizes simplicity. The Hebrew and English names of the dead, dates of birth and death, and certain Hebrew letters are gener-ally included. These letters are the initials of the words in the phrase *tehei nishmato/nishmatah tzereurah bitzror ha-yahim* (May his/her soul be bound up in the bond of life). Respect paid to the memory of the dead is not confined to the site where the earthly remains are interred. But as the grave does symbolize a memorial for the dead, it is an appropriate place for family and friends to gather in respect. The formal unveiling, or posting on-line itself, is a symbol signifying that we open our hearts to the memory of the dead, to the meaning of their lives, to their influence upon us, and to appropriate ways of perpetuating their devotion. Jewish custom indicates that stones, picked up at the gravesite, may be placed as a memorial sign on the tombstone. Cyber graves allow you to do the same. People who want to express their respect and their sympathy in a tangible way should contribute to a favorite cause of the deceased. Mourners generally prefer being notified of charitable contributions made in memory of the dead rather than receiv-ing flowers or specially prepared baskets of food or sweets. Jewish tradition has always emphasized concern for the living, helping the needy in this world. This is also a way of extending the influence of the deceased after he or she is no longer walking this earth. Cyber obituaries can provide direct links to the charitable institutions of the deceased choice. It is proper that the name of the deceased loved one be permanently linked to the synagogue, the House of God. Virtual monuments may include links to the synagogue. Synagogues may want to provide a virtual memorial plaque recording the Hebrew and English name. Memorial plaques are grouped by the Hebrew months. In the course of the year, new plaques are dedicated on the eighth day of Pesach and on the eighth day of Sukkot, Shemini Atzeret (Nielsen et al., 1983).

Cemeteries can be seen as one of our most valuable windows to the past. A cemetery may be a place for burying the dead, but it is also a place for uncovering a wealth of genealogical data. This may be of interest to individuals of various religions and cultural backgrounds, but may be of particular interest to Mormons; Scientologists may find cyber monuments highly suitable (Davies, 1998); while Native Americans living the Indian Way may find virtual obituaries helpful in communicating information about a wake (Arviso Alvord, 1999). Changes in our understanding of death and grief have changed our ritual responses to death. Protestant, Catholic, and Jewish communities have developed new funeral services in the past few decades and will be influenced by the Web in the future (Habenstein & Lamers, 1996).

FEATURES AND COSTS

Some commercial Web cemeteries offer visitors a chance to send e-mails and even virtual flower arrangements. Some Web sites are simple: one photo, dates of birth and death, maybe one line from the Bible or the deceased's favorite song. Many are yearbook-like reminiscences. Others are full of links to other Web sites, music, and video. They contain detailed, personal, sometimes humorous biographies. Standard memorials are created from an inventory of designs or designs supplied by the customer to create a memorial containing all the standard elements of traditional memorials, including the publishing of a digital image or images, other graphic icons, and a Condolence/Visitors page. Deluxe memorials are more elaborate than a Standard Memorial, and may contain different features. These can consist of several Web pages with extensive graphics or even a 3-D Virtual World. They could also be single or double page memorials with distinctive graphic or design requirements. The creation of a deluxe memorial may not be automated and may require individual programming and design. New features may be added, such as an anniversary reminder, automated anniversary mailings to a group of people, or other features which may enhance the value of the memorial such as links to physical monuments or Web-site access at the grave site via a solar powered LCD display in the monument, or a personal tablet PC with a wireless connection, allowing visitors at the grave to surf the Net. Another possibilities are on-line wills, which will be executed by a trustee, and e-mails to be sent to a mailing list notifying selected individuals of one's death.

There is a growing number of virtual cemeteries, which charge a fee for the simple act of posting a brief memorial. Others believe the Internet should remain an open and free place to share one's loss, and therefore there are no costs associated with the basic listings on the Web. These sites are either servers operated by individuals or non-profit organizations, or commercial Web sites which make their money by selling banner advertisements or other services. Others may charge from $10 for a virtual obituary to $1,000 for a complete multimedia package—including text, poems, bible verses, photographs, virtual flowers and candles, audio, video, and a guest book with automatic e-mail forwarding. The lower end of the scale usually offers fewer features on their site, and a longer wait to get the site up. While others have fully automated Web-sites which allow customers to design and update their sites on-line and post them directly on the Web. Some companies offer longer contracts and perpetual memorials. The perpetual nature of these sites is highly questionable, how will the sites keep up with the ever-changing technology. What will the Internet look like in 30 years? These costs are hard to forecast and one wonders how you will be able to view these sites. Will the html code pass away like the eight-track records did? Yet the Web is a low cost alternative to a physical monument, at a price tag ranging from free to a thousand dollar. Many fear that as the social equity in our communities decreases, family members will decide to spend grandma's inheritance money on the education of the grandchildren rather than on her funeral. One could also argue that the Web offers a new dimension to a monument which a physical monument could not offer in the past. Virtual memorials are currently more of an add-on sale to newspaper obituaries or physical monuments.

VIRTUAL CEMETERIES, MEMORIALS, AND OBITUARIES

The following are a few sample sites, from the United States and Canada, which provide a mixture of the good, the bad, and the ugly. You can find these sites on-line. Don't be surprised if you cannot locate them, if it is past the year 2000, some may already be gone and others may have joined in. The dynamic nature and velocity of e-commerce make some of these sites extremely vulnerable.

Angels Online Memorial Pages	Internet Obituary Network
Arrangements.com	Legacy Archives
Cyber Cemetery	Living Memory
Cybermourn	Memorial Gardens
Dearly Departed	Memoriam
Digital Milestones	Obituaries Worldwide, Inc.
E Memoriam, Ltd.	The Obituary Daily Times
E-Obit.com	Obit Details
Eternal Monuments In Cyberspace	The Obituary Page
Eternal Surf	Passedaway.com
Family Cemetery	Perpetual Memorials
Forever Memorials	Remembrances
FuneralTribute.com	Simplex Knowledge Company—
Garden of Remembrance	"The Virtual Funeral"
Heartland Hills Memorial Gardens	Virtual Memorial Company
Heavenly Door	Virtual Memorials
Imminent Domain	The Virtual Memorial Garden
Immortality Inc. (Living Tributes)	WebObits.com
In Memory	The Web Memorial
In The Memory Of	World Gardens: The Virtual Cemetery
In Memoriam	WorldMemorial.com
Internet Memorials	The World Wide Cemetery

THE PRESENT AND FUTURE OF
ON-LINE MEMORIALS

When you are in the process of your grief, a properly designed virtual memorial can give you refuge and companionship. Web sites with bereavement chats and message boards can create a strong and supportive community. For those who are not yet ready to interact, Web sites of others who have experienced loss may be rich with empathy. The anonymity of the Web allows one to visit 24/7, 365 days a year the graves of loved ones. It crosses geographic boundaries and one is able to view it virtually from anywhere in the world. Another important aspect is that one can visit sites without being seen. This may be especially important for the bereaved whose relationship with the deceased officially ended or never officially existed, such as lovers, mistresses, and ex-spouses. Creating a Web site is similar to drawing one's feelings, ending with a positive scenario, which gives the opportunity to have one's feelings acknowledged. This in itself is a very soothing interaction. The design of a Web site offers this type of interaction even to people who are less talented with pencil and paper.

It is difficult to get an accurate count of how many people are currently memorialized on the Web. Our latest count showed approximately 2,500 memorials of various forms. Current virtual memorials are growing slowly through words of mouth in the Internet world. But the number will be growing as the Web becomes more a part of our daily life, deathcare industry experts say. Cyber cemeteries will die or flourish in the future depending on the amount of money which can be made with these on-line testimonials. So far no large companies have entered the virtual cemetery market. This market has great potentials for the traditional players in the deathcare industry. Funeral homes, cemeteries, casket and monument companies, as well as secondary suppliers to the death care industry like florists and newspapers, will either want or be forced to provide on-line services of various kinds to compete in the new e-economy. The big breakthrough will come when some major Internet companies target this market either from a technology, transaction handling, or Web content aspect.

REFERENCES

Arviso Alvord, L. (1999). *The scalpel and the silver bear—The first Navajo woman surgeon combines Western medicine and traditional healing.* New York: Bantam Books.

Baden, M. (1989). *Unnatural death: Confessions of a medical examiner.* New York: Ivy Books.

Bermann, E. (1973). *Scapegoat—The impact of death-fear on an American family.* Ann Arbor, MI: University of Michigan Press.

Borg, S., & Lasker, J. (1981). *When pregnancy fails—Families coping with miscarriage, stillbirth, and infant death.* Boston, MA: Beacon Press.

Davidson, J., & Doka, K. (1999). *Living with grief—At work, at school, at worship.* Washington, DC: Hospice Foundation of America.

Davies, R. (1998). *The Lazarus syndrome—Burial alive and other horrors of the undead.* New York: Barnes & Noble Books.

Habenstein, R., & Lamers, W. (1994). *Funeral customs the world over.* Milwaukee, WI: Bulfin Printers Inc.

Habenstein, R., & Lamers, W. (1996). *The history of American funeral directing.* Milwaukee, WI: National Funeral Directors Association.

Jackson, E. (1957). *Understanding grief—Its roots, dynamics and treatment.* Nashville, TN: Abingdon.

Kübler-Ross, E. (1969). *On death and dying—What the dying have to teach doctors, nurses, clergy and their own families.* New York: Touchstone Book—Simon & Schuster.

Murphy, E. (1995). *After the funeral—The posthumous adventures of famous corpses.* New York: Barnes & Noble Books.

Nielsen, B., Hein, N., Reynolds, F., Miller, A., Karff, S., Cochran, A., & McLean, P. (1983). *Religions of the world.* New York: St. Martin's Press.

Raether, H. (1994). *The American funeral.* Milwaukee, WI: National Funeral Director Association.

Wilkins, R. (1996). *Death—A history of man's obsessions and fears.* New York: Barnes & Noble, Inc.

CHAPTER 9

Violence is the Dark Side of Spirituality

John D. Morgan

There are many reasons for violence: economic reasons, overcrowding, mental and emotional illness, or long-term hostilities. In this chapter, I want to explore a different perspective. I want to look at the spiritual roots of violence. Violence occurs within the context of a belief system. I will begin by discussing the uniqueness of the person; second, the impact of death on the human condition; third, what constitutes spirituality and how spiritualities differ; and finally, how the person in the face of death uses violence.

THE PERSON IS A UNIQUE SUBSTANCE

If I were to hand you something that you might not recognize, you would look at it, see what it does, and eventually figure out that it is, perhaps, a magnifying glass. We discover what something is by what it does. Actions flow from the essence (Wuellner, 1956): A thing is what it does. We can tell what a human being is, by looking at what he or she does.

There is, however, a difference between looking at chalk and seeing what it does, and looking at human beings and seeing what they do. Chalk is an individual, that is one out of many (Reese, 1980, p. 250). If I need a piece of chalk to write on the board, any one of them will do as long as it is long enough for my fingers. If I need a human being, it isn't a situation in which any one will do. In that sense, human beings are not individuals, they are persons (Ortega y Gasset, 1957, p. 140). We misuse the term "individual" all of the time. An individual is simply one out of the group. When we complain that we are not being treated as individuals, we in fact are being treated as "one out of the many." Any one will do. What we are really complaining about, and what we should say, is that we are not being treated as persons.

What is it to be a person? Fundamentally, a person is a subject (Morgan, 1993, p. 4). A subject is that which has powers. The term power is not used here in any political sense, or sense of power over others. Rather it is being used in its root sense of "the capacity to do." Some such powers are the power to see, or the power to taste. A subject is a potential seer but unless there is a colored object (the lining of my tie) the subject will not see. We use the term "object" for these things that activate our powers (Morgan, 1993, p. 4). The colored object (my tie) has made the power to see, the subject, specific. A subject is a potential seer of any color whatsoever, but becomes an actual seer of a specific colored object. A subject is a potential hearer of any sound, but because of the object, now hears a specific sound. Objects get their meaning and value from subjects. Color would be meaningless if there were no seeing creatures in this world. Sounds and odors would have no meaning if there were no sensate creatures in the world.

Unfortunately, we often think of persons, ourselves and others, as objects. It was not too long ago that our understanding of a woman was that she was "somebody's daughter," then "somebody's wife," then "somebody's mother," and then eventually "somebody's widow." A woman was defined in terms of somebody else. She was thought of objectively, that is, as a thing which gets meaning from outside. When we think of persons primarily as their sex, their race, their religion, their nationality, their career, their sexual orientation, we think of them as objects, as that which gets meaning from without. But a person is not an object. The person is a subject, that which creates meaning.

If I ask you "who are you?" you might respond by giving a name, "I'm Jane." But "Jane" is just a sound. If you say "I'm a student," I still do not know who you are. You could respond with a very long list of categories, and I still would not know who you, the person, really is. Eventually we come to the realization of "Yes, but . . . !" "Yes, I'm a student"; "yes, I'm nineteen"; "yes, I'm a woman"; "yes, I'm a Canadian"; "yes, I'm a mother"; but these categories do not begin to describe who one is. No list of categories ever defines a person.

A subject is the one who says "yes, but." This "moment of subjectivity" (Sartre, 1957, p. 15) is the realization that no list of categories could possibly ever describe the person. The moment of subjectivity is the moment in which one realizes that never before in the history of the universe did s/he exist, never again will s/he exist. Each person is a once-in-the-lifetime-of-the-universe event. In 1960, when the World's Fair was held in New York, the Vatican allowed Michelangelo's great statue *The Pieta* to be brought to New York. People were concerned because, although boats don't sink very often, they sometimes do. Had the boat sank, that statue would be lost. But Michelangelo made several copies of *The Pieta*, and each was literally cast in stone. Michelangelo's statue does not grow or develop or learn or create value systems. Each subject, however, each person, is a unique self-creation. The important lesson we learn from life, and from death, is that the death of any person is a far greater loss than the destruction of Michelangelo's statue. Persons create knowledge and values. Persons create themselves.

A person is a unique substance of a rational nature (Reese, 1980, p. 424); a unique source of knowing and valuing; a once-in-the-lifetime-of-the-universe event. Each of us is a unique being, never before in the history of the universe did any of us exist.

DEATH ALWAYS WINS

Each person is unique, yet destined to cease to be. Nothing makes the person more conscious of his/her uniqueness than death. No one has said this better than Ernest Becker.

> It is a terrifying dilemma to be with and to have to live with . . . to live a whole lifetime with the fate of death haunting one's dreams and even the most sun-filled days. (Becker, 1973, p. 27)

This ambiguity is the fate of being human. We are unique; yet we know that we will go into the ground to rot forever. Each of us is a special self-creation, but as far as nature is concerned, we are nothing but body (Becker, 1973, p. 31). Once we have passed our genes onto the next generation, we have done our evolutionary work. The awareness that we are nothing but bodies and bodies die, forces us to ask the question, "what kind of God would make such fancy worm food?" (Becker, 1973, p. 26).

Let me stress this point. We are unique beings, never before in the history of the universe did any one of us exist. But each of us is going to go into the grave to rot forever. Each of our loved ones are unique creations, and they too, will go into the grave to rot forever.

How do we live with this terrible awareness of death? Becker says that there are three responses to death. The first is the one that most of us play all of the time, "I will deny that it is going to happen." I'll just pretend that if I don't think about it, it isn't going to be there. If I don't think about it, it won't happen for another couple hundred thousand years to me or anybody I love. We spend our life just pretending that it isn't going to happen. So what are the consequences of the denial of death? An example that I like to use is: think of the nastiest thing you've ever done in your life. Think of how much energy we spend in suppressing these thoughts. We don't want to think about the fact that we did X because if we think about it, we might accidently blurt it out and everyone would know what terrible persons we are. So we spend much of our lives suppressing this knowledge about our fundamental failures. We walk on eggshells because we are afraid. This is what our culture teaches us to do about death! It has the same effect. We walk on eggshells all the time because we're afraid that doing something might remind us about death. That's what Becker calls the normal response (Becker, 1973, p. 23).

The second response is referred to as the neurotic (Becker, 1973, p. 23). People become so wrapped up in their fear of death that they refuse to play by society's rules. They refuse to play games. Becker believes that Freud missed the point in his discussion of anality and the Oedipus Complex (p. 31). The most fundamental repression is not of sexuality, but of the consciousness of mortality (p. 31). We avoid messiness because messiness reminds us of decay. We desire after our opposite sex parent not because of sexual jealousy, but because we wish to be *causa sui,* our own parent. That way, we can then be assured of protection from death (p. 107).

The third response to the term of death is illustrated by that woman over in Calcutta who died a couple of years ago. By standards of our culture Mother Teresa was obviously a nut. She went out into the streets and found old, smelly, dirty beggars and brought them into her house. Why in the world would anybody do that? By the standard of our culture no one would have expected Jesus of Nazareth to die a natural death. He annoyed the power structure. These persons did what they perceived needed to be done in spite of personal costs or community values. This is what Becker (1973) calls the hero. "Man must reach out for support to a dream, a metaphysic of hope that sustains him and makes his life worthwhile" (Becker, 1973, p. 275). Most of the persons reading the chapter may not consider themselves heroes, but they are. When you go home at night and your children say, "Mommy, read to me," the last thing you want to do is read to your kids when you've had a long day at work; but you do it. Saturday morning, "Daddy, I need a ride to the rink." You don't want to get up on a Saturday morning and drive the kids to the rink but we do it. Why? Why do we do such things? Why did Mother Theresa do what she did? Why did Jesus annoy everybody that He knew was going to kill him? What is the secret of the hero? Becker says the hero takes death seriously (p. 11). S/he knows that death is going to happen one way or the other. The hero says "I'm going to die, so I might as well die having lived well." That is really what true humanity is about. The heroic person is the one who realizes this is the one shot we've got at living life. I might as well live well to do what needs to be done. I'm going to die one way or the other, I might as well live well.

SPIRITUALITY IS ESSENTIAL LONELINESS

"Spirituality" is a term used often today but we didn't discover it. Thinkers since Plato (1920, p. 449) have written about the basic idea. Spirituality refers to the ability of the human mind to transcend, to step beyond, space and time (Aquinas, 1945, p. 750). What does that mean? It doesn't mean that you and I are going to fly off to Mars right at this second. Consider the following true statements. Anselm (cited in Armstrong, 1993, p. 202) wrote his proof for the existence of God in Paris in the 12th century. Jack Morgan taught Anselm's proof for the existence of God in Los Angeles in 1960. Jack Morgan taught Anselm's proof for the existence of God in San Diego in 1963. Jack Morgan taught Anselm's proof for the existence of God in Montreal in 1973. Jack Morgan taught Anselm's proof for the existence of God in 1983 in London, Ontario. The words used, the ideas referred to are all very understandable. Twelfth century, 1960, 1963, 1973, 1983, Paris, Los Angeles, San Diego, Montreal, London. In understanding these words, the body remains in the place and time indicated by a year to date calender and a properly set clock. Yet our minds have the ability to understand outside this immediate time and this immediate place. A dog, a cat, an elephant is only aware of its immediate surroundings. You and I can go beyond.

Students spend literally thousands of dollars, an enormous amount of time and energy to strive for something that does not exist: Their degree. The degree does not yet exist, it won't exist until they walk across the stage at graduation. But look how much money they have spent on it, look at how much time they have put into it. They have some ability of knowing something that is not physically present to them.

If I ask you, "Do you like beer?," whether you do or not, you know what I am talking about. You understand it, even if you do not have any beer on your tongue right at this moment. I did not ask you if you like "this beer" the one on your tongue right now. But I asked do you like beer, any beer at all. None of us have ever tasted "any beer at all." We have all tasted individual sips of beer at specific moments in time. Yet we understand the question "Do you like any beer at all." There is something about the human mind that is not limited to this moment, right here and now. This is spirituality, the ability of the mind to transcend immediacy.

This ability of the human mind to transcend the immediacy is the basic meaning of spirituality but it doesn't stop there. When we look over the history of thought, we can see what many people have told us what it is to be a human being. Plato (1920) tells us that we are a spirit captured in a body (p. 449). Aristotle (1941) tells us that we are a union of body and soul (p. 538). The person is social according to Rousseau (1972, p. 291). Not social according to Hobbes (1958, p. 107). The person is dual according to Descartes (1995, p. 164); a worker according to Marx (1995, p. 256). We could look at each one of those theories and say, "he has a point." Each of these theories makes sense or it never would have lasted. Each of these theories is a good theory about what it is to be human. But we say, "yes, but." Yes we are workers, yes we are sexual beings, yes we are spirits, yes we are social, but that doesn't begin to describe who I am. Spirituality is our ability to integrate these various identities. I have an identity of myself as a child of God, I have an identity of myself as a worker, I have an identity of myself as a will to power, I have an identity of myself as a social construct. Spirituality is seen in my integration of how I take the data of life, the data of experience, the data of education and I put it together to get the person, who I am. The subject that I am draws from objects and creates the self.

"Spirituality refers to the ability of the human person to chose the relative importance of the physical, social, emotional, religious, and intellectual stimuli that influence him or her and thereby engage in a continual process of meaning-making" (Morgan, 2002). Each of us has been raised in a tradition of some sort, whether that tradition is Buddhism, Christianity, consumerism, or hedonism. Each of us decides how much of that tradition s/he is going to adopt. Spirituality is our ability to decide for ourselves how much I'm going to take from A, from B, from C, from D, and try to put it together in some sort of consistent whole. The philosopher Ortega y Gasset (1957) describes the human person as a drama, an actor (p. 50). We find ourselves on the stage of life. The difficulty is that no one ever told us what the script is. No one ever told us what role we are playing. We ad-lib our way through life.

One thing we know is that there is a final curtain. When we become conscious of the limits of our time, we start being self-consciously spiritual. Spirituality is the ability to self-create, this ability to decide who I want to be, who I am. And we draw from our various experiences and make as good a picture as we can. Sometimes we don't do it very well, sometimes we do it pretty well. Buddhism is a spirituality,

Christianity is a spirituality, so is consumerism, so is Marxism. All of these are meaning systems that someone has formulated. The question is whether the meaning system is always going to be helpful. When one is young, bright, sexy, healthy, almost any meaning system works. One of the advantages of the major religious traditions is that they are also helpful in crisis moments of life.

In our consciousness of our spirituality we realize that our ego boundaries become permeable (Klass, 1993, p. 52), we realize that there is more out there than the individual person. I am on this stage of life but I am not alone. I respond to other people with their spiritualities. I become aware of the connection with other persons, with the environment, with our God (Graydon, 1996, p. 326).

If we look at the major religious traditions, we'll see that what seems to be common among the major religious traditions is that all of them say that in some how or another we're self-creations (Smith, 1986, p. 480). One group may call it virtue, somebody else might call it responsibility, one might put the emphasis on positive action, somebody else might now have a lot of the "thou shalt nots," but in the long run all of the major religious traditions reinforce our self-creation. The major religious traditions reinforce that reality is much more than tables and chairs and rocks, that there is more to reality than meets the eye, that we are more than a physical, biological entity, that we are part of a larger wholeness (Smith, 1986, p. 480). We may differ as to how we might call that: the Marxist might call that the classless society, being part of the larger wholeness; someone else might call that the Kingdom of God; someone else might call it the One that is beyond all things. They all agree that we are part of a larger wholeness. And whatever we are, we become fully who we are by being related to others. Whatever we are we need forgiveness, we need peace with ourselves. These are the lessons of the great tradition.

Becker says that with consciousness comes anxiety. This is found clearly in the story of Abraham and Isaac (Genesis, 22, 1-8). Abraham was wandering through the deserts and he made this deal with God. God said, "You preach me as the one God and I will make you the father of a vast nation." Sounds like a good deal. The problem was his wife was long past child-bearing age, he was an old man, and this was long before Viagra. But Sarah gets pregnant. They have this kid and they are happy, Abraham is now on the road to having this vast family, this vast nation. All of a sudden somebody comes, an angel, a messenger, and taps him on the shoulder and says, "Abraham, God would like you to do a little something for him. God would like you to do a little thing." "Sure, anything God wants." "God would like you to sacrifice Isaac." Well, I don't know about you but I would want to see his angel union card myself. I would want a hand-written note from God.

Abraham is the archetype of the loneliness of being a person. We have the revelation to Abraham in the desert. We have the revelation through Jesus. We have the revelation through Mohamad. We have the revelation through Buddha. Each of us has to decide for ourselves. And that's what Abraham had to do. Abraham is the archetype of the hero. The person who says, this is my one shot at life and I'm going to do it as well as I can. We know that the story has a happy ending, but the happy ending is almost irrelevant. What was important was his willingness to follow his conscience, his spiritual creation.

The increasing anonymity caused by industrialization, technology, and over-population makes it vastly more difficult for any of us to act in a significant way or to believe in the importance of our uniqueness (Gray, 1970, p. 11).

We live in a culture that is so falsely individualistic. There is no realization of community, of connection. If we look at the new religious interests, the new interest in spirituality, it's my spirituality with my God and my religion and so on, that it doesn't include community at all. It doesn't include the dream of Abraham, it doesn't include the dream of the great spiritual teachers. Contemporary persons are highly skeptical, anxiety-ridden, consumer material oriented, immediately oriented and fascinated by the unusual (Irion, 1993, p. 96). As Gerry Cox mentions in his chapter, as Native peoples and the Black peoples become more integrated into our con-sumerist culture, the higher the suicide rate. So they had their communities focus on spirituality. As they become part of the dominant culture, they've lost that focus and the suicide rate has gone up.

VIOLENCE IS CLEANSING THE WORLD OF TAINTED ONES

Personal choice of values in a limited life is the root of spirituality and also the root of the violence. Ernest Becker holds that the fall into self-consciousness has given us dread or anxiety. "It makes routine, automatic, secure, self-confident activity impossible" (Becker, 1973, p. 60). Animals are spared the awareness that they must create themselves; and the awareness that they have a limited time in order to do it; and the knowledge that no matter how well they do it, death is still one per customer and one per every customer.

Each of us creates a sense of personal identity and set of values. Then we meet someone with a different sense of identity or a different sense of values. How do we handle that? Here I am raised as a Catholic and so on, and now all of a sudden I meet you, who is a Hindu, or you as a Protestant, or you who is Black, or you who is gay. I have created my spirituality and now all of a sudden, my fundamental anxiety, my fundamental ambiguity with myself is reinforced because you're out there and you've got a different value system. The evil that troubles us most, according to Becker, is our own vulnerability (Becker, 1975, p. 12). None of us are throughly convinced of our values. We are convinced of our positions but only to a limited degree. When another comes along with another position, that's pretty threatening. If I can prove that my God is bigger than your God, then I feel a little safer. If I can prove that my God can beat up your God, then I feel a little bit safer. "No wonder men go into a rage over fine points of belief. If your adversary wins the argument about truth, you die" (Becker, 1975, p. 64).

There is a film called *Licence to Kill Homosexuals* (Arthur Dong Film, 1997). It consists of interviews with people who had killed homosexuals. In it, many people think it is perfectly alright to kill these people who are contaminating our good culture. I'm sure that we could have found such films about Blacks, about Jews, about Muslims, about communists, about capitalists. When we are sufficiently insecure, we can convince ourselves that everyone else contaminates our culture. If I can get rid of them, I can protect myself from them, then I'm safe. The arguments about capital punishment are similar. All we have to do to have a safe community is kill a few people. If I can get rid of that guy, and that guy, and that guy, then life will be beautiful. Sometimes we don't even have to kill them, I can ostracize them by not publishing their books, I can ostracize them in many other ways. But if I can protect myself from their influence, then I'm going to be safe. As Ernest Becker (1975) says, evil comes from our urge to victory over evil (p. 136).

The root of evil, it seems to me, is far deeper than economic. Evil is rooted in the anxiety each of us feels because we are alone in the cosmos. If somehow or other I can be protected from that aloneness, by building defenses, then that makes it easier. Each of us is a self-creation facing annihilation and we know that this is our one shot, you don't get a second chance. And so we feel vulnerable, we feel weak.

Killing is a symbolic solution of a biological limitation (Becker, 1975, p. 99). I can prove that I am no longer biologically as limited if I can control life and death. If I can kill somebody, than obviously I have control. Sacrifice is what Louis Mumford said it was, an admission of our pitiful finitude of powerlessness, in the face of the tremendous mystery of the universe (Becker, 1975, p. 101). We sacrifice because the universe is so awe-inspiring. Again, look at the story of Cane and Abel (Genesis, 4, 1-16). Abel sacrificed his vegetables and the fruit, in the name of his God. And Cane was a little scared that maybe Abel's sacrifice was better than his. So he'd solve that problem by killing the threat. Everyone feels dissatisfied with him/herself, and so there are two things one can do with this dissatisfaction. One can accept the blame him/herself, or can blame it on the other. Guess who's going to get it? Who is responsible for my failure as a human being? Either you are, or I am. So I am going to prove that you're at fault. Men and women kill to cleanse the earth of tainted ones.

PERSONS NEED TO BE COMFORTABLE
IN THEIR OWN SKINS

Others have written about the importance of limiting gun access, or reaching out to the disenfranchised, reaching out to the alienated. I think that we also have to consider that even if guns were not as readily available, even if we reached out to the disenfranchised, we are still going to have our fundamental insecurity of life. Each of us is this unique being who has to make sense out of life and do it on our own. We stand on the shoulders of giants, but we still have to do it on our own as Abraham did. And that's scary.

Those who are uncomfortable with ambiguity, uncomfortable in their own skins may believe that they need to be protected from others. To protect myself from your influence, I may want to kill you. Because if I can kill you, that just proves how much power I have.

What we have to try to do is find some way of helping each other be comfortable in our own skins. What we have to do is find some way of helping people face a life that includes death. Enjoying a donut that includes a hole in it. Facing a life that includes pain.

Each of us has the realization that everyone that I love is going to die. I've got a lot of choices, I can pretend that it is never going to happen, or I can take the energy caused by this realization and perhaps try to make a better world. The great work that the Bereaved Families of Ontario, Compassionate Friends, the Candlelighters, or Mothers Against Drunk Driving has done, is that they have made meaning out of chaos. There is another alternative to violence: not to deny that my loved ones will die, not to deny that I'm going to die, but try to make some sort of meaning out of this chaos. Reduction of violence is going to take more than just simply changing laws about firearms. It's going to take a whole new approach of our culture, a whole new approach of our educational system.

We need to somehow or other try to create a culture in which meaning might triumph over chaos.

Once you face death, nothing else matters. Once you come to terms with ultimate reality, nothing else matters anymore. I am reminded of the line from Terrence, "I am human, nothing human is foreign to me" (Terrence, 1966). Death has the ability to teach us to accept reality in its fullness. To accept the limits of what it is. This is the work of death education, palliative care, bereavement service. We have to try to make other people comfortable in their own skins.

REFERENCES

Aquinas, T. (1945). Summa theologica, I, Q. 79, A. 4. In A. C. Pegis (Ed.), *Basic writings of Saint Thomas Aquinas*. New York: Random House.

Aristotle, de Anima (1941). In R. McKeon (Ed.), *The basic works of Aristotle*. New York: Random House.

Armstrong, K. (1993). *A history of God: The 4,000 year quest of Judaism, Christianity and Islam*. New York: Ballantine.

Becker, E. (1973). *The denial of death*. New York: Free Press.

Becker, E. (1975). *Escape from evil*. New York: Collier-Macmillan.

FitzGerald, D. J. (1995). Rene Descartes: The human person as dualism. In H. Brown, D. L. Hudecki, L. A. Kennedy, & J. J. Snyder (Eds.), *Images of the person: The philosophy of the human person in a religious context* (pp. 147-181). Chicago, IL: Loyola.

Genesis, 4, 1-16. *The Jerusalem Bible*. Garden City, NY: Doubleday.

Genesis, 22, 1-8 (1966). *The Jerusalem Bible*. Garden City, NY: Doubleday.

Gray, J. G. (1970). On understanding violence philosophically. In J. G. Gray, *On understanding violence philosophically and other essays* (pp. 1-35). New York: Harper and Row.

Graydon, D. (1996). Casey house hospice: Caring for the person living with HIV/AIDS. In J. D. Morgan (Ed.), *Ethical issues in the care of the dying and bereaved aged* (pp. 323-334). Amityville, NY: Baywood.

Hobbes, T. (1958). *Leviathan*. Indianapolis, MN: Bobbs Merril.

Irion, P. E. (1993). Spiritual issues in death and dying for those who do not have conventional religious belief. In K. J. Doka & J. D. Morgan (Eds.), *Death and spirituality* (pp. 93-112). Amityville, NY: Baywood.

Klass, D. (1993). Spirituality, protestantism, and death. In K. J. Doka & J. D. Morgan (Eds.), *Death and spirituality* (pp. 51-73). Amityville, NY: Baywood.

Licence to Kill Homosexuals (1997). Deep Force Productions, Arthur Dong Film, 1997.

Morgan, J. D. (1993). The existential quest for meaning. In K. J. Doka & J. D. Morgan (Eds.), *Death and spirituality* (pp. 3-9). Amityville, NY: Baywood.

Morgan, J. (2002). Dying and grieving are journeys of the spirit. In R. Gilbert (Ed.), *Health care & spirituality: Listening, assessing, caring.* Amityville, NY: Baywood.

Ortega y Gasset, J. (1957). *Man and people.* In R. Trask (Trans.), New York: Norton.

Plato, Phaedo (1920). In B. Jowett (Ed.), *The dialogues of Plato* (Vol. I, pp. 441-501). New York: Random House.

Reese, W. L. (1980). *Dictionary of philosophy and religion: Eastern and Western thought.* New Jersey: Humanities.

Rousseau, J. J. (1972). The social contract. In A. Fagothey (Ed.), *Anthology of right and reason* (pp. 291-297). St. Louis: Mosby.

Ryan, M. T. (1995). Karl Marx: The human person as worker. In H. Brown, D. L. Hudecki, L. A. Kennedy, & J. J. Snyder (Eds.), *Images of the person: The philosophy of the human person in a religious context* (pp. 251-293). Chicago, IL: Loyola.

Sartre, J.-P. (1957). Existentialism. In J.-P. Sartre (Ed.), *Existentialism and human emotions* (pp. 9-51). New York: Philosophical Library.

Smith, H. (1986). *The religions of man.* New York: Harper & Row.

Terrence, Heuton Timorumesnes, I, i, 25 (1966). In *The Oxford dictionary of quotations.* London: Oxford.

Wuellner, B. (1956). *Summary of scholastic principles.* Chicago, IL: Loyola.

CHAPTER 10

Native American Grief and Loss: Conceptualizations of Disenfranchised Grief and Historical Trauma at Individual and Community Levels

Steven R. Byers, Theresa T. Erdkamp, and Lisa Byers

INTRODUCTION

Various forms of unresolved grief affect American Indian and Alaska Natives. However, problems and issues in Native American communities are seldom conceptualized as resulting from a grief and loss perspective. It is arguable that the majority of symptoms and psychological dynamics observed by clinicians and researchers can be interpreted as resulting from the traumatic and oppressive historical encounters of American Indian and Alaska Natives with European colonizers. This chapter posits that the majority of individual, family, and community problems in the Native American population should be addressed from a disenfranchised grief and trauma perspective. Not taking disenfranchised grief into consideration when working with Native American groups is problematic. Interventions, therapy, and research that omit predication of disenfranchised grief will lack ecological and contextual validity. This is problematic given the need many problems and issues in Native Americans need to be addressed. For healing to be achieved within communities, more information pertaining to Native American individual, community, and family issues needs to be accomplished. As an entrée into conceptualizing Native grief and loss as disenfranchised and cast in the context of oppression and resistance, this chapter examines and applies the concept of disenfranchised grief formally and conceptually to Native grief, loss, and trauma. The authors propose guiding principles for interventions based on addressing the effects of oppression in Native communities.

Native American mental issues, individual and family coping problems, and community needs argue for those in the social sciences and mental health professions to apply themselves in a massive effort to assist indigenous groups in the United States.[1] However, the history of the behavioral sciences relationship with Native Americans is problematic. Multiple cases of failure, distrust, and poor interactions between Native Americans and the behavioral sciences have occurred (Rogler, 1999).

While the behavioral sciences have much to offer ethnic and culturally different populations, more needs to be done to accomplish culturally and ecologically valid practices on behalf of the research and counseling practitioner (Ziemba, 2000). Work in the grief and loss field affords examples of concepts and practices that can enhance conceptualization and practice within Native American communities. As an initial effort toward more culturally and ecologically efficacious theorizing and conceptualizations, this chapter presents an application of the concept of disenfranchised grief to Native American family, community, and individual psychological issues. The authors have concluded, based on their work with Native Americans as social workers, psychologist, and researchers, that more needs to be done to effect positive change and healthier coping styles in Native America. Also, based on reviews of historical and contemporary relations between Native Americans and the U.S. society, it is evident that applying concepts derived from the grief and loss field to Native American struggles, losses and patterns of grief would be more efficacious than previous treatment of these issues. The authors also feel that approaching problems Native people face from a grief and loss perspective constitutes a radical departure from past approaches applied in the social science and counseling fields. Typically, Native American issues and problems have been viewed through the lenses of Euro-American theories and frameworks that are largely contextually irrelevant to indigenous people's histories and problems. To demonstrate the efficacy of our views we open this chapter with a brief overview of the historical context (past and recent) that would argue for considering Native American psychological issues from a grief and loss perspective.

HISTORICAL CONTEXT

Native American and Alaskan Natives have experienced high levels of loss and trauma (Brown, 1970). Various campaigns have been mounted to eradicate or assimilate the U.S. indigenous groups. Early relations between invading Europeans and Native populations were typically disastrous for Native groups. Jaimes (1992) characterizes early relations between Native and invading groups as largely genocidal, comparing death and trauma to modern day warfare and ethnic cleansing campaigns. Attempts to eradicate Native People from the U.S. continent began when Columbus encountered the North American continent in the 1400s and continued into the late 1800s with U.S. army campaigns designed to exterminate the Apache of

---

[1] In this chapter references to behavioral science or scientist is used in an inclusive sense, referring to mental health workers, social workers, counseling and clinical psychologists, and social science researchers.

New Mexico and the Sioux Tribes of the Northern plains. Also, many instances of collective loss and trauma occurred through forced re-locations and assimilation tactics practiced by church, state, and local entities across and within many Native groups into the late 1800s (Bordewich, 1996).

After the military campaigns came a wave of assimilation policies and programs extending well into the 1900s. While direct attempts of extermination gave way to policies of assimilation, the disruption, pain, and trauma for Native People continue well into the present day. Some authors point out that the psychological pain and displacement resulting from formal policies that ended in this century are problematic and pronounced in indigenous communities and families (Kessler, Cleary, & Bourke, 1985). Urbanization policies and boarding school programs designed to assimilate Native people have directly affected the lives of a majority of indigenous people living today.[2]

THE CONCEPT OF
DISENFRANCHISED GRIEF

Doka (1989) developed the concept of disenfranchised grief during the late 1980s. The concept met with wide approval and led to various re-conceptualizations in grief and loss treatment and research projects. Many counseling approaches to bereavement were altered to address the disenfranchised elements of grief and loss in various marginalized groups. However, a systematic and thorough application of this concept to the U.S. indigenous population has yet to be accomplished. Years, if not decades, of work are necessary to accomplish a theoretically, scientific, and clinically robust application of the disenfranchised grief concept to Native American experience. However, initial steps in such a program begin with conceptualizations and the delineation of research and treatment foci derived from the application of the concept. What follows is a presentation of the original concept, a summary of a recent project relevant to applying the concept of disenfranchised grief to Native populations, and suggestions for future work in the area of bereavement studies and grief and loss treatment with Native groups.

DISENFRANCHISED GRIEF: CONCEPT
AND APPLICATIONS

Doka (1989) defined disenfranchised grief as grief that individuals experience "when they incur a loss that is not or cannot be openly acknowledged, publicly mourned, or socially supported." He also noted that disenfranchised grief can occur and can be maintained in three primary ways: 1) the relationship is not acknowledged or recognized; 2) the loss is not acknowledged or recognized; and 3) the grief stricken is not recognized.

---

[2] For a more extensive account of the traumatic relations between Native Americans and the United States, see Nabokov, P. (1995).

According to Doka (1989), disenfranchised grief is typified by relationships that are "hidden" or unrecognized in that the dominant group or society does not accept or appreciate the relationship wherein the loss occurs. Therefore, loss and pain derived from the disenfranchised relationship is not acclaimed as appropriate for bereavement. Also, disenfranchised grief is often not viewed or legitimized due to the societal context. In other words, loss and associated bereavement is minimized or ignored by the broader social context. Current societal examples would include the loss of a beloved pet or perinatal loss.

NATIVE AMERICANS: GRIEF AND LOSS

Based on the overview of the disenfranchised concept provided above and review of the historical relations between Native Americans and the U.S. society and government, one can appreciate the concept's relevance to Native Americans at the collective and individual levels. Collectively, Native Americans have suffered the loss of their homeland. As noted above, early encounters with the invading parties often resulted in indigenous groups being dislocated and driven from homeland bases. Through systematic maneuverings on behalf of the U.S. government, Native Americans were forcibly removed form their homelands. The removals often took place under harsh physical conditions resulting in the death of a significant number of tribal members. Those who survived were separated from traditional sources of food, medicine, and spiritual sites (Obrien, 1992). From the late 1700s to the late 1900s Native parents and extended families have unwillingly encountered programs sanctioned by the United States and state governments designed to remove their children from their homes. Even during the late 1900s and into the new millennium, social service agencies routinely work in opposition to Native American families and children, traumatizing families and removing children from birth parents and extended families (Halvorson, Puig, & Byers, 2001). Ketcher (1999) provides accounts of blatant violation of Native American family values and views in routine and uninformed operations of urban and reservation social service agencies. Often these actions result in the unwarranted out-of-home placement of Native American children, disrupting and traumatizing children and families.

Further evidence for viewing Native American communities from a grief and loss perspective can be found in health and wellness data derived from Indian Health Services records. Table 1 depicts multiple contemporary problems regarding Native American health and wellness status.

Other data points to a current set of problems resulting from an embattled and traumatic history. High school and college dropout rates indicate a culturally stressful context operative for Native Americans (Byers & Forward, 2000; Byers, Yang, & Ullstrup, 2000; James, 2000; Oetting & Beauvais, 1990). Treatment of Native children within school systems often continues to be negative and discriminatory (James, Chavez, Beauvais, Edwards, & Oetting, 1995).

Health care and school systems are frequently stressful and therefore avoided within Native communities and families (Robbins, 1992). Economic and

Table 1. Contemporary Health Status of Native Americans

☑ Age Adjusted Death Rates 35% higher than U.S. All Races
☑ Years of Potential Life Lost 73% higher than U.S. All Races
☑ Alcoholism 579% greater
☑ Suicide 70% greater
☑ Accidents 212% greater
☑ Diabetes Mellitus 231% greater
☑ Tuberculosis 475% greater
☑ Pneumonia/Influenza 61% greater
☑ Shorter Life Expectancy that average U.S. resident
☑ Increased Rate for accidental injury
☑ Increased Rate for suicides
☑ Increased Rate for homicides
☑ The Highest Infant Mortality Rate
☑ The Highest Rate of Mortality from Infectious Diseases of Any Ethnic Group
☑ Mortality Rate Higher for Tuberculosis, Influenza, Pneumonia, Renal Disease, and Diabetes

Source: Trends in Indian Health (1997) by Indian Health Service.

environmental conditions are problematic in many reservation and urban communities (James, Wolf, Lavato, & Byers, 1995). Incest and sexual abuse rates have been reported as not only high, but often denied with Native communities (Hodgson, 1997). Incarceration rates for American Indian males are disproportionately high for the population and gender (Jaimes, 1992). Drug and alcohol use and abuse rates are also challenging in both reservation and urban Indian communities (Oetting, Beauvais, & Edwards, 1990).

Multiple family, community, and individual dynamics limit Native American lives. What is critical to consider is that the majority, if not all, of the traumata and losses within the Native American populace have occurred with little or no attention paid to their impact. Additionally, some argue that assimilation policies and practices (coupled with views of Native people as less than human), grief and loss rituals and coping mechanisms were also targeted for elimination (Yellow Horse Brave Heart, 1995). Campaigns to eradicate or assimilate Native Americans by the dominant group acted as disruptions and displacements of culturally sanctioned methods of coping with grief and loss. The Euro-American social context, in both distant past and present manifestations, has mitigated against Native American cultural continuance and coping. A framework predicated on disenfranchised grief emphasizes that various dimensions of a given social context may deny recognition, legitimization, and support of loss and trauma. In the case of Native American culture and the Euro-American based dominant social context we clearly have an example of this phenomena.

HISTORICAL TRAUMA: AN APPLICATION OF GRIEF CONCEPTS TO NATIVE AMERICAN LOSS

In Yellow Horse Brave Heart (1995) study of Native American grief response she identified salient dynamics germane to the study of Native American grief and loss. Her work should be understood as an initiatory effort in the cultural study of disenfranchised grief and loss.

Yellow Horse Brave Heart (1995) conducted an intervention with North American Plains Tribal members. She also assessed participants' views and satisfaction with the intervention. Yellow Horse Brave Heart found a high level of satisfaction with the intervention given it replicated traditional plains tribes methods and practices associated with healing and restoration of spiritual balance at the collective and individual levels as regards grief and loss.

Yellow Horse Brave Heart's clinical intervention and research are noteworthy on many counts. First, she utilizes a culturally efficacious healing ceremony to permit both collective and individual grief. Researching traditional Lakota ceremonial practices pertaining to trauma and loss, Yellow Horse Brave Heart found that grief within the Sioux tribes affected more than the individual sufferer of the immediate loss or pain (the individual is traumatized). The trauma, loss, or hurt also affects multiple relations of the bereaved (i. e., relatives and the spiritual forces operative in one's environment). In order to grieve appropriately, the bereaved must engage in ceremonial practices that permit acknowledgment and appropriation within the individual and the collective (all of those affected by the loss or trauma not recognized in the present and the past from family, band, and tribe). In other words, appropriate grieving must occur through ceremony and engagement with an entire community affected by the loss or trauma. Affective coping must include appropriation and inclusion of the collective in the physical world *and those deceased.*

It is critical to note that not only have the Sioux encountered multiple instances of loss and trauma, but in many instances have been acutely traumatic given the violence incurred. The Sioux's tribal history includes multiple engagements with the Euro-American social order and military that included personal violence, rape, and murder. Perhaps the most notorious event was the massacre of Sioux tribal members at Wounded Knee, South Dakota in 1877. Also, during the 1960s and 1970s multiple deaths occurred on the Sioux reservations in South Dakota. During the 1970s, American Indian activists demonstrated multiple cases of police brutality, rapes, murders, and related traumata dealt to the Sioux and other tribal members in U.S. reservations and cities. At various times during the 1970s death due to violence among the Sioux tribes in South Dakota exceeded the death rate of the entire state (Vizenor, 1990).

It is also critical to note that the Sioux were not permitted to engage in their traditional ceremonies until 1978. Ceremonies designed to engage the collective toward a healing and restoration of balance were not permitted until 1978 and have continued to be debated as efficacious in the U.S. Congress until present day. Yellow Horse Brave Heart learned that the key to healing from trauma dating back centuries is derived from collective and culturally sanctioned healing practices that she replicated in her research. Balance and release of pain cannot, according to Sioux tribal custom, result until souls and spirits of the deceased are addressed and their trauma and loss acknowledged through collective ceremony. The impact of this disenfranchised grief is exacerbated each day and hour that it goes unacknowledged. The intervention utilized in the Yellow Horse Brave Heart intervention was therefore developed to include acknowledgment and appropriation of those involved and release of pain and depersonalization of ancestors.

IMPLICATIONS AND CONSIDERATIONS FOR NATIVE AMERICAN GRIEF AND LOSS

Yellow Horse Brave Heart's study highlights what can be accomplished when practitioners adopt a culturally driven model of intervention and research. As an initial effort it highlights the importance of culture operative in marginalized grief among Native People. Obviously, more needs to be done in the research area on Native American grief and loss. Yellow Horse Brave Heart worked within only one tribal culture. It would be interesting to see if her intervention methods are efficacious across the multiple tribal cultures and contexts that exist in the United States.[3] Each tribe has its history and its current contextual dynamics affecting life. As an example, it is estimated that 60-70 percent of the U.S. Indian population permanently resides in urban areas. Also, economic dynamics affect Native American life. Some reservations experience high unemployment and poor economic outlooks (James et al., 1995). Other reservations have good economies and have developed sophisticated economic development plans.

Other contextual determinants operative in Native America include: 1) various levels of assimilation; 2) varying histories of trauma and loss within Native communities; 3) varying levels of awareness of grief and loss; and 4) various levels of distrust of Euro-American organizations such as the health care, mental health care, and social work systems. We discuss each of these contextual influences separately.

DYNAMICS OF ASSIMILATION

As a result of the various types of relationships and reactions to the U.S. social order and government systems (state, county, federal), American Indians have

---

[3] Currently 511 tribes are listed as federally recognized tribes within the United States. It has been estimated that another 383 tribes are recognized at the state level. Certainly, future clinical work and behavioral science research should work to achieve an appreciation of the diversity within Native America.

assimilated to Euro-American values and social practices. While an expose on the effects of assimilation on American Indian behavior and personality is well beyond the scope of this chapter, it should be noted that various levels and types of bi-culturalism are operative in Native America. In their respective professional practices, the present authors have encountered clients and communities struggling with bi-cultural or assimilation issues. A body of research does exist that examines the function of ethnic and cultural identity (see Phinney, 1990, for summaries of this research) that corroborates the degree of struggle and challenges that result from culture identification and character. Advances in clinical work and research on disenfranchised grief within Native American contexts must assess these dynamics in order to realize efficacious treatment and research outcomes. Assuming normative reactions or universal patterns in grief and loss reactions should be avoided until more data can be gathered to address the variations in level and type of assimilation and how it influences coping and adaptation.

VARIATIONS IN TRAUMA AND LOSS HISTORIES

Again, based on a tribe's relationship with the U.S. social order and government systems, various levels and types of trauma exist within tribal communities. Some tribes were targeted for extermination into the late 1800s. Others were not. Some tribes were viewed as "more civilized" by U.S. policy makers and agencies than others and therefore treated differently. Some tribes have within their histories literal massacres. Others have longer, more protracted histories involving extermination policies and actions. Tribes on the eastern U.S. coast are typically less in numbers, having fought with invading parties for longer periods of time. Also, some tribes adopted legal methods (trained in U.S. legal customs) as a way to battle for their rights. These are just some examples of the differences that exist.

It is critical for researchers and practitioners to appreciate the diversity in historical trauma legacies. Assessing individuals, families, and groups with the variations in trauma legacies must be accomplished at both intervention and research practices. Some, based on their individual efforts to heal and address trauma, may have come to a point of healing that has dealt with their disenfranchised grief. Others may have healed to the point where they are just beginning to acknowledge their loss and grief. Others, given the denial of grief and loss, may not have accomplished much healing. The present authors advocate for sustained and systematic research and intervention efforts that research, document, and utilize information and techniques based on an appreciation of the diversity of histories within Native America.

LEVELS OF AWARENESS OF DISENFRANCHISED GRIEF WITHIN INDIGENOUS GROUPS

It is critical to appreciate that Native Americans are often not aware of the effects of the trauma and loss in their lives. Based on our clinical work and research projects with American Indian persons and groups, the effects of disenfranchised grief and trauma are largely not recognized, let alone addressed. Indeed, given the definition of disenfranchised grief, it is logical to assume that those affected by it are unaware of its influences. Research and counseling work must address the lack of awareness and the affects resulting from the marginalization and denial of loss, trauma, and grief.

HISTORICAL DISTRUST IN NATIVE AMERICAN COMMUNITIES

Finally, across all tribes, services and programs designed to assist or work with tribes have met with limited successes. Many tribal communities have been under-served by health care, mental health care, and family services. Halvorson, Puig, and Byers (2000) point out that many tribes distrust social workers, psychologists, and health care professionals. Deloria (1992) points out that researchers have a history of assessing "Indian issues" from a Euro-centric perspective that has resulted in a profound level of mistrust and avoidance of anthropologists, demographers, and social scientists. While we cannot provide the reader with a full treatment of the distrust and avoidance dynamics, we wish to highlight some of the contextual backdrops for this phenomenon.

First, government programs and allocation of monies designed to assist American Indian communities have largely been culturally incongruent or insufficient in amounts. Programs on behalf of the U.S. government divisions intended to assist Native People have typically been based on Euro-centric concepts of health, care, and service delivery. Recently, reports to Congress completed by Indian Health Services have emphasized the need to rectify this situation by incorporating more culturally efficacious concepts and service delivery methods. Related, the historical relationship between the Bureau of Indian Affairs and tribes has been estranged as a result of the Bureau's insensitivity and Euro-centrism. It is the informed view of the present authors that both Indian Health Services and the Bureau of Indian Affairs operate from a paternalized and dehumanized framework. Both evolved to manage tribal matters in a manner that assumed indigenous people as unable to manage their own affairs. From inception to present day manifestations, the two entities designed to alleviate problems and suffering with Native communities have operated organizationally in dehumanizing ways. The result: distrust of systems and practices on behalf of the U.S. government, practitioners (medical staff, social workers, psychologists, etc.), and researchers.[4]

While policies and viewpoints regarding American Indians have changed and evolved over the past centuries (from extermination to assimilation and then to assistance), ideological presuppositions and associated practices have not. The

---

[4] Records indicate forced sterilization of Native American women based on policies of Indian Health Services and Public Health Services occurred from 1972-1976. With policies such as these in place, it is not surprising that Native Americans have come to distrust services and research projects. For a more detailed account of such policies see American Indian Policy Review Commission's Report on Indian Health, American Indian Journal of the Institute for the Development of Indian Law, February 1977.

contextual situation in the United States pertaining to Native Americans and their histories involves trauma and loss, the disenfranchisement of the trauma and loss, plus research, programming, and services that have routinely failed. Service utilization records and research data indicate Native People often ignore or avoid programs and research designed to alleviate individual and group problems (Robbins, 1992). After centuries of grief, loss, and trauma, programs and institutions that have interfaced with American Indians have largely resulted in more problems, losses, and trauma. This must be recognized and addressed in order to enlist indigenous individuals and communities in efforts to address a primary contributor to current and future problems: delegitimized grief and loss.

SUMMARY OF LOSS AND GRIEF DYNAMIC: THE FORMAL CASE FOR DISENFRANCHISED GRIEF IN NATIVE AMERICA

The present authors conceived this chapter as a way of directing attention to the loss and trauma in Native America. Our audience is primarily the professional grief and loss community in the United States. Our main purpose driving this chapter is to focus attention on conceptualizing and reconceptualizing individual, family, and community issues in American Indian communities from a grief and loss perspective. By utilizing Doka's concept of disenfranchised grief, we argue that much can be accomplished. Clinical and counseling work with Native Americans, is in our opinion, needed. However, barriers noted earlier must be addressed if ecologically valid work is to be realized. We also wish to emphasize that grief and loss research projects need to be completed with indigenous communities. We view counseling practice and research work as two areas of professional practice that can inform one another toward a deeper appreciation of Native American loss, trauma, and grief. Hopefully, professionals conducting research and working in the counseling fields will be stimulated by the present offering and a dialogue can ensue, one that addresses the issues pertaining to the marginalization of grief reactions in Native American groups. The present authors endorse professional symposia and conferences that would directly assess and work on conceptualizations and future directions in counseling practices and research efforts dealing with Native American grief and loss.

U.S. social science research, theory, and clinical practice have evolved to include various techniques and concepts that emphasize cultural dynamics addressing Native American issues and topics. However, on the whole, these fields of professional conduct have not included formal and systematic conceptualizations predicated on grief and loss theory, let alone the concept of disenfranchised grief. Yet, as this chapter has demonstrated, many of the problems and issues with Native American populations can be illuminated if addressed from the concept of disenfranchised grief.

Native American communities, families, and individual lives are affected by disenfranchised grief, loss, and trauma. Research, theory, and practice focused on Native American topics that omit an emphasis on disenfranchised grief, we argue, will be erroneous. We view disenfranchised grief as a concept that permits research, theory, and practice to advance toward a more ecologically valid conceptualization of what has occurred within American Indian communities at the micro-, meso-, and macro-contextual levels. Some issues, problems, or dynamics operative in Native communities may not be influenced or affected by disenfranchised grief. However, we posit that we will be more effective in our research and clinical work if it is an assumed priori that disenfranchised grief is operative. At the minimum, predicating disenfranchised grief as an important consideration in working with Native Americans permits a check on the pathologizing and assumption that symptoms and problems are driven by individual dynamics. How can Native American symptoms and issues be construed as the result of individual pathology with all the evidence to the contrary?

Considering the mandated operations to eradicate and assimilate Native Americans along with the contemporary demographics that point to embattled relations for Native Americans, the present authors advocate predication of disenfranchised grief as explanatory in a majority of dynamics in Native America. It is a culturally appropriate concept applicable in clinical work and social science research on a majority, if not all, of the issues influencing Native Americans.

We have argued for application of this concept in Native American research and clinical work. Now we will discuss some of the most prominent benefits of utilization this concept.

First, as Yellow Horse Brave Heart's (1995) research indicates, the losses and the traumata Native Americans have endured do not necessarily fit dominant Euro-American social science models of grief and loss. We argue in this chapter from a conceptual viewpoint and her work provides research evidence that Native American's ancient methods of coping and grieving are understood and sanctioned in current times. Disenfranchised grief and the transmission of disenfranchised grief function to limit life and potential at multiple levels. Yellow Horse Brave Heart's research provides preliminary confirmation that researchers and practitioners should not assume Euro-American psychological and group dynamics are operative in Native American's reactions to loss.

Further, appreciation of the marginalization and denial of loss and trauma with Native American communities prompts the practitioner to consider alternate treatment and research methods when working with Native People. Practitioners are more prone to be creative and develop alternate cultural models of research and treatment if they appreciate the efficacy of culture and history vs. individualistic theories and models predicated on pathology of psychological problems. We view this as critical to valid and efficacious research and treatment practices. Reviewing the concepts of disenfranchised grief and the history of Native Americans lead to an innovative and powerful treatment and healing technique in Yellow Horse Brave Heart's work.

Second, the distrust of Euro-American research and clinical work may be lessened, if not thoroughly removed, if those trained in mainstream clinical and research programs begin to consider symptoms and pathology in terms of contextually determined outcomes that are affected by the disenfranchisement of trauma and loss. Surely, approaching Native American issues and concerns from a vantage point that emphasizes the centuries of struggle, trauma, and resistance will go much farther in terms of effective treatment and research within indigenous groups. Approaching communities that have been marginalized and traumatized by dominant cultural and societal contexts may also permit partnerships being built between the practitioner and the disenfranchised community. Stellar examples of clinical and research practitioners and aboriginal groups have recently proven efficacious and have lead to important advances in conceptualizations and treatments of disenfranchised grief in Australia (McKendrick &Thorpe, 1998).

Third, helping research and clinical theory to progress should not be the only consideration in re-conceptualizing marginalized communities' issues and problems. Enhancing the welfare of the marginalized and disenfranchised, an original intent of Doka's pioneering work, should receive direct and sustained attention. Adopting a praxis model of scholarly conduct will likely result in advancing the treatment and researching of grief manifestations in Native America. Research and clinical work should be conceived as a partnership with the marginalized community in mind. Related, the phenomenology and experiential dynamics of disenfranchised grief and trauma are critical to appreciating the full impact of the marginalized and oppressed. We would argue that research and clinical work may need to take on a social justice orientation when attempting to engage oppressed or marginalized communities, especially when dealing with the types of loss and trauma the U.S. indigenous groups have encountered.

For example, recent work with aboriginal cultures in Australia has lead to findings that have resulted in challenge and provocation of the Australian government. Bird's (1998) compilation of narrative accounts of those victimized by the Australian boarding schools has permitted a wave of struggle and healing within the aboriginal population as a number of individuals accounted the abuse, loss, and trauma while involved with the boarding school programs (deleted words). The narratives revealed a program that functioned to de-personalize the aboriginal groups through physical and sexual abuse in the guise of government sanctioned programs designed to "better" the Australian aboriginal populations. Accounts shared in the text are chilling and traumatic to read or hear. However, appreciating the concept of disenfranchised grief and bereavement theory argues for the documentation and struggle with the atrocities in the Australian boarding schools as a critical step toward coping and healing.

It is not untenable that a similar outcome could result if practitioners began to document and research in a systematic fashion, the grief and loss experiences of Native Americans in U.S. boarding schools. However, we emphasize that the "uncovering" or bringing to light of traumata within a marginalized group must be accomplished or else the grief will remain disenfranchised, further complicating the liberation and healing that could occur.

Re-conceptualizations are necessary if Native Americans are to benefit from treatment and research. We argue that re-conceptualizations are key to moving the behavioral and clinical sciences toward more contextually and culturally efficacious ground. Until recently, dominant research and treatment modalities and theories were predicated on Euro-centric and individualistic views of coping, stress, and pathology. The medical model of disease and pathology greatly limited the contextual renderings of symptoms and problems within marginalized groups in the United States. Through applications such as the ones examined in this chapter, we argue clinical work and behavioral science can only change for the better. Certainly the fields of grief and loss counseling and research have encountered other examples of denial and resistance with perseverance and commitment to addressing difficult and disenfranchised loss. Native Americans, continuing to struggle in the United States, will be better served if their history and contemporary issues are addressed from more valid treatment and research frameworks.

We would like to make one final point. This chapter was written from the perspective of the practitioner. The authors are currently involved in counseling work, academic research, and social work. However, we do not mean to limit the suggestions to practitioners in social work, psychology, and academic research. We feel what has been developed in this chapter is also applicable to other professions who routinely interface with U.S. indigenous communities (i.e., attorneys, health care professionals, human service agencies). Due to the historical context, Native American's interface with a multitude of practitioners, often with professionals from fields not typically incorporating grief and loss theory and concepts. To affect the broad based change needed to address disenfranchised grief and loss within indigenous populations, all practitioners, we argue, need to practice from a more efficacious location; one that emphasizes the loss and trauma in Native life.

REFERENCES

Bird, C. (1998). *The stolen children: Their stories.* Australia: Random House.

Beauvais, F., Chavez, E. I., Oetting, E. R., Deffenbacher, J. L., & Cornell, G. R. (1996). Drug use, violence, and victimization among White Americans, Mexican Americans, and American Indian dropouts, students with academic problems, and students in good academic standing. *Journal of Counseling Psychology, 43*(3), 292-299.

Bordewich, F. M. (1996). *Killing the white man's Indian: Reinventing Native Americans at the end of the twentieth century.* New York: Dell.

Brown, D. (1970). *Bury my heart at Wounded Knee.* New York: H. Holt Publishers.

Byers S., & Forward, J. (in press). Native American transition to higher education: A case for cultural displacement. *Journal of American Indian Education.*

Byers, S., Yang, R., & Ullstrup, K. (2000). Native American college students & cultural conflict. Manuscript submitted to *Journal of American Indian Education.*

Deloria, V. (1992). Trouble in high places: Erosion of American Indian rights to religions freedom in the United States. In M. A. Jaimes (Ed.), *The state of Native America,* Boston, MA: South End Press.

Doka, K. J. (1989). Disenfranchised grief. In K. J. Doka (Ed.), *Disenfranchised grief: Recognizing hidden sorrow* (pp. 3-11). Lexington, MA: Lexington Books.

Halvorson, K., Puig, M. E., & Byers, S. (2001). Culture loss: American Indian family disruption, urbanization and the Indian Child Welfare Act. *Journal of Child Welfare,* Hunter College School of Social Work, Hunter New York.

Hodgson, M. (1990). Shattering the silence: Working with violence in native communities. In T. A. Laidlaw & C. Malmo (Eds.), *Healing voices: Feminist approaches to therapy with women.* San Francisco, CA: Jossey-Bass.

James, K. (2000). Social psychology: American Indians, science, and technology. *Social Science Computer Review, 18*(2), 196-213.

James, K., Chavez, E., Beauvais, F., Edwards, R., & Oetting, G. (1995). School achievement and dropout among Anglo and Indian females and males. *American Indian Culture and Research Journal, 19,* 181-206.

James, K., Wolf, W., Lavato, C., & Byers, S. (1995). *Barriers to workplace advancement experienced by Native Americans: A U.S. Department of Labor Glass Ceiling Commission Monograph,* No. BP434093.

Jaimes, M. A. (1992). Sand Creek: The morning after. In A. James (Ed.), *The state of Native America: Genocide, colonization, and resistance.* Boston, MA: South End Press.

Kessler, L. G., Cleary, P. D., & Bourke, J. D. (1985). Psychiatric disorders in primary care: Results of a follow up study. *Archives of General Psychiatry, 42,* 583-587.

Ketcher, R. G. (1999). Personal communication. Denver, Colorado.

McKendrick J. H., & Thorpe, M. (1998). The legacy of colonization: Trauma, Loss and psychological distress amongst aboriginal people. *Grief Matters, 1*(2).

Nabokov, P. (1995). *Native American testimony: A chronicle of Indian-White relations from prophecy to present.* New York: Penguin.

Obrien, E. M. (1992). American Indians in higher education. *Research Briefs, 3*(3), 1-16.

Oetting, E. R. & Beauvais, F. (1990). Orthogonal cultural identification theory: The cultural identification of minority adolescents. *The International Journal of Addictions, 25,* 657-687.

Oetting, E. R., Beauvais, E., & Edwards, R. (1990). Adolescent drug use: Findings of national and local surveys. *Journal of Consulting & Clinical Psychology, 58*(Aug), 385-394.

Phinney, J. S. (1990). Ethnic identity in adolescents and adults: Review of the research. *Psychological Reports, 108,* 499-514.

Robbins, R. L. (1992). Self-determination and subordination: The past, present, and future of American Indian governance. In M. A. James (Ed.), *The state of Native America: Genocide, colonization, and resistance.* Boston, MA: South End Press.

Rogler, L. H. (1999). Methodological sources of cultural insensitivity in mental health research. *American Psychologists, 54*(6), 424-433.

Vizenor, G. (1990). *Crossbloods: Bone courts, bingo and other reports.* Minneapolis, MN: University of Minnesota Press.

Yellow Horse Brave Heart, J. M. (1995). *The return to the sacred path: Healing from historical trauma and historical unresolved grief among the Lakota.* Dissertation Abstract. Northhampton, MA: Smith College for Social Work.

Ziemba, S. (2000). *Barriers to mental access among the urban poor.* Unpublished thesis manuscript. Colorado State University, Fort Collins, Colorado.

CHAPTER 11

In the Aftermath of Columbine: Tragedy as Opportunity for Transformation

Kevin Ann Oltjenbruns, Steven R. Byers, and Suzanne Tochterman

INTRODUCTION

April 20, 1999!—a day that none of these authors will ever forget! Each of us works at Colorado State University (CSU), located in Ft. Collins, Colorado. Fort Collins is a community located about 1½ hours drive north of Columbine High School in Jefferson County. In the days following the massacre of 13 individuals at the hands of two students who then killed themselves, we had various opportunities to interact with and provide support to community members. We interacted with students at CSU who were themselves alumni of Columbine High School; talked to local high school teachers who were troubled by instituting their own "lock down" procedures, corresponded with social workers and grief counselors directly involved in the Denver community. Throughout the entire Rocky Mountain Front Range community, the authors encountered an intense reaction to the Columbine tragedy. A sense of shock and emotional numbing marked our own interactions with others in response to the killings.

The authors found themselves conducting research shortly after the Columbine tragedy that engaged their intellects and their emotions in a way none had encountered previously. As we collected data and synthesized codes and counts, we found ourselves reacting and responding to our data at both the cognitive and emotional levels. No other research in our collective work afforded us the opportunity to research and assess the reactions and responses to a national tragedy so near to our own communities. As we worked through the various stages of our research, we simply could not divest of the sense that a type of innocence was being replaced with a new realization among our subjects.

Our experiences surrounding the Columbine shootings resulted in the collection of two data sets.

When Dr. Oltjenbruns was asked to speak at the May 1999 King's College Conference focusing on children and bereavement, she had planned to discuss a number of contextual variables that have an impact on individuals' ensuing grief process. Given that these school shootings had taken place only a month before, she chose to spend much of her time talking about the influence of violence. She and Dr. Byers had received permission from Dr. Jack Morgan to give a survey to those participants attending this particular King's College who agreed to do so. The survey was entitled *In the Aftermath of the Columbine Shootings—Reactions of Grief Professionals.* Eighty people completed the survey—59 women and 21 men; 54 percent of the respondents lived in the United States and 45 percent lived in Canada.

When Dr. Tochterman, a faculty member in the School of Education at CSU, entered the local high school where 25 pre-service teachers in training had been placed for practicum work, she was struck by the degree of upheaval. Working at a local high school with college students who were preparing to be teachers, she found it necessary to support not only the pre-service teachers, but the practicing "mentor teachers" as well. Both of these groups of teachers seemed to be in shock; both groups needed to be heard. Additionally, the high school students who attended school an hour and a half north of Columbine were also affected.

In the pre-service seminar on teaching, in the faculty lounge, in the hallways, conversations seemed to center on the reality of school violence. Realizing that a school-wide forum had not yet been held, Dr. Tochterman gathered pre-service teacher candidates, teachers currently working at the high school, and high school students. As part of the processing, each group was asked to respond to an open-ended question "How did the recent events at Columbine affect you as a student/teacher in the public schools today?"

Responses were gathered on April 28, 1999, one week after the shootings at Columbine. Ninety-four people responded: 24 pre-service teachers (college students); 32 in-service, practicing teachers; and 38 high school students. A similar question was asked one year later to a like group of pre-service teacher candidates, practicing teachers, and high school students.

As we examine various reactions to the events at Columbine, we utilized data sources derived from the school-related contexts just described and from the participants of the 1999 King's College Conference, held one month following the tragedy.

CRISIS AND SPIRITUAL CHANGE

Many authors in this edited volume address spirituality as it pertains to "meaning." Events in our lives can result in significant reflection and shifts in our psychological and spiritual frameworks. Some of the most profound events are due to their import: the power they have to challenge or disrupt long-standing views of the world. Human beings often face obstacles in their lives or challenges to their worldviews. However, when an event is traumatic or extremely violent, existential, psychological, and spiritual meanings can be challenged. Our relationship to our world can be challenged based upon how violence and trauma challenge our values and what is meaningful to us.

Violence of the magnitude of the Columbine killings confronts us on multiple levels. It asserts another context—another reality that demands explanation. Questions result based on the motives of the killers, the reactions of the victims, the survivors, as well as the manner and methods in which information on the violence reaches us. When violence occurs as it did at Columbine, the frameworks and values we hold are in essence disputed to the extent that they cannot assimilate the events.

Balk (1999) argues that crises trigger spiritual change—but only those crises that: "(a) allow time for personal reflection, (b) whose aftermath is forever colored by the experience of the crisis, and (c) that create a psychological imbalance or (psychological) disequilibrium that resists readily being stabilized" (p. 486). To set the context for this particular chapter, we shall briefly highlight concepts of crisis, meaning, and transformation.

The shots at Columbine High School were truly shots "heard around the world." Hundreds personally knew those who were killed and were devastated by the traumatic end to their lives. Many more were impacted as children and adults alike questioned the safety of the world they live in. Many experienced a shift in their personal worldview—that the world is a safe place, filled with much positive promise or that parents can protect children from the evil in the world. A sense of invasive psychological trauma resulted from the shootings. The views of life and world were altered based on the violence and its aftermath at Columbine.

To others, the meaning of the Columbine shootings was significantly different, but nonetheless a possible impetus for spiritual change. Some questioned why there was so much emphasis given to providing resources to this particular community when many others are devastated by violence occurring within their borders on a regular basis, with community members left to feel that no one cares about what occurs in some segments of our society. Some drew a contrast to the numbers who died at Columbine (15) to the millions killed during the Jewish Holocaust or the annihilation of Native American peoples, and more recently, to the numbers killed on September 11th. Yet others noted the expectation that members of the military, depending on their assignments, are expected to face the real possibility of massive death tolls as they engage in conflict. It is important to recognize the absolute legitimacy of those reactions—each of us, given our own life circumstances, will arrive at different meaning about an event such as the Columbine killings. Each of these subjective reactions to the slaughter at Columbine would bring with it a personal meaning.

> Personal meanings are subjective meanings associated with objective death. . . .
> can involve positive or negative consequences for the individual. If positive, they
> can . . . be comforting. If negative, they can be disorderly and disturbing and lead
> to emotional turmoil . . . can similarly involve consequences for individuals' own
> lives; such consequences can be positive or negative. (Circelli, 1998, p. 714)

The bridge between a definition of meaning and spiritual development may be found in the four tasks identified in Figure 1; these tasks help define a process of spiritual transformation resulting from a significant loss. Restoration provides a test of the

---

Tasks

- Experience the pain
- Understand and transform suffering
- Make a connection/heal relationships
- Find meaning in life

Figure 1. Tasks helping to define a process of spiritual transformation.
Adapted from Longaker (1997) and Worden (1991).

meaning we construe as we deal with the loss, as we construct a new life following the loss. Restoration involves a transformation. If an authentic restoration ensues, the change involves a renewal to our lives (Balk, 1999, p. 491).

Viewing loss in terms of its spiritual change dimension is very important. Often ignored in the professional helping professions and in social science research, recent work emphasizes the importance of spirituality to the human being. As noted earlier, Balk's conceptualizations are informative when considering the spiritual dimensions associated with loss and trauma. Related, a crisis that involves spiritual change must allow time for personal reflection. This would imply spiritual change is an ongoing active process, not a single event. One may describe that process using many different models. This particular chapter uses a model adapted from Longaker (1997) and Worden (1991), which is summarized in Figure 1.

We would not expect that a process of spiritual growth would be linear, but would assume that there would be a shifting of orientations, similar to what is described in Stroebe and Schut's (1999) dual process model of coping. This model assumes an oscillation between a loss orientation and a restoration orientation. Further, losses may be re-grieved over a lifetime as new meanings are developed.

FINDINGS

Adopting the above framework permitted us to approach the data sources we had gathered from a theoretically and conceptually robust framework. Using the methodology summarized in the introduction of this chapter, the authors were able to find poignant examples of each of the four tasks depicted in Figure 1 (experience the pain, understand and transform suffering, make a connection/heal relationships, find meaning in life).

While many examples of each were found to illustrate each task, only subsets are recorded in Tables 1 through 5. Each table identifies the source of the comments; the responses included in italics in each table are verbatim.

Table 1. Experience the Pain

King's College Participants, data collected May 1999

Common Themes—Affective

Fear

Of future

- *Worry about the future of my young children—fear that they could be victims someday or even the thought what if they (my own children) ever did something like this*

- *Fear for my own daughter as she moves toward adolescence*

For safety

- *I suddenly became aware of how unsafe we all are, and I am fearful*

Anger

- *Anger at the media for inappropriate/sensationalist coverage*

- *Anger at gun lovers—both sides of the border*

Note: When asked on the survey which of their own responses following Columbine most surprised them—most responded in regard to anger: at the school administration, at the parents of the two perpetrators, at the media, at the police.

Sadness

- *I felt so very sad for all of those families. My heart just ached . . . I felt such a heaviness for the parents.*

- *I was concerned and sad and felt helpless that this type of incident and others could not be prevented (e.g., copycat in Alberta) and that helpless children were victimized by angry, isolated peers. Part of that helplessness is a feeling of failure.*

- *As a parent, I felt so connected to the pain. I could feel myself related to the parents. Also, I realized that I have lost my sense of this event being something that happens elsewhere. I believe now that if it could happen in Colorado, it could happen anywhere—even in my little Canadian town. At one point, I felt more of a buffer zone from this—even though I knew it was not a real one.*

Common Themes—Cognitive

Disbelief

- *Disbelief. Inability to accept. Inability to comprehend how and why.*

Table 2. Experience the Pain

Practicing Teachers

- *We have students here who are capable of these atrocities . . . I wonder could it happen here.*

Pre-Service Teachers

- *I sat in the parking lot for the longest time today, staring at the students walking in the building. I sat for over twenty minutes and my hands were shaking so much I could not even open the car door. My heart was racing and my throat was tight. I felt like I would cry but all I did was shake. I did not think I would have the energy or the will to get out of my car and go in the school building.*

- *I was sitting in the back of the classroom watching my match up teacher and this is going to sound awful but this is what I felt—I just saw bloody kids lying all over the room. I saw them bleeding at their desks. My mind was playing tricks on me.*

- *I don't think I want to teach anymore. What is the point? We get paid next to nothing, get treated like second class citizens in our society and now we are victims of shootings . . . I would be putting myself in danger by choice . . . I will tell you I don't want to die for this cause.*

High School Students

- *I feel endangered almost all of the time. When I walk down the hall I find it difficult to look at people as I pass them. I feel knots in my neck and a pit in my stomach.*

- *In my mind's eye, I feel like I have a bull's eye painted on my forehand.*

- *The tears I have cried keep coming and don't seem to wash away the despair.*

Table 3. Understand/Transform Suffering

King's College Participants, data collected May 1999

Not included—the only data set collected was done so one month following the shootings. Authors do not believe that sufficient time had transpired to allow a "transformation."

Data below collected April 2000—one year later . . .
Practicing Teachers

- *I have never before felt such a reaffirmation of my desire to be a teacher. If this mass murder doesn't tell teachers that they are needed, I am not sure what would.*

- *I want to be a teacher who realizes the influence that I have over kids. I want to communicate with my students. I want to be proactive and share the pride I have in their achievements. It is our job as teachers to reach out to each and every child we meet.*

Pre-Service Teachers—data collected April 2000—one year following shootings

- *I don't know how we as teachers can break down the barriers between cliques and encourage marginalized groups to feel a sense of belonging but we have to. It is a cycle that we need to break. How do you dissolve the barriers and the boundaries between our young people? I don't know, but, together, we need to figure it out.*

High School Students—data collected April 2000—one year following shootings

- *I feel I should be safe in this school. I am no longer scared to go into the cafeteria or the library. I trust that I am a good person, am good to other people and that this school is a safe place. Even though a year ago I was shell shocked, I am over it for the most part now.*

Table 4. Make a Connection/Heal Relationships

King's College Participants, data collected May 1999

- *I took guilt upon myself, despite the fact that I have always been active in the lives of the teenagers around me. I keep wondering what more I should be doing with them.*

- *My rage toward the "killers" changed as I began to see them as victims also.*

- *I have begun meeting with people in the community to initiate a program to involve "youth on the edge"—academically, legal, socially to be mentors and assistant to children and youth who are obviously disenfranchised.*

- *I felt compelled to write a letter to my 3-year-old daughter about this incident. Although she is blissfully unaware of Columbine, I needed her to know that impact it had at the time . . . the letter went into her baby book, with other letters I have written her about significant moments in her life.*

- *I told her (my eight-year-old granddaughter) to be herself. To continue to be the kind and sensitive child she is and that her mommy, daddy, grandpa and I would do everything in our power to always keep her safe.*

Data below collected April 2000—one year later . . .

Practicing Teachers

- *I believe that my job is primarily that of an advocate for children—someone who fosters a sense of self worth and importance, and the idea of infinite possibility to every child. The subject that I teach is far less important than the young men and women I teach.*

Pre-Service Teachers

- *I want to be a teacher even more. I want to be a good role model.*

- It has instilled in me a deep desire to teach, but to help students shape themselves into productive and creative and enlightened citizens in society.

High School Students

- *When there is someone at school who I don't like—instead of telling them, I just don't say anything to make them mad or hurt their feelings, and I still try to be nice to them.*

- *I don't pick on the nerds any more.*

- *It opened my eyes to the people who were once mere shadows in my life.*

- *Even though I am only 15, I may not be here forever. What I mean is that I could go at any time. Or a loved one could go at any time, so have been telling the important people in my life just how important they are to me.*

Table 5. Find Meaning in the Loss (April 2000)

King's College Participants, data collected May 1999

- *I felt an affirmation of the goodness of most young people mixed with a concern about the inevitability of more violence. There was also a concern that we must teach tolerance and empathy to you youth.*

- *I felt perhaps like the students who wanted to repair the school—I wanted to repair my life and do what I can do for others. Not to let violence win and control the focus of my life.*

- *(We must learn a lesson) I preached a sermon on the stoning of Stephen and reminded my congregation that we have taught our young people that they should join in the throng of throwing stones. We make comments in front of our children, which have allowed them to believe that it's okay to taunt and insult others.*

Data below collected April 2000—one year later . . .

Practicing Teachers

- *I have never before felt such a reaffirmation of my desire to become a teacher of high school students. If this mass murdering at Columbine does not tell teachers that they are needed, I am not sure what would. Students need role models and caring and dedicated adults in their lives more than ever.*

- *I don't believe the world has ever been a safe place. Violence is by no means a twentieth century creation. But I used to believe that there were safe places in the world and school was one of them. The public schools are an integral piece of the problem, but therefore are also a part of the solution. As I am an integral part of the system, I too become responsible for helping to stop the violence, in any way that I can.*

Pre-Service Teachers

- *I am trying to get the students to interact more with one another. I am stressing more about students' commonalities than their differences. Instead of appreciating how we are all different . . . I am trying to use cooperative methods in my teaching so that students call all interfaces and learn that the stranger sitting across from them is much like them.*

High School Students

- *I can speak for myself and for my friends. We won't hurt or inflict pain on others, especially not in school. It really just gives kids a bad name in general.*

SUMMARY/CONCLUSIONS

The findings presented in this chapter underscore the importance of the spiritual meaning in reactions to a national tragedy. Our participants were not psychologically close to those killed at Columbine, yet they expressed deep and abiding questions pertaining to their spiritual views and values in relation to the meaning of the tragedy. Many respondents openly detailed reactions similar to reactions that victims or victims' relatives typically experience in reaction to trauma and violence.

It is noteworthy that some emphasized that what occurred at Columbine should not be viewed as any more critical than atrocities that occur daily, that often occur outside of the media's emphasis. The respondents that emphasized other violent occurrences provide us with a contextual and historical reminder: violence, death, loss, while not always making the papers and television coverage, occur with great frequency. Perhaps the violent incidents reported as a part of high-visibility media coverage needs to be a reminder of the issues and dynamics of normative violent contexts. Perhaps, if one ponders the meaning of these reactions in terms of their import, they stand as a reminder of the level and depth of trauma in populations that are marginalized, discounted, or disenfranchised.

Reviews of the responses to these Columbine surveys point out that those in the professional human services and teaching fields struggle with attributing meaning to acts of senseless violence also. While others look to the professional for assistance in times of tragedy, it is important to appreciate the impact of loss and trauma due to violence on the professionals. Perhaps sharing the impact of the events with clients may work to enhance and humanize the grief and loss counseling process.

Finally, the violence that occurred at Columbine resulted in intense reactions all across the county and the world. The visibility of the event was due in part to the assumed safety and trust attributed to affluence and privilege. When violence and death occur within areas such as the Columbine community, we pause and react in a manner predicated on shock because *we assumed it would not happen there.*

REFERENCES

Balk, D. Guest Editor. (1999, September). *Death Studies: Special Issue—Spirituality and Bereavement.*

Circelli, V. G. (1998). Personal meanings of death in relation to fear of death. *Death Studies, 22,* 713-733.

Harvey, J. H. (Ed.). (1998). *Perspectives on loss: A sourcebook.* Brunner/Mazel.

Longaker, C. (1997). *Facing death and finding hope: A guide to the emotional and spiritual care of the dying.* New York: Doubleday.

Stroebe, M., & Schut, H. (1999). Dual process model of coping: Rationale and description. *Death Studies, 23,* 197-224.

Worden, J. W. (1991). *Grief counseling and grief therapy: A handbook for the mental health practitioner* (2nd ed.). New York: Springer.

SECTION IV

Professional Caregivers and Spirituality

When a Patient Dies: Meeting Spiritual Needs of the Bereaved in a Health Care Setting

Fran Rybarik and Diane Midland

Over half of all deaths in the United States occur in acute care hospitals (Kaufman, 1998). Approximately 780,000 individuals die annually in short-stay hospitals in the United States (National Center for Health Statistics, 1999). When one considers the number of family members and friends touched by these deaths, the figures become unimaginable. All too frequently, loved ones feel abandoned by health care providers when the status of the patient's care changes from full, aggressive treatment to comfort care, or when the patient dies. Health care has traditionally been focused on "curing" and, as such, has not done well in the area of supporting dying patients and grieving friends and family. Spiritual care is a key component of that support.

In general, spirituality refers to one's beliefs, values, sense of purpose, direction, and one's relationship to a larger whole. The spiritual dimension allows humans to attach meaning to the life experiences they encounter. Attaching meaning is a way to understand and cope with the losses one experiences through the death of another. Recent studies support the hypothesis that intrinsic spirituality aids bereavement—that individuals who apply their belief system to experiences like bereavement seem to cope more adaptively (Easterling, Gamino, Sewell, & Stirman, 2000).

In the early 1980s, Gundersen Lutheran Medical Center in La Crosse, Wisconsin, developed a program to support and facilitate the grief of parents whose baby died during pregnancy, at birth, or shortly after birth. As the RTS (formerly known as Resolve through Sharing) program was established on the units were perinatal and newborn death occurred, it became evident that these same premises of sensitive, compassionate care could—and *should*—be practiced throughout the entire health care environment.

An interdisciplinary committee comprised of physicians, nursing, social service, and pastoral care was organized to define what a comprehensive bereavement program might look like within a health care organization. The ultimate result of this committee was the establishment of *Bereavement: Guidelines for Care* (Midland, 2002) that would provide consistent care no matter where a patient died in the medical center. The guidelines are divided into three main categories: anticipatory grief support; care at the time of death; and follow-up with a bereaved family member. The guidelines are based not only on the experiences and mission of Gundersen Lutheran Medical Center, but also on international, national, and regional research and standards (Corr, Morgan, & Wass, 1994; Discher & Haggerty, 1994; Joint Commission on Accreditation of Healthcare Organizations, 2000; Roberg, 1993; Witter, Tolle, & Moseley, 1990). Excerpts from the guidelines are in Table 1.

ESTABLISHING A TEAM APPROACH

Throughout the *Bereavement: Guidelines for Care* (Midland, 2002), it becomes evident that care of the dying patient and his/her significant others is best accomplished through a team approach. Although there may be a natural tendency to think that no one can perform a task as proficiently as I can (or perhaps another person from my discipline), the reality of health care and bereavement care is that collaboration and consultation are imperative. No one individual or discipline can do it alone. It truly takes a "team" effort to provide the best service and avoid staff "burnout" or "compassion fatigue." Each discipline has their unique area of expertise that will enhance the total outcome of the care provided.

TEAM DEVELOPMENT

Keep in mind that teams do not develop overnight. They require nurturing and restructuring as changes occur within the setting. Feedback is necessary between team members so that there are opportunities to learn—to evaluate what works, what doesn't work. A team is defined as "a group of people who are committed to the attainment of a common objective, who work well together and enjoy doing so, and who produce high quality results" (Team Building: Measuring Success, 1998). To be a team, there must be shared goals, interdependence, commitment, and accountability for the outcome. There must also be room for conflict, challenge, failure, and mutual respect.

Working together as a team requires going through various stages of development, sometimes described as the life cycle of a team. One model defines five stages of a team life cycle: Forming, Storming, Norming, Performing, and Adjourning (Team Building: Measuring Success, 1998). Some common experiences of team members at each stage of team development are listed in Table 2.

Teams may find that they move between the various stages at any given time. As the composition of the team changes—a member leaves and a new person comes onboard—the team returns to a forming stage and repeats some of the behaviors of each stage during the process of redesign. Teams that provide bereavement support at the bedside within the health care environment seldom reach the adjourning stage. Each time a patient is near death or dies, an interdisciplinary team is involved in assisting and supporting the survivors. The make-up of the team will be as unique as each patient and family. Team members may experience some of the characteristics of each stage as they work on a bereavement team.

Within the hospital setting, care for dying patients and their family or friends is generally provided by physicians, nurses, social workers, and chaplains or clergy. This is not to exclude the potential value of a host of other professions who may come into contact with the significant others of a dying/deceased patient. For example, a respiratory therapist who has daily contact with the family of a comatose ventilator patient may be viewed by the family as someone who is especially sensitive to their situation and needs. Patients with breast cancer may see a genetic counselor as a primary team member. Designated organ/tissue requesters may play a significant role in helping families deal with the options available to them. In other health care settings such as a nursing home, certified nursing assistants may play a key role in a resident's care at the end of life. This is why it is so important for all health care employees to have at least a basic introduction to the premises of bereavement care and know about the bereavement program within their health care setting.

PRIMARY BEREAVEMENT TEAM ROLES

The following are some suggested tasks assumed by the various disciplines that provide bereavement care.

Physician

- keep family informed of patient's condition and/or death
- involve family in decision making
- assure family that appropriate treatment was provided
- answer questions
- provide information about autopsy
- assure that family receives autopsy results in an understandable and sensitive manner
- be available to the family to address concerns that may arise following the death

Nursing

- facilitate referral to other disciplines as appropriate
- contact designated organ/tissue procurement organization (OPO) at or near the time of death
- take care of the body after death, i.e., bathing, positioning
- assist with death notification and autopsy request, when appropriate
- offer options of seeing, spending time with, and touching the deceased
- assure privacy for the bereaved
- provide emotional support to grieving survivors
- reinforce physician's explanations as needed
- complete necessary forms and documentation

Table 1. Bereavement Guidelines for Care

I. ANTICIPATORY GRIEF SUPPORT

   A. Provide timely information to patient/loved ones regarding patient's condition.

- Offer interdisciplinary care conference; maintain open communication between disciplines
- Provide booklets about the dying process, like *Gone From My Sight* (Karnes, 1995) or *A Time for Peace* (Discher & Klos, 1997), when appropriate
- Respect cultural differences in communication
- Recognize that alternative communication methods may be necessary to inform significant others of patient's status (i.e., telephone calls, interpreters)

   B. Assure that all attempts are made to keep the patient comfortable, taking into account the diagnosis

- Assess need for fluid/food (include option of withdrawal of fluid/food)
- Manage pain at patient's level of need
- Assess need for emotional/spiritual comfort (offering sacrament of the sick for Catholic/Episcopal patients, etc.)
- Provide for support of chaplain/social worker
- Share alternative coping tools such as music, relaxation techniques, visualization, and massage

   C. Promote a comfortable environment

- Turn lights down/up
- Role model touching and talking with patient
- Remove unnecessary barriers to allow loved ones closeness

   D. Give loved ones support

- Offer option to assist with care
- Provide information regarding food/fluid withdrawal

   E. Encourage open communication and ventilation of feelings

- Allow for privacy with patient and separate gathering space for loved ones
- Recognize there may be a wide emotional reaction of patient/loved ones

II. CARE AT TIME OF DEATH

   A. Use door card to protect family and help all staff provide compassionate care

   B. Offer refreshment bereavement tray

   C. Follow death notification policy

   D. Provide emotional comfort to loved ones

- Offer time alone with the deceased
- Offer to assist with contacting others in their support systems
- Allow loved ones time to process the news of the death before discussion about organ /tissue donation, autopsy, and funeral arrangements
- Provide Pastoral Care support to loved ones
- Be sensitive to personal language of the bereaved—how do they refer to the deceased?

Table 1. (Cont'd.)

E. Physical care of body

- Create a private space (i.e., move roommate to different room)
- Offer options of family participating in care of body or family watching care, or family not present at time of body care
- Offer option of viewing body before/after removing medical devices, give anticipatory guidance of what body will look like
- Elevate head of bed, place body in good alignment, make hands accessible for touching
- Create warm environment (i.e., lights down, bed rails down)
- Give family permission to touch body if they desire
- Offer mementos (lock of hair, handprint, jewelry)

III. BEREAVEMENT FOLLOW-UP

A. Pastoral Care to provide book *Don't Take My Grief Away From Me* (Manning, 1979)

B. Death information pamphlet to be given at the time of death

C. Sympathy cards to be sent

1. Signed and sent by staff
2. Signed and sent by physician

D. Invite loved ones to hospital memorial service

E. Invite loved ones to grief education support group

F. Make bereavement follow-up calls

G. Send grief information packet

Source: Excerpts from *Bereavement: Guidelines for Care.* Copyright 2000 Gundersen Lutheran Medical Foundation, La Crosse, Wisconsin. Used with permission.

Social Service

- assist in assessing family needs (psychosocial, family systems)
- advocate for the family
- counsel family regarding areas of concern
- liaison with community resources
- make referrals, when appropriate

Pastoral Care/Chaplain

- assess level of bereavement
- assist family and patient with expression of feelings
- liaison with parish clergy
- respond to spiritual, religious, and faith needs of family and patient

Table 2. Stages of Team Development

Forming Stage—the "polite" stage—team output is low

- members want to make a positive first impression
- there is mild to moderate enthusiasm
- members have positive expectations about anticipated outcomes

Storming Stage—the "purpose" stage—team output is low

- members ask, "Why are we here?"
- exploration about what members are supposed to do
- discrepancy between initial hopes/expectations and the reality of the situation
- some conflict begins to surface
- members begin to shed assumptions as they get to know each other

Norming Stage—the "power" stage—team output is moderate to high

- team comes together (team and individual power bases are established)
- resolution of differences between initial expectations and realities goals and objectives are agreed to and owned by members

Performing Stage—the "synergy" stage—team output is very high

- team identity is complete
- members have a positive feeling about the team
- members work well together and are confident about outcomes

Adjourning Stage—frequently the forgotten stage

- goals of the team are achieved
- team recognizes accomplishments and celebrates
- others may reward the team
- the team disbands

Source: *Team Building: Measuring Success,* 1998.

- assist with "finding meaning" in this loss
- assist with rituals of dying
- officiate at funeral, memorial service, blessing, or baptism
- provide ongoing pastoral support following the death

These are merely suggested tasks. You may find that within each organization disciplines have very different assignments. It is important, however, to not overlook the potential influence that these groups, and others, might have as a part of your bereavement team. Depending on the circumstances, it may be more appropriate for disciplines to share in these role expectations, to cross the line into another discipline's area. Team members must communicate with one another so that all are aware of what is being done. The paramount need is that of the patient and family, not who is supposed to do what. This is not a time for territorial conflicts to surface and impede the care given to families. Meeting the spiritual needs of the dying patient and his/her family is an excellent example of care that goes across disciplines, and works best with an interdisciplinary team approach.

AN INTERDISCIPLINARY APPROACH

Although the terms interdisciplinary and multidisciplinary are sometimes used interchangeably to describe a team, distinctions should be noted. Multidisciplinary care involves less communication between disciplines. Each discipline performs a separate consult and either gives recommendations directly to the patient and/or family or to one physician who manages the patient's care. In a multidisciplinary model, responsibility for responding to the spiritual needs of the dying patient and grieving family would fall to the chaplain or clergy person. In some care settings, the services of a chaplain or the clergy are not readily available, and spiritual needs of a bereaved family may not receive equal attention to physical or emotional needs.

In an interdisciplinary model, the care is more holistic. The basis of an inter-disciplinary team is integrated clinical care, open communication among team members, and mutual respect for each other (Grant, 1995). Although the primary responsibility for responding to the spiritual needs of the patient and/or family still falls to pastoral care, other disciplines could meet parts of this need. Other health care professionals may use their listening skills to help the patient or family discern the meaning of this experience to them. A nurse may complete a spiritual assessment. All can offer their presence or participate in prayer at the patient's or family's request. Professionals who work with the bereaved are recognizing the role of spirituality across the continuum of care—from referral through treatment of the patient and throughout follow up with the bereaved family. In an inter-disciplinary team, members collaborate and negotiate with one another so that the patient and family receive consistent information and integrated care. The model in Figure 1 shows the patient and family in the center of the circle where "tasks" or work overlap among the disciplines.

ADVANTAGES OF AN INTERDISCIPLINARY, COLLABORATIVE APPROACH

Collaboration is a learned art that must be developed, practiced, and continually fine-tuned. There are three variables that are essential to collaboration with an interdisciplinary approach:

- There must be recognition of the common goals for the patient and family;
- There must be mutual support of each member of the interdisciplinary patient care team; and

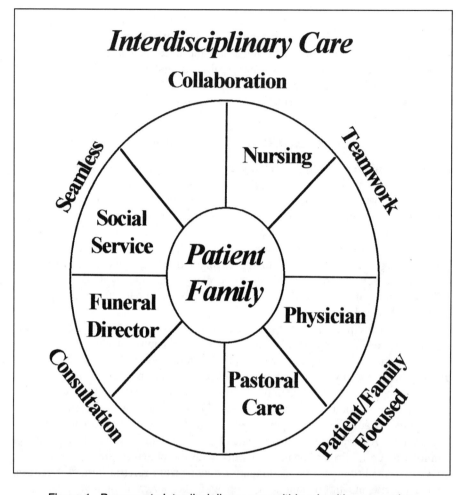

Figure 1. Represents interdisciplinary care within a health care setting
(Midland, Gensch, & Rybarik, 2001). Patient and family are the center of all care
provided by various disciplines. Other disciplines may be added to the circle.
The interdisciplinary team remains patient/family focused, provides seamless
services requiring teamwork and ongoing collaboration.

• There must be a balance of power—each profession must recognize the value
of the other's role (Grant 1995).

Developing an interdisciplinary team approach initially takes much time and
effort, but the benefits far outweigh the disadvantages. There are benefits to patients
and their families, as well as to caregivers and health care organizations.

The benefits to patients and families initially appear to occur with increased care
coordination and integration, which also benefit caregivers and the organization.

When patients and families are treated as members of the interdisciplinary team, they are empowered to be partners in the process, rather than passively having care "done" to them. Interacting with members of an interdisciplinary team helps serve patients and families of diverse cultures, because different members of the patient's family may "connect" with different members of the interdisciplinary team. Having a connection and hearing the same message from different team members who cared for the deceased enhances the communication, trust, and relationship building with individual family members at a very significant time.

CASE STUDY

Less than two months into a new job in the Trauma/Emergency Center, a social worker sat with a mother whose clothes were soaked with the blood of her three-year-old daughter who had been hit by a car. As any mother would have done, she had cradled and rocked the little girl in her arms until the ambulance arrived. By the time they reached the hospital the child was in full cardiac arrest and mom was blank and numb. The two sat and waited for other family to arrive, or for the doctor to come and say that everything was okay. It seemed like hours. Finally the physician slowly appeared at the door to the consultation room and, as he entered and sat down with them, the social worker knew that the little girl had died. This is how she described the experience:

> Although I felt unprepared for being with this particular family, I recognized the value and necessity of my presence—to help with phone calls, arrange for a quiet place for the family to gather, create time for them to hold and say "good-bye" to the child who would never again run and play. I soon realized that there were no words that would make everything better or any answers to those parent's pleadings of "How could God let this happen?" I, along with the physician, nurses and chaplain, was merely available to be with them as they began the painful journey of reconstructing their lives without their daughter. I could not have functioned independently of the other health care team members. We each had a role to fulfill and were a piece of this family's tragedy.

CONCLUSION

We seem to have traveled full circle in the area of death, dying, and bereavement. We have gone from caring for the dying person at home to denying the existence of death by "doing everything possible" to sustain physical life. When a patient dies in a hospital, nursing home, or other health care setting, an interdisciplinary bereavement team creates an opportunity to meet the physical, emotional, spiritual, and social needs of that patient's family and friends consistently and professionally. We now recognize the profound impact that we can have on individuals and families who are encountering death as a part of life, and grief as a normal response to that person's death. It is truly a privilege to be allowed to share in this milestone experience with another.

REFERENCES

Corr, C. A., Morgan, J. D., & Wass, H. (Eds). (1994). *Statements on death, dying, and bereavement*. London, Ontario: King's College.

Discher, T. M., & Haggerty, P. A. (1994). *The bereavement needs of family members in a hospital setting*. Unpublished master's thesis. Winona State University, Winona, MN.

Discher, T. M., & Klos, M. J. (1997). *A time for peace*. La Crosse, WI: Gundersen Lutheran.

Easterling, L. W., Gamino, L. A., Sewell, K. W., & Stirman, L. S. (2000). Spiritual experience, church attendance, and bereavement. *Journal of Pastoral Care, 54*(3), 263-275.

Grant, R. (1995). *Interdisciplinary collaborative teams in primary care: A model curriculum and resource guide*. San Francisco: Pew Health Professions Commission and California Primary Care Consortium.

Joint Commission on Accreditation of Healthcare Organizations. (2000). *Comprehensive accreditation manual for hospitals*. Oakbrook Terrace, IL: Author.

Karnes, B. (1995). *Gone from my sight* (tenth printing). Stilwell, KS: Author

Kaufman, S. R. (1998). Intensive care, old age, and the problem of death in America. *The Gerontologist, 38*(6), 715-725.

Manning, D. (1979). *Don't take my grief away from me*. Springfield, IL: Human Services Press.

Midland, D. (Ed.). (2002). *Compassionate bereavement care: A model for program growth*. La Crosse, WI: Gundersen Lutheran Medical Foundation.

Midland, D., Gensch, B., & Rybarik, F. (Eds.). (2001). *RTS bereavement training in pregnancy loss, stillbirth, and newborn death*. La Crosse, WI: Gundersen Lutheran Medical Foundation.

National Center for Health Statistics. (1999). National hospital discharge survey: Annual summary, 1997. *Vital and Health Statistics, 13*(144), 10, 26.

Roberg, S. (1993). *Staff survey* (unpublished). La Crosse, WI: Gundersen Lutheran.

Team building: Measuring success. (1998). La Crosse, WI: Gundersen Lutheran.

Witter, D. M., Tolle, S. W., & Moseley, J. R. (1990). A bereavement program: Good care, quality assurance, and risk management. *Hospital & Health Services Administration, 35*(2), 263-275.

CHAPTER 13

An Exploratory Study of the Spirituality of Clergy as Compared with Health Care Professionals

David W. Adams and Rick Csiernik

In North America prior to the twentieth century, both instrumental and spiritual counseling were almost exclusively the domain of the clergy. When people were in difficulty it was often the clergy who were most familiar with their congregants and, often, with the community at large. Ministers, pastors, priests, and rabbis were frequently viewed as trustworthy, readily accessible counselors who did not levy charges for their services and did not turn away people in need. The clergy were accepted by most people as the link to a greater power, interpreters of the meaning of life and death, and respected authorities concerning spiritual beliefs and religious practices.

For those who were elderly, ill, or dying at home or in hospital, the clergy were mobile and readily granted access. Jails, prisons, and other public facilities welcomed the clergy to tend to the spiritual and emotional needs of anyone requiring their wisdom and guidance. In health care, hospitals were not only accessible to the clergy but were often founded and operated by religious orders and sects. Association with various religions still continues as part of prominent health care institutions. For example, some are named after saints attesting to affiliation with the Roman Catholic or Protestant faiths or bear names associated with the Jewish faith such as Mount Sinai and Beth Israel. Today many of these institutions are funded through a variety of public and private sources. At the same time, a plethora of other health care facilities have evolved from federal, state, and municipal governments, and private business interests and trusts. Even in those facilities that have retained their religious affiliations, much less patient care is provided by nuns, brothers, or others functioning as part of a specific religious faith. The same holds true for the administration as most chief executives are professional health care administrators with specialized training.

HELPING PROFESSIONALS VERSUS
THE CLERGY

Despite this move away from being a major power in the health care industry, the clergy were left the dominion of spirituality and spiritual care of both the living and the dying. However, within the last two decades other groups have gradually encroached on the realm of the clergy and incorporated both spirituality and spiritual care into their practice principles. Competition has arisen from a variety of fronts such as psychiatry, psychology, social work, and even nursing and other medically related professions. Non- clergy helping professions taking a holistic view of counseling and embracing a wellness approach (Csiernik, 1995), are no longer merely content with providing for a patients' physical, psychological, and social health and well-being but have also become actively involved in the provision of spiritual support and care. So much have other professions risen to prominence and dominated what was once the realm of the clergy that Specht and Courtney (1994) referred to psychotherapists as "contemporary secular priests."

THE BROADER CONTEXT OF SPIRITUALITY

It appears that in health care this gradual expansion in the practice of helping professionals was accompanied by greater recognition of the importance of spirituality, a broader definition of its meaning, and for some, a deeper understanding of spirituality as an integral component of their own and their patients' lives. Included in this expansion were:

1. A tendency to move away from the traditional perspective that linked spirituality solely with religion and religious practices.
2. Recognition that spiritual concerns were no longer reserved for those living with life-threatening or terminal illnesses or bereavement.
3. A shift to spirituality as a concern of wellness as opposed to a concern of illness.
4. A perspective of spirituality that included living in a manner that incorporated maximizing one's potential; adapting to and managing challenges in changing environments and situations; maintaining social responsibility and actions; and integrating the mind, body, and spirit (Ardell, 1977; Dunn, 1961; Sefton et al., 1992; Adams & Csiernik, 2002; de Veber, 1995; Morgan, 1993).

From the literature and our clinical experience we could speculate that for at least some helping professionals, spirituality has become more personalized and associated with:

- purpose and meaning;
- an ability to reflect upon and seek a greater personal understanding and acceptance of oneself;
- an integration of facts and ideas concerning situations that evoke spiritual concerns;

- positive connections to others and the environment in a framework of culture, community, and caring;
- meaningful linkages to one's origins and the influence of greater powers;
- motivation, energy, and drive;
- continuance through time (Adams & Csiernik, 2002; de Veber, 1995; Morgan, 1993).

However, such speculation simply piqued our curiosity. We needed to understand what spirituality meant to different sub-groupings of health care professionals and, ideally, to the clergy as well. We needed to determine:

1. How they defined spirituality.
2. The importance of spirituality in their personal and working lives.
3. Their level of comfort with their own spirituality.
4. How their spiritual needs were met.
5. How their spirituality was strengthened and/or changed.
6. What impeded their ability to fulfill their spiritual needs.
7. The consequences of not meeting one's spiritual needs.
8. The impact of spirituality on one's work.
9. How clients/patients were helped to meet their spiritual needs.

METHODOLOGY

This study was an exploratory examination of spirituality among clergy and health care professionals. Participants were grouped into four sub-categories: clergy, nurses, physicians, and other helping professionals (OHP). The latter included occupational therapists, physiotherapists, psychologists, and social workers. Professionals working within a formal institution, in a community-based setting, or in a private practice were all included in the study.

In formulating the study, no existing instrument examining the nine areas of interest was discovered. Consequently, a new eight page descriptive questionnaire constructed specifically for this investigation was employed. It was developed, pre-tested, and modified with the assistance of eight clinical and academic key informants. The first page, Part A, consisted of six closed ended demographic questions. Part B made inquiries about the respondents' spirituality through 14 open ended questions. Part C asked two closed ended questions relating to how participants helped patients meet their spiritual needs while the last two pages, Part D, inquired about how respondents helped their co-workers meet their spiritual needs. The questionnaires were distributed to counseling professionals attending a conference on death, dying, and bereavement in London, Ontario and to a random selection within the Regional Municipality of Hamilton-Wentworth, in Ontario, Canada. A total of 149 questionnaires of 686 were returned for a response rate of 21.7 percent. Thus, the following results provide only a preliminary glimpse into the issue of the spirituality of clergy compared with other helping professionals.

RESULTS

Twenty of the 149 respondents (13.4 percent) were clergy, 45 (30.2 percent) were nurses, 22 (14.8 percent) were physicians while the remaining 62 individuals (41.6 percent) were other helping professionals (OHP). Nurses (93.2 percent) and OHP (85.5 percent) were predominately female, while the majority of physicians (63.6 percent) and clergy (55 percent) who replied were male (Table 1).

Approximately two-thirds of the survey participants identified themselves as Christian, 4 percent stated they were Jewish, while another 4 percent responded that they were Unitarian. Twenty-three persons (15.4 percent) stated that they had no religious affiliation (Table 2). Clergy were predominately Christian, 70 percent Protestant and 15 percent Roman Catholic with only one Rabbi participating in the study. Over 40 percent ($n = 53$) of respondents attended religious services more than once per month though nearly one quarter ($n = 30$) reported never attending in the past year. Not surprisingly, clergy were the group with the greatest regular attendance while half of all physicians reported no attendance at religious services in the year prior to the survey (Table 3). In considering who shaped their spirituality, most helping professionals replied that it was a member of their family of origin. The exception to this were the clergy, for whom it was another member of the clergy or a teacher (Table 4).

The Meaning of Spirituality

The conceptualization of spirituality took on a multiplicity of meanings (Table 5). The three most common answers were all reported by between 45 percent and 40.9 percent of respondents. The most frequent reply was relating to inner self, which included having a sense of wholeness, fulfillment, and inner peace. The second most frequent answer was caring for others followed by a belief in or having a relationship with a supreme being. Other replies included a search for meaning in their lives (20.1 percent), a connection with the soul and an eventual transcendence from life on earth (8.7 percent), and an appreciation of, and connection to, the creative self (1.3 percent).

However, the different sub-groups had quite distinct interpretations of this open ended survey question. For clergy, the existence of a supreme being was the most dominant response (75 percent), though 55 percent of clergy also defined spirituality

Table 1. Sex of Respondents

	Clergy	Nurse	Physician	OHP	Total
Male	11 (55%)	2 (4.4%)	14 (63.6%)	7 (11.3%)	34 (22.8%)
Female	9 (45%)	42 (93.2%)	4 (18.2%)	53 (85.5%)	108 (72.5%)
No response	0	1 (2.2%)	4 (18.2%)	2 (3.2%)	7 (4.7%)
Total	20 (100%)	45 (100%)	22 (100%)	62 (100%)	149

Table 2. Religious Faith of Respondents

	Clergy (n = 20)	Nurse (n = 45)	Physician (n = 22)	OHP (n = 62)	Total (n = 49)
Protestant	14 (70%)	22 (48.9%)	9 (40.9%)	29 (46.8%)	74 (49.7%)
Roman Catholic	3 (15%)	10 (22.2%)	5 (22.7%)	79 (11.3%)	25 (16.8%)
Jewish	1 (5%)	3 (6.7%)	1 (4.5%)	1 (1.6%)	6 (4%)
Unitarian	0 (0%)	1 (2.2%)	0 (0%)	5 (8.1%)	6 (4%)
Atheist/Agnostic	0 (0%)	0 (0%)	1 (4.5%)	1 (1.6%)	2 (1.3%)
Other	2 (10%)	2 (4.4%)	1 (4.5%)	7 (11.3%)	12 (8%)
None	0 (0%)	7 (15.6)	4 (18.2%)	12 (19.3%)	23 (15.4%)
No response	0 (0%)	0 (0%)	1 (4.5%)	0 (0%)	1 (0.7%)

Table 3. Attendance at Religious Services

	Clergy (n = 20)	Nurse (n = 45)	Physician (n = 22)	OHP (n = 62)	Total (n = 149)
More than 1/month	20 (100%)	22 (48.9%)	4 (18.2%)	27 (43.5%)	73 (49%)
1/month	0 (0%)	2 (4.4%)	3 (13.6%)	4 (6.5%)	9 (6%)
1/quarter	0 (0%)	3 (6.7%)	1 (4.5%)	5 (8.1%)	9 (6%)
Sacred holiday—1/year	0 (0%)	4 (8.9%)	2 (9.1%)	3 (4.8%)	9 (6%)
Never	0 (0%)	6 (13.3%)	11 (50%)	12 (21%)	30 (20.1%)
Other	0 (0%)	8 (17.9%)	1 (4.5%)	10 (16.1%)	19 (12.8%)

Table 4. The Person Who Influenced My Spirituality Most Was:

	Clergy (n = 20)	Nurse (n = 45)	Physician (n = 22)	OHP (n = 62)	Total (n = 149)
Family of origin	6 (30%)	19 (42.2%)	8 (36.4%)	21 (33.9%)	54 (36.2%)
Teacher/clergy	11 (55%)	13 (28.9%)	3 (13.7%)	17 (27.4%)	44 (29.5%)
Nuclear family	0 (0%)	1 (2.2%)	1 (4.5%)	7 (11.3%)	9 (6%)
Friend	1 (5%)	2 (4.4%)	2 (9.1%)	3 (4.8%)	8 (5.4%)
Religious/biblical figure	2 (10%)	0 (0%)	0 (0%)	1 (1.6%)	3 (2%)
Other	0 (0%)	7 (15.6%)	4 (18.2%)	7 (11.3%)	18 (12.1%)
No response	0 (0%)	3 (6.7%)	4 (18.2%)	6 (9.7%)	13 (8.7%)

Table 5. Conceptualization of Spirituality

	Clergy (n = 20)	Nurse (n = 45)	Physician (n = 22)	OHP (n = 62)	Total (n = 149)
Relates to inner self	11 (55%)	20 (44.4%)	8 (36.3%)	28 (45.2%)	67 (45%)
Caring for others	7 (35%)	22 (48.8%)	9 (40.9%)	25 (40.3%)	63 (42.3%)
Supreme being	15 (75%)	21 (46.6%)	4 (18.8%)	21 (33.9%)	61 (40.9%)
Search for meaning	3 (15%)	11 (24.4%)	4 (18.8%)	12 (19.4%)	30 (20.1%)
Soul/transcendence	3 (15%)	4 (8.8%)	0 (0%)	6 (9.7%)	13 (8.7%)
Creativity/art	0 (0%)	1 (2.2%)	0 (0%)	1 (1.6%)	2 (1.3%)
No response	0 (0%)	1 (2.2%)	4 (18.8%)	2 (3.2%)	7 (4.7%)
Average number of responses	2	1.8	1.4	1.6	1.6

in relation to their inner self. Reference to a supreme being was made by 47 percent of nurses, one third of other helping professionals, and less that 20 percent of physicians. For the latter two groups, caring for others and a personalized relationship with their spirituality were both reported more frequently than having a relationship with or an understanding of God. Of the seven persons who did not reply to this question four were physicians.

The Importance of Spirituality in Personal and Work Life

Survey participants were next asked to rate the importance of spirituality in their lives, the importance of having their spiritual needs met, and the importance of meeting their patients' and colleagues' spiritual needs. A 5-point Likert scale was utilized, with 1 representing little importance and 5 being extremely important. Clergy had the highest rating in three of the four areas, with replies ranging from 4.1 for helping meet their colleagues' spiritual needs to 4.8 for importance of spirituality in their own lives. The nurses who responded to the questionnaire had the highest score in respect to having their own spiritual needs met, 4.9 compared to the clergy's score of 4.5, OHPs' 4, and physicians' 3.8. Nurses consistently rated the role of spirituality higher than other helping professionals with physicians having the lowest ratings across all four questions (Table 6).

Personal Comfort With Spirituality

Almost all respondents (91.9 percent) documented comfort with their personal spirituality (Table 7). The primary reason for this was their inner self. They felt at peace with how they perceived their spirituality and their spirituality provided them with a sense of wholeness. Approximately 31 percent of respondents, led by clergy

Table 6. Role of Spirituality

	Clergy (n = 19)	Nurse (n = 45)	Physician (n = 22)	OHP (n = 62)	Total (n = 148)
Importance of spirituality in my life	4.8	4.7	3.8	4.6	4.5
Importance of having my spiritual needs met	4.5	4.9	3.8	4.0	4.3
Importance of meeting the spiritual needs of patients	4.5	4.0	3.6	3.8	3.9
Importance of helping colleagues meet spiritual needs	4.1	3.4	3.0	3.3	3.4

Table 7. Comfort with Personal Spirituality

	Clergy (n = 20)	Nurse (n = 45)	Physician (n = 22)	OHP (n = 62)	Total (n = 149)
Yes	16 (80%)	43 (95.5%)	21 (95.5%)	57 (92%)	137 (91.9%)
No	4 (20%)	2 (4.4%)	0 (0%)	4 (6.5%)	10 (6.7%)
Undecided	0 (0%)	0 (0%)	1 (4.5%)	1 (1.5%)	2 (1.3%)

at 44 percent, replied that they simply felt secure in their current beliefs, while 38 (27.7 percent) claimed that spirituality helped them to problem solve. The leap of faith that led to a belief in a higher power provided comfort for 34 (24.8 percent) persons. Interestingly, the belief in a higher power was more frequently a comfort for nurses than clergy. Also of interest was the fact the 42.4 percent of physicians (n = 9) did not answer this question (Table 8).

The Meeting of Spiritual Needs

Not surprisingly, the majority (65.1 percent) of health care professionals in the survey stated that they met their spiritual needs through their religious practices. Again, the highest response was from clergy at 90 percent and the lowest from physicians at 31.8 percent. Other frequent responses to how spiritual needs were

Table 8. Reasons for Comfort with Spirituality

	Clergy (n = 16)		Nurse (n = 43)	Physician (n = 21)	OHP (n = 57)	Total (n = 137)	
Personal inner self	8	(50%)	22 (51.2%)	8 (38.1%)	25 (43.9%)	63	(46%)
Feel secure in beliefs	7 (43.8%)		16 (37.2%)	5 (23.8%)	14 (24.6%)	42 (30.7%)	
Helps solve problem	6 (37.5%)		9 (20.9%)	7 (33.3%)	16 (28.1%)	38 (27.7%)	
Belief in higher power	4	(25%)	16 (37.2%)	2 (9.5%)	12	(21%)	34 (24.8%)
Allows to care for others	7 (43.8%)		8 (18.6%)	6 (28.6%)	4	(7%)	25 (18.3%)
Connection to world	0	(0%)	1 (2.3%)	2 (9.5%)	2 (3.5%)	5	(3.6%)
Connection to soul	0	(0%)	1 (2.3%)	0 (0%)	1 (1.8%)	2	(1.5%)
No response	2 (12.5%)		11 (25.6%)	9 (42.4%)	10 (17.5%)	32 (23.4%)	
Average number of responses	2.1		2.6	2.5	1.6	1.8	

met included reflection (53 percent), interpersonal communication (36.2 percent), caring for others (25.5 percent), and interaction with nature (25.5 percent) (Table 9). The most prominent method through which physicians met their spiritual needs was by caring for others, a factor that was rated fourth by nurses and fifth by both clergy and OHP. Clergy had the greatest number of responses per respondent to this question averaging 3.4 answers each, substantially more than the other three groups.

The Strengthening and Changing of Spirituality

Also anticipated was the discovery that the health care professionals' spirituality was strengthened most by religious experiences (46.2 percent) and relationships (38.3 percent). These two items were the most frequent responses for all respondents (Table 10) followed by time alone (18.8 percent), interaction with nature (15.4 percent), creative expression (11.4 percent), and work including interaction with co-workers (10.7 percent) which rated above caring for others (9.4 percent). When asked which life event changed their spirituality the most, the most common and significant reply was no response. One third of the nurses, 24 (38.7 percent) of OHP, one half of the physicians, and one member of the clergy chose not to or were unable to provide a response. The next most frequent answer related to death and loss of relationships though no group replied at a frequency of greater than 30 percent. Six of the 20 clergy (30 percent) did state that it was a general life event such as marriage or birth of a child that had the most significant impact upon their spirituality (Table 11).

Table 9. How Personal Spiritual Needs are Met

	Clergy (n = 20)	Nurse (n = 45)	Physician (n = 22)	OHP (n = 62)	Total (n = 149)
Religious practice	18 (90%)	30 (66.7%)	7 (31.8%)	42 (67.7%)	97 (65.1%)
Reflection	12 (60%)	18 (4%)	10 (45.5%)	39 (62.9%)	79 (53%)
Communication	10 (50%)	13 (28.8%)	7 (31.8%)	24 (38.7%)	54 (36.2%)
Caring for others	6 (30%)	12 (26.6%)	9 (40.9%)	11 (17.7%)	38 (25.5%)
Through nature	5 (25%)	13 (28.8%)	3 (13.6%)	17 (27.4%)	38 (25.5%)
Passive diversion	7 (35%)	9 (20%)	3 (13.6%)	15 (24.2%)	34 (22.8%)
Creative diversion	5 (25%)	6 (13.3%)	1 (4.5%)	8 (12.9%)	20 (13.4%)
Physical exercise/ recreation	3 (15%)	3 (6.6%)	1 (4.5%)	8 (12.9%)	15 (10.1%)
Living by one's values	1 (5%)	6 (13.3%)	3 (13.6%)	3 (4.8%)	13 (8.7%)
Positive thinking and acts	0 (0%)	3 (6.6%)	2 (9.1%)	2 (3.2%)	7 (4.7%)
No response	0 (0%)	1 (2.2%)	3 (13.6%)	3 (4.8%)	7 (4.7%)
Average number of responses	3.4	2.5	2.2	2.8	2.7

Impediments to Meeting One's Spiritual Needs

Factors that survey participants stated as most frequently preventing them from meeting their spiritual needs were a lack of self-discipline (57 percent), fatigue and stress (30.2 percent), and relationship problems (20.1 percent). These three responses were common to all four groups, though again many participants (15.4 percent) gave no reason (Table 12).

Consequences of Not Meeting One's Spiritual Needs

There were many consequences associated with not being able to meet one's spiritual needs, as illustrated in Tables 13 and 14. The feeling most commonly expressed by clergy was emptiness (65 percent), while for nurses the common feelings were emptiness (37.8 percent), depression (37.8 percent), and confusion (33.3 percent). Over one-third of physicians stated that depression was their most

Table 10. Spirituality Strengthened Most By

	Clergy (n = 20)	Nurse (n = 45)	Physician (n = 22)	OHP (n = 62)	Total (n = 149)
Religious experience	14 (70%)	20 (44.4%)	7 (31.8%)	42 (67.7%)	97 (65.1%)
Relationships	7 (35%)	16 (35.6%)	8 (36.6%)	39 (62.9%)	79 (53%)
Time alone	5 (25%)	8 (17.7%)	3 (13.6%)	24 (38.7%)	54 (36.2%)
Nature	2 (10%)	7 (15.5%)	3 (13.6%)	11 (17.7%)	38 (25.5%)
Creative expressions	1 (5%)	6 (13.3%)	1 (4.5%)	17 (27.4%)	38 (25.5%)
Co-workers/work	3 (15%)	4 (8.8%)	4 (18.1%)	15 (24.2%)	34 (22.8%)
Caring for others	3 (15%)	4 (8.8%)	2 (9.1%)	8 (12.9%)	20 (13.4%)
Positive feelings	1 (5%)	1 (2.2%)	1 (4.5%)	8 (12.9%)	15 (10.1%)
Problem solving	0 (0%)	1 (2.2%)	0 (0%)	3 (4.8%)	13 (8.7%)
Life purpose	1 (5%)	0 (0%)	2 (9.1%)	2 (3.2%)	7 (4.7%)
No response	2 (10%)	4 (8.8%)	6 (27.3%)	3 (4.8%)	7 (4.7%)
Average number of responses	2	1.6	1.7	2.8	2.7

common feeling though, yet again, over one-third did not reply. For the OHP group, anger was the most common emotional reaction (45.1 percent).

In examining actions arising from the inability of helping professionals to have their spiritual needs met, there was no dominant theme. Slightly more than one quarter of respondents stated that they stepped back when this occurred, took time for themselves, retreated from the world or slept more. Approximately one in five stated they practiced their faith to a greater degree, or asked for more guidance when this occurred while 19.5 percent engaged in self-care behaviors. Of the four groups, clergy were the least likely to practice self-care when unable to meet their spiritual needs. Other behaviors included taking a positive action such as setting a goal related to their spirituality. This included problem solving (18.1 percent), communicating their concerns to others including clergy, family, and friends (13.4 percent), or becoming angry with the situation (13.4 percent). The second most frequent reply for clergy was to engage in negative acts (25 percent), a response which ranked eighth overall and was given by only one nurse and no physicians.

Table 11. Life Event that Changed Spirituality

	Clergy (n = 20)	Nurse (n = 45)	Physician (n = 22)	OHP (n = 62)	Total (n = 149)
Death/loss	5 (25%)	13 (28.9%)	3 (13.6%)	9 (14.5%)	30 (20%)
Religious experience	4 (20%)	2 (4.5%)	0 (0%)	9 (14.5%)	15 (10.1%)
General life events	6 (30%)	2 (4.5%)	1 (4.5%)	4 (6.5%)	13 (8.7%)
Aging	0 (0%)	8 (18.2%)	1 (4.5%)	2 (3.2%)	11 (7.4%)
Personal illness	1 (5%)	2 (4.5%)	1 (4.5%)	3 (4.8%)	7 (4.7%)
Positive relationship	1 (5%)	0 (0%)	1 (4.5%)	5 (8.1%)	7 (4.7%)
Family responsibility	1 (5%)	3 (6.9%)	0 (0%)	1 (1.6%)	5 (3.4%)
Other	1 (5%)	0 (0%)	4 (18.2%)	5 (8.1%)	10 (6.7%)
No response	1 (5%)	15 (33.3%)	11 (50%)	24 (38.7%)	50 (33.6%)

Table 12. Factors Preventing the Meeting of Spiritual Needs

	Clergy (n = 20)	Nurse (n = 45)	Physician (n = 22)	OHP (n = 62)	Total (n = 149)
Lack of self-discipline	16 (80%)	29 (64.4%)	8 (36.6%)	32 (51.6%)	85 (57%)
Fatigue/stress	6 (30%)	15 (33.3%)	8 (36.6%)	39 (30.2%)	45 (30.2%)
Relationship problems	7 (35%)	10 (22.2%)	0 (0%)	26 (20.1%)	33 (22.1%)
Intense emotions	2 (10%)	3 (6.7%)	2 (9.1%)	4 (6.5%)	11 (7.4%)
Problems with organized religion	2 (10%)	4 (8.8%)	0 (0%)	4 (6.5%)	10 (6.7%)
Materialism	0 (0%)	3 (6.7%)	1 (4.5%)	3 (4.8%)	7 (4.7%)
Isolation	2 (10%)	1 (2.2%)	0 (0%)	4 (6.5%)	7 (4.7%)
Uncaring world	1 (5%)	0 (0%)	0 (0%)	0 (0%)	1 (0.7%)
No response	1 (5%)	6 (13.3%)	9 (40.9%)	7 (11.3%)	23 (15.4%)
Average number of responses	1.9	1.7	1.5	1.4	1.5

Table 13. When I am Unable to Meet My Spiritual Needs I Feel:

	Clergy (n = 20)	Nurse (n = 45)	Physician (n = 22)	OHP (n = 62)	Total (n = 149)
Empty/unfulfilled	13 (65%)	17 (37.8%)	2 (9.1%)	22 (35.5%)	54 (36.2%)
Angry/frustrated	5 (25%)	14 (21.1%)	5 (22.7%)	28 (45.1%)	52 (34.9%)
Depressed	5 (25%)	17 (37.8%)	8 (36.4%)	16 (25.8%)	46 (30.9%)
Confused	5 (25%)	15 (33.3%)	4 (18.2%)	19 (30.6%)	43 (28.9%)
Agitated/anxious	4 (20%)	6 (13.3%)	3 (13.6%)	19 (30.6%)	32 (21.5%)
Isolated/lost	10 (50%)	6 (13.3%)	1 (4.5%)	10 (16.1%)	27 (18.1%)
Inattentive to my needs	1 (5%)	5 (11.1%)	1 (4.5%)	9 (14.5%)	16 (10.7%)
Guilty	0 (0%)	1 (2.2%)	1 (4.5%)	4 (6.5%)	6 (4%)
Hopeful of doing better	1 (5%)	0 (0%)	0 (0%)	1 (1.6%)	2 (1.3%)
No response	1 (5%)	5 (11.1%)	8 (36.4%)	10 (16.1%)	23 (15.4%)
Average number of responses	2.3	1.9	1.5	2.2	2.0

Table 14. When I am Not Able to Meet My Spiritual Needs I:

	Clergy (n = 20)	Nurse (n = 45)	Physician (n = 22)	OHP (n = 62)	Total (n = 149)
Step back/away	8 (40%)	14 (31.1%)	6 (27.3%)	11 (17.7%)	39 (26.2%)
Practice my faith	4 (20%)	13 (28.9%)	3 (13.6%)	13 (21%)	33 (22.1%)
Engage in self-care	1 (5%)	10 (22.2%)	4 (18.2%)	14 (22.6%)	29 (19.5%)
Take positive actions	3 (15%)	6 (13.3%)	4 (18.2%)	14 (22.6%)	27 (18.1%)
Become angry/irritable	6 (30%)	2 (4.4%)	1 (4.5%)	11 (17.7%)	20 (13.4%)
Communicate with others	3 (15%)	11 (24.4%)	3 (13.6%)	3 (4.8%)	20 (13.4%)
Exercise/turn to nature	1 (5%)	3 (6.7%)	4 (18.2%)	8 (12.9%)	16 (10.7%)
Engage in negative acts	5 (25%)	1 (2.2%)	0 (0%)	7 (11.3%)	13 (8.7%)
Use my creativity	1 (5%)	4 (8.9%)	1 (4.5%)	2 (3.2%)	8 (5.4%)
Endure	1 (5%)	2 (4.4%)	2 (9.1%)	3 (4.8%)	8 (5.4%)
Become sad	0 (0%)	4 (8.9%)	0 (0%)	4 (6.5%)	8 (5.4%)
Feel uncertain	3 (5%)	2 (4.4%)	0 (0%)	2 (3.2%)	7 (4.7%)
Care for others	0 (0%)	0 (0%)	1 (4.5%)	1 (1.6%)	2 (1.3%)
Neglect my spirituality	1 (5%)	0 (0%)	0 (0%)	0 (0%)	1 (0.7%)
No response	1 (5%)	6 (13.3%)	7 (31.8%)	8 (12.9%)	22 (14.8%)
Average number of responses	1.9	1.7	1.6	1.7	1.7

Impact of Spirituality on Work

The last area to be reviewed was the impact of spirituality on the quality or effectiveness of work. Not surprisingly, all clergy respondents stated that spirituality had an impact on their work. What was unexpected was that nearly 91 percent of other helping professionals stated that spirituality was an important dimension of their practice (Table 15). Sixty-five percent of clergy stated that their supervisor or manager supported their efforts in helping meet not only clients' spiritual needs, but also the spiritual needs of colleagues. This was also true for 38.8 percent of non-clergy (Table 16).

How Clients/Patients were Helped to Meet Their Spiritual Needs

Clergy most frequently assisted their clients' efforts to meet their spiritual needs through listening (4.8 on a 5-point scale), praying with them (4), praying for them (3.9), and discussing the impact of a personal or family crisis on one's perception of spirituality (3.7). Non-clergy were also most likely to assist their clients in meeting their spiritual needs through listening (4.7), followed by sharing information (3.8), and discussing the impact of crisis on spirituality (3.2). Praying with clients was the lowest ranked response for non-clergy (1.8) though praying for clients was ranked in the middle of the eight options and also in the middle of the 5-point scale (Table 17).

Table 15. Does Spirituality Affect the Quality or
Effectiveness of Your Work?

	Clergy ($n = 20$)	Non-Clergy ($n = 129$)
Yes	20 (100%)	117 (90.7%)
No	0 (0%)	8 (6.2%)
No response	0 (0%)	4 (3.1%)

Table 16. Does Your Manager/Supervisor
Support Your Efforts in Helping Colleagues
Meet Their Spiritual Needs?

	Clergy ($n = 20$)	Non-Clergy ($n = 129$)
Yes	13 (65%)	50 (38.8%)
No	2 (10%)	14 (10.8%)
Not applicable	5 (25%)	39 (30.2%)
No response	0 (0%)	26 (20.2%)

Table 17. I Help My Clients Meet Their Spiritual Needs Through:

	Clergy (n = 20)	Non-Clergy (n = 129)
Listening	4.8	4.7
Sharing information	3.5	3.8
Telling them about my spirituality	3.0	2.3
Telling them about my religious beliefs	3.0	1.9
Helping them clarify their own spiritual beliefs	3.6	2.7
Praying with them	4.0	1.8
Praying for them	3.9	2.5
Helping them recognize that a crisis may change one's spirituality	3.7	3.2

DISCUSSION

As with any exploratory study there are distinct limits to making general inferences from the data. Nonetheless, the study did yield some interesting differences between the groups, some that could have been predicted and others that were unexpected. It was not surprising that clergy in the study:

1. Attended church services more regularly and frequently than members of other helping professions.
2. Had their spiritual understanding influenced by fellow clergy as teachers and mentors more so than their family of origin. This result is congruent with the intensity of spiritual study required to become a clergy practitioner.
3. Incorporated a relationship with a supreme being, introspection, and caring for others as major components in defining their spirituality. However, it is surprising that only 75 percent cited the relationship with a supreme being as a major component and only 55 percent included introspection while only 35 percent suggested that caring for others should be included. Perhaps this reflects a diversity in the definition of spirituality that the clergy shares with other disciplines.
4. Had their spiritual needs met through religious practices, reflection, and communication with others.

5. Were strengthened spiritually by religious experiences, relationships, and time alone. However, it was again surprising that only 70 percent cited religious experiences, only 35 percent listed relationships, and only 25 percent noted the importance of time alone, especially as the other groups recorded an equal or greater response concerning the importance of relationships and a very similar response to time alone.
6. Encountered changes in their spirituality through death/loss, religious experiences, or general life events. However, only a small percentage of the clergy answered this question.

Less predictable were the clergy's:

1. Lack of comfort with their own spirituality. They were less comfortable than either of the three sub-groups, perhaps because of their continuing quest for understanding and the continual need to field and reflect upon the spiritual questions of others.
2. Reasons for being unable to meet their spiritual needs. This included the majority's recognition that lack of self-discipline was a major factor. Other reasons such as relationship problems (35 percent) and fatigue/stress (30 percent) were important but far less prevalent. Explanations may be linked to the potential lack of rigor in the scheduling practices of some clergy such as hospital chaplains and the crisis orientation in service delivery which may lead the clergy to give the needs of others a higher priority than their own.
3. Reactions to being unable to meet spiritual needs. These included feeling empty/unfulfilled (65 percent), isolated/lost (50 percent), depressed (25 percent), angry/confused (25 percent), and agitated (20 percent). Each of these responses reflect the intensity of emotion associated with their personal spirituality and its importance in being connected to others and feeling fulfilled. Feeling empty/unfulfilled and isolated/lost were cited far more frequently by clergy than other health care professionals.
4. Actions when their spiritual needs could not be met. This included stepping back/away (40 percent), engaging in negative acts (25 percent), becoming angry and irritable (30 percent), and on a positive note, practicing their faith (20 percent). The latter action was taken more often by nurses and almost equally as often by OHPs. In addition, the clergy tended to engage the least in self-care (5 percent) when compared to the other three groups (average 19.5 percent).

In the workplace, it was no surprise that all clergy valued how much spirituality affected the quality or effectiveness of their work. Where applicable most found their manager/supervisor supported their efforts to help colleagues meet their spiritual needs. However, how they helped their clients meet their spiritual needs was less predictable. Beyond commonalties with all other disciplines in respect to listening and sharing information, the clergy clearly demonstrated differences in their approach. They were much more likely to pray with and for their patients; help patients to clarify their spiritual beliefs; and tell them about their own spirituality and spiritual beliefs. The clergy were also slightly more apt to help patients recognize that a crisis may be a stimulus to change one's spirituality.

When we contrasted the clergy with other disciplinary groups in respect to their spirituality, maintenance of their spiritual beliefs, and their spiritual practices in the workplace, we were tempted to re-examine our earlier perceptions regarding the spirituality of the other disciplinary groups and how they have impinged upon the roles of the clergy. For example, the importance of spirituality in their lives and having their spiritual needs met were key concerns of nurses to an equal or greater extent than the clergy themselves. However, meeting the spiritual needs of patients was slightly less important for nurses and meeting of the spiritual needs of colleagues was even less important. OHPs also valued their spirituality highly but were somewhat less concerned about having their own spiritual needs or the spiritual needs of their patients met and much less concerned about helping their colleagues meet their spiritual needs. Physicians ranked well behind other groups in all areas. However, physicians cited that caring for others was as important as meeting their spiritual needs.

Traditionally, the clergy in health care as deliverers of pastoral care and related services have been expected to be a calming and reassuring influence. It is anticipated that they will ally the fears of the ill and dying and by so-doing remove some of the strain on other professional caregivers enabling them to focus on their core mandates. Consequently, the clergy are expected to be:

- clear about their spiritual beliefs and religious practices;
- able to understand the spirituality and religious faith of others;
- capable of defining and interpreting the meaning of life, death, and in some situations, life beyond death;
- able to unite families in spiritual understanding through discussion or the use of religious rituals or other tools of the trade;
- connectors linking patients and their families to faith communities external to the health care institutions;
- facilitators of interdisciplinary communication and esprit de corps, and in some instances, teamwork.

Our findings do not negate any of these expectations. In fact, the workplace data reflects support of the clergy's role and functions. Listening, praying, focusing on spiritual concerns, clarifying understanding, and sharing personal or secular beliefs, all fit traditional expectations. However, our study also demonstrates that other disciplinary groups are concerned about spirituality. They are grappling with their own spirituality and are directly involved in the spiritual care of their patients. Their interest may, however, reflect a generalist approach to spirituality as opposed to the specialist approach of the clergy. In discussing the business world, Rutte (1999) suggests that as this century winds down a spiritual reawakening has begun, a reawakening that is associated with general principles of belief and conduct as opposed to in-depth specifics of spiritual definition. This spiritual movement is emphasized by:

- humanity and caring;
- understanding human needs;
- rebuilding interpersonal connections; and,
- respecting each other and ourselves (Rutte, 1999).

Although each of these components is readily identified in health care today, the concept of a spiritual reawakening may be inappropriate. Rather, we may be witnessing an expansion of spiritual awareness, understanding, and integration into patient care, and expansion that can be, and needs to be, delivered through a multidisciplinary team. While the clergy in the foreseeable future will remain the focus and foundation of spiritual care within this team, they are no longer alone in meeting the spiritual needs of the ill and the dying. Are the clergy, as Specht and Courtney (1994) suggest, inundated or overwhelmed by "secular priests" or other competitors in such a setting? Or, are the clergy strengthened in influence and effectiveness by an alliance with spiritually knowledgeable health care professionals? Although further study is warranted, the latter seems to be the reality.

REFERENCES

Adams, D., & Csiernik, R. (2002). A beginning examination of the spirituality of health care practitioners. In R. Gilbert & J. Morgan (Ed.), *Health care and spirituality: Listening, assessing, caring.* Amityville, NY: Baywood.

Ardell, D. (1977). *High level wellness.* Emmasus, PA: Rodale Press.

Csiernik, R. (1995). Wellness, work, and employee assistance programming. *Employee Assistance Quarterly, 11*(2), 1-13.

de Veber, L. L. (Barrie). (1995). The influence of spirituality on dying children's perceptions of death. In D. Adams & E. Deveau (Eds.), *Beyond the innocence of childhood: Helping children and adolescents cope with life threatening illness and dying.* Amityville, NY: Baywood.

Dunn, H. (1961). *High level wellness.* Arlington: R. W. Beatty.

Morgan, J. (1993). The existential quest for meaning. In K. Doka & J. Morgan (Eds.), *Death and spirituality.* Amityville, NY: Baywood.

Rutte, M. (1999, June). Spirituality in the workplace. Lecture given at Hamilton Health Sciences Corporation, Hamilton, Ontario, Canada.

Sefton, J., Wankel, L., Quinney, H., Webber, J., Marshall, J., & Horne, T. (1992, March). Working towards well-being in Alberta. In *National Recreation and Wellness Conference,* Corburg, Australia.

Specht, H., & Courtney, M. (1994). *Unfaithful angels: How social work has abandoned its mission.* Toronto: Maxwell Canada.

CHAPTER 14

Living, Dying, and Grieving in the Margins*

Rev. Richard B. Gilbert

DEFINITIONS

"Disenfranchised" is a word that has taken on significant meaning these days, especially at the time of this writing. Many still talk about the recent election of the President of the United States and whether or not their vote was counted.

For the bereaved, and for those of us who provide care and support for them, disenfranchisement is not new. Kenneth Doka (1983) brought credibility to this concept in his pioneer work. Doka writes, "In self-disenfranchised grief, incipient grief is not recognized or is covered over, much the same as in socially disenfranchised grief . . ." (p. 25). The discussion that follows heightens the despair that can follow, with guilt and shame rampant, as people are disenfranchised, cut off within and without from their right to grieve in self-determined ways so they can come to terms with their world as it now is.

Some debate the use of "healing" when speaking of the anticipated outcome of grief's work. The opposition is rooted in faulty or limited definitions, suggesting that implicit in healing is the absence of "sickness," and that grief is not a sickness. This is true. Grief is a normal part of our investment in life and love that comes when life events and relationships are interrupted by loss. Still, healing as goal persists. Healing is the integration of the whole self, emotionally, socially, physically, sexually or with some expression of intimacy, and spiritually. There can be no wholeness if we are unable to come to terms with our losses and what life has become for us.

Betty Davies, writing from a nursing perspective, states (Rando, 2000), "When patients cannot redefine themselves, they experience anger, feelings of worthlessness, and persistent frustration with their altered situations" (p. 139).

*This chapter was prepared for a forthcoming Baywood Publishing publication based on many of the presentations at the Bereavement Conference at King's College, London, Ontario, 1999.

Tom Attig (2000) writes, "Our lasting love affirms the enduring meanings of their lives, meanings not canceled by death. Lasting love consoles us and moderates our suffering as their legacies enrich our lives" (p. 7). Death interrupts. Lasting love sustains. To be disenfranchised is to not only to have the significance of our loss diminished, but also the questioning of the very love that sustains and guides us. Without this love and without a sense of meaning or purpose in the midst of loss there is no healing or wholeness, a person set adrift in the sea of meaninglessness, hopelessness, and complication.

In Doka's ongoing work with disenfranchisement we have sensed a pall of things secret or otherwise unapproved that leaves a person disenfranchised. A person in a Gay relationship grieves in silence, hidden, without support except, perhaps, in his or her own community, because he or she dare not reveal the nature of the relationship and the pain of the loss. The risk is too great. The person hides, struggles privately and painfully, and often healing does not come. As DeSpelder and Strickland (1999) remind us, "When grief is disenfranchised, either because the significance of the loss to the survivor is not recognized or because the relationship between the deceased and the bereaved is not socially sanctioned, the person suffering the loss has little or no opportunity to mourn publicly" (p. 257).

The bitter taste of disenfranchisement effects many others who are simply cut off for reasons that do not fit the common approach used in this discussion. Some are denied their public forum and yet in no other way are judged. These are the *marginalized*. Often because of ignorance (by others) or indifference, or simply because those closest to the bereaved have chosen not to "understand," many become marginalized. Sometimes it is the nature of the loss or the relationship. Often it is because we are functioning in normal and healthy ways and others around us (or even ourselves) do not understand that "functioning appropriately" is not a pass key out of the long tunnel of grief's sorrow. Many are marginalized because society fails to come to terms with uniqueness associated with gender (Martin & Doka, 2000). We might argue that victims of domestic violence, often wrapped in stigma and shame, are disenfranchised. That generally is true. They also can be marginalized (Miles, 2000) because we put roadblocks in their way because of our inability to see ourselves as part of the problem. A victim of domestic violence may rethink definitions of spirituality in order to preserve safety. We marginalize them when we offer only one pathway or set of spiritual definitions.

When my mother died I experienced a profound sadness and a deep struggle with abandonment. My wife and sister offered sensitive caring and support, but, based on the reactions of most, I was marginalized. Does that make my story shady or questionable? What hooked me was my own adoption and the sudden reality that I had not lost two parents, but four. That overwhelming sense of loss sent me into emotional crisis that still leaves some bitter moments and painful scars. I felt dismissed, misunderstood, and frequently patronized, but I did not consider myself disenfranchised.

The nature of the relationship is important in determining factors of disenfranchisement. They also can produce marginalization. As a chaplain I work very closely with the sick and dying. Many patients want me to do their funeral.

Oftentimes a stranger is asked because the family or the funeral director may not know of this bonding. "I was just doing my job." Of course, there is the often not-so-subtle notion that funerals are to be done by "real ministers." Nurses frequently speak of feeling "out of the loop" because the patient they so cared for died when they were off duty. "I was not there for them when they needed me the most."

Marginalization can be a choice. For others, it is a reality set by others. Some are derailed, denied their public due because of the actions of others. Many of the marginalized find a subculture, an alternate presence or community in which to grieve. One of the taped interviews for this seminar was with a member of my monastic community who works with the deaf community. Himself hearing impaired, Br. Peter Christopher chastises the church for thinking that just by providing an interpreter they have done enough. He reminds us that entire thought processes must be changed before we can even begin to communicate with a person who is deaf. When he signs at a liturgy he not only must do tremendous preparatory work, in a sense "rewriting the Bible in a new language with new images," he must first be within their community and their stories if he is to speak to them anew. Because, in this case, the hearing choose to marginalize rather than relate, the hearing impaired find new ways, new communities, "life within the margins," in order to live, celebrate, and heal.

The educators and pioneers quoted at the outset of this chapter have drawn us into an experience of the roadblocks that confront many as they grieve. We must continue to meet the marginalized. Marginalization can and often does emerge as the result of prejudice, ignorance, insensitivity, or fear. Sometimes it happens simply because we are not aware (and may also be unwilling to learn) about other individuals, groups, or communities that come together because of like needs or rituals.

For some who are marginalized, the effects, processes and feelings may be much the same as for the disenfranchised. We continue to be drawn into that perspective as we see the continued (and growing) racism that exists worldwide. Others who are marginalized simply create their own ways, finding what works for them. They seem to do just fine without us. The problem is that a wall has been built and we are lesser people because of their absence. The community is not complete, and, in fact, may not be a community at all. To marginalize is to relegate or set apart a person, issue, group, or cause to a lesser or unimportant place or position within that society, community, or group.

We have already cited general areas that would concern us, including beliefs, victimization, gender and professional challenges, or circumstances. Because this conference has been concerned with the spiritual dimensions and expressions of bereavement, we will limit ourselves to those dimensions. Still we must ask or otherwise use as our assessment tools (well beyond discussions only of spirituality and/or religion) these questions:

1. What is marginalization?
2. Who are the marginalized?

3. Do we heighten the marginalization or become more aware and more present?
4. What are the spiritual issues that surround, confront and are confronted by margins?
5. What becomes the bereavement challenges for us and for the marginalized?

SPIRITUAL AND RELIGIOUS PARAMETERS

In his chapter, "Re-Creating Meaning in the Face of Illness" (Rando, 2000), Doka writes,

> Spirituality is a concept that we understand and acknowledge but find hard to define. Part of the trouble lies in the fact that spirituality is distinct from religion. The latter can be more readily recognized as an institutionalized set of beliefs or dogma shared by a defined group. Spirituality, though, is broader than that. Though religion certainly may be part of spirituality, it does not encompass it. (p. 104)

Spirituality is about meaning. Like grief, it is its own journey, its own unfinished product. Because it often feels as vulnerable or at risk as any other part of our story or experience, it can suffer hardship, loss, and redefinition (because of the crisis of loss) at a time when we thought we could depend on its absoluteness for us. Spirituality can shrink to just another set of problems at a time when we can ill afford such a disruption to our inner harmony.

Meaning is what keeps us focused and able to move forward in our journey. Meaning may, at best, be about trust, about our willingness to risk. It is seldom about making sense. Suffering is the timeless struggle for all believers, of all spiritual backgrounds. Spirituality that is healthy has to be open to all of our questions, uncertainties, and frustrations, including the rougher edges of some very tough feelings. What happens when the very feelings we would express are challenged. "Shame on you for not believing in the power of the Risen Christ." This was shared with me about one minister. Others hear over and over again that anger is a sin. Many are sabotaged by the notion that we are supposed to rejoice in our suffering, that God *gave* us this suffering for a reason. What peril emerges for our understanding of God with this kind of practice?

The marginalization continues. Our spirituality is twisted and turned, or otherwise we rush through it because of the deeper pain of the loss. For others our spirituality is reasonably intact, but we are sideswiped by religion or our religious affiliation. We come to our religious leaders (assuming they are even available to us) and expect them to understand something about grief. Because many of them have yet to deal with their own grief issues, coupled with a lack of a training, we are forced to deal with less than helpful leaders who then marginalize us because we feel either shut out or now required to seek out a new community. Moe, in his important, yet often brutal discussion of pastoral care and pregnancy loss (1997) reminds us,

> Most religious leaders today do not mean to be insensitive to those suffering from pregnancy loss. Unlike the religious leaders in the Good Samaritan parable who saw suffering and ignored its victims, most church leaders today are caring

people who do not minister because they are completely unaware that any suffering is involved with pregnancy loss. They may see the symptoms of suffering and grief but never understand that actual suffering and grief are taking place. (p. 1)

Moe states further, "Churches are often considered as places where families come to celebrate. Those who are not able to celebrate may find the church a difficult place to enter" (p. 25). While the marginalized experience these problems in different ways and with different impact, McBride (1998) places before us the great risk that is always just around the corner and which must concern us as caregivers. "Until the trauma story is told and the emotions reconnected, a person is often spiritually arrested developmentally, and has difficulty looking at spiritual issues from any other focus than the one that was present when the trauma occurred" (p. 19).

In his pivotal work on Alzheimer's disease and those caring for loved ones with Alzheimer's, Earl Grollman (1996) with Kenneth S. Kosik, M.D., sums up well the struggle that can emerge in a new pathway to meaning and hope if we allow it and, at times, if others get out of our way (pp. 112-113):

"Dear God, why me? Why us?"

It may be not only a question but also your cry of distress, your plea for help.

When unexpected crises shatter life, and anxiety and grief become the fabric of your days, your faith may flicker low and become extinguished.

However, for some, facing illness can also be a religious pilgrimage.

Faith can somehow be strengthened through the painful struggle, and both comfort in spiritual beliefs and a holiness—in Hebrew, *Kedusha*—with deeper insights and new understandings can be found.

Faith may help you accept the unacceptable, giving you courage and compassion as you support your loved one through the limbo of this disease.

Through prayers, simple or formal, you can release your feelings, and utter your secret concerns and fears.

In the darkness of your anguish, you may discover a measure of solace and peace, a sense that even as you struggle, you do not struggle alone.

The Professionally Marginalized

In the class setting we presented an interview with The Reverend Dr. Paul Wolkovits, a Roman Catholic priest serving in the Archdiocese of Los Angeles. He currently is studying in Rome. He came to the priesthood, to his "call," as a career change after a number of years working internationally in the financial world. He was asked to speak about the marginalization of priests, particularly, and clergy, generally. As a side note, some found it difficult to hear him because they have felt so marginalized by the Roman Catholic Church. Their comments would suggest that they have been so traumatized that they cannot believe there are others who are marginalized, possibly traumatized, and still manage to stay reasonably healthy in that denomination and even bring about significant accomplishment. While Ritter and O'Neill (1996) have devoted an entire book to a very significant study of the unique risks for abuse present within Roman Catholicism and "fundamentalist Protestantism," both Wolkovits and this author would insist that all religious groups and denominations are open to these criticisms and must address these concerns.

Shaky Foundations and Insufficient Skills and Leadership

Clergy walk a very fine line between the human and the divine. In my work as a chaplain I am regularly pulled in and pushed away around the humanity of others. Many delight in my willingness to be open with them, appropriately playful, even open to some of their at least slightly savory stories. Others, when observed from the distance, are having a grand time, but they quickly shut down as I approach because of their general perceptions (or personal responses to) of clergy or what one physician pointed to "My divine nature among them which should not be embarrassed by their playfulness." I wonder what would happen if we discussed God's sense of humor.

Wolkovits (in the tape, which is available from this author) cites several important factors for our discussion here. In the discussion he identifies his marginalization by the very religion (denomination) and people he has come to serve. He suggests that the very fabric of what it means to be a priest (or another term to suit other religious groups) has been ripped apart by the lack of proper (and realistic) seminary training and unhealthy leadership that often becomes a preventative rather than a proactive force in the lives and work of the clergy.

Walmsley and Lummis (1997) support these claims, identifying how basic seminary training leaves us ill-equipped for the ministry. We do not enter the ministry workplace with a healthy self-concept that determines to do healthy self-care, personal spiritual care (which is much different than feeling every spiritual devotion needs to be fit into some sermon or program), the ability to draw boundaries between reasonable and unreasonable expectations. We don't learn how to say "no." Those unhealthy dynamics are often fostered by congregational and synodical leaders because they, too, suffer the marginalization that sets them apart from healthy goals, spiritual refreshment, and good self-care practices. When some of our judicatory leaders are in more "trouble" than the sheep of their flock (the clergy and the congregations), how can they possibly contribute in healthy ways?

The study by Walmsley and Lummis (1997), while primarily within the structures and unique concerns of the Episcopal Church in the United States, offers important observations of the marginalization processes that occur for religious professionals and how it impacts personally and professionally on these workers, on their families or close circle of friends, the congregation (or other workplace), and the larger denomination. They offer this alternative.

> Judicatories and denominations can promote the spiritual, emotional, physical and vocational health of clergy and spouses through creating health-sustaining resources, providing constructive support, and instilling the importance of using preventative measures. Doing this effectively requires that a diocese know the particular issues and problems its clergy and spouses encounter in the different

areas of their lives and circumstances, and what resources programs best fit with the needs and interests expressed. A diocese must then know how to communicate and deliver resources so that they are accepted and utilized by clergy, or by their spouses. Effective programming and resource provision also involves taking into account realities of geography, proximity of clergy to one another, financial and personnel assets of the diocese, and other such exigencies. (p. 112)

Marva Dawn and Eugene Peterson (2000) speak of the "unnecessary pastor." Like Wolkovits, they remind us that we are marginalized by unrealistic expectations from within ourselves or by those imposed upon us. We will only become "necessary" again when we rediscover the call to ministry. To do this means not only radical surgery on our part, but the very "system" we call the church (or organized religion). The hazardous waste of this kind of management and leadership is an affront to the goals of any religious community committed to forgiveness, mercy, and peace. Marva and Pederson suggest, "Churches find themselves powerless in the world and not able to invite our neighbors into the faith because we do not live in ways that give any warrant for belief" (p. 161).

Personal Integrity and Integration

The interview then explored the marginalization that comes with the denial of our humanity. Some seem to thrive, codependently fitting into own delusions, on this sense of holiness about themselves. Again we cite the fabric of the "system" that eats away at the minister's own humanity. Wolkovits, at the time of this interview, was serving a parish in Los Angeles with over 17 active cultures and languages, an average Sunday attendance of 12,000, and two priests. There were also the demands of an elementary school and a high school, and a culturally mixed community rife with problems, including gangs.

In the interview he spoke of his personal frustration with trying to take a day off, even a few hours away, when another hospital calls, someone is knocking at the door for counsel and support, one more purposeless meeting, or another wedding or funeral. His denomination often renders lip service to active lay ministries and ministers. Even though there is relief in active lay members doing their responsible share for the religious community (assuming there are healthy clergy available to encourage this), it comes with its own price for clergy. Clergy must find the time to train and supervise these ministries, or find the funds to hire someone who can. They get some relief from this ministry format, but, if they are doing their work, they tend to find more people in need of pastoral care. In addition, the minister finds himself (or herself) in a tension between the pressures of the larger denomination that can easily thwart (marginalize) those who develop creative partnerships in ministry, and what about the lay people who still expect their ministers (and judicatories) to have a word for every situation, see everyone in the hospital, visit in all of the homes, attend all of the meetings, show up at every school program, be always out doing ministry while, at the same, always in the office waiting for someone to stop by . . . somehow while managing to stay healthy and holy in the mess that these attitudes and practices create.

Clergy of all denominations must come to terms with their very real marginalization. We must fight for change, do our bereavement work (within our own loss experiences), but also commit to the health and well-being that *we* must foster and maintain in organizations that talk the talk about such inclusiveness but often do not walk the walk. Some, like John P. Egan (1998), had to leave the priesthood in order to maintain the larger priesthood that is his as a child of God called to serve God in the world. He had to escape the margins in order to address them.

> Presented here are reflections on a journal written over the course of more than eight years. They were years of intense personal struggle, as I became more and more keenly aware that the hierarchical priesthood to which I was ordained was built on a dangerous lie.
>
> I had come to realize that Catholic hierarchical priesthood gave religious legitimacy to the false and deadly concept that there were superior and, therefore, inferior humans; that the "superiors" had a divine mandate to lord it over the "inferiors." Such a lie violates our radical equality and makes community with each other and Mother Earth impossible. (p. 5)

Daniel Langford (1998) explores these issues of self-integrity and personal health in ministry as they impact on, and thus can marginalize, clergy spouses. His study is essential if we are to bring about any solution to the marginalization among clergy. He cites how clergy spouses can be marginalized by the congregation, by stereotypes, even by their own ministers/spouses. He writes, here quoting Roy Oswold,

> Clergy wives are usually a talented, creative, dedicated group of Christians. When they are relegated to being "non-persons," when their point of view is never taken seriously . . . the church as a whole is diminished.
>
> If in any way their lives are made miserable through attitudes and actions on behalf of church members, that negative energy spills over and adversely affects the parish's life. (p. 28)

Those Marginalized as They Search for an Open Community

The course offered several other recorded interviews which addressed issues of marginalization. We already mentioned the needs of the deaf community and how they are often marginalized by the religious establishment that can easily marginalize the deaf and the hearing impaired because of its unwillingness to adjust its language, definitions, values, and methods to meet the needs of another group of people. That group then is marginalized. The disenfranchised would be at risk for shutting down, for profound complications in their need for public support as they mourn. The marginalized often follow a pathway of co-existence. They are the church, for example, but it all becomes a religious community divided because of margins. All "compartments" are wounded by the others, a symptom of marginalization, and all are new mourners who must come to terms with what they are not receiving (the blessings of community) from those they have marginalized. We thus become the marginalized as much as we are the ones who marginalize.

Healing must work in all directions.

The second interview was with Br. Ronald Francis, who presides (by election) over the Mercy of God Community. I am privileged to be an associate in that community. Those who seek more information about this community or non-residential community living and sharing can contact MGC at PO Box 41055, Providence, RI 02940. Your inquiries are welcomed.

Throughout the Bible we meet a God who invites, who welcomes, who defies marginalization and welcomes communion and community. It is a sad story that the communities that represent this God often contradict God by their judgments and practices. Many in the Gay community will state that there is no organization more homophobic than the church. The Episcopal Church continues to be divided and threatened with further division over this one issue, thus reminding us that there are no quick solutions to the behaviors and teachings (or perceived teachings) that marginalize others. Yet the church must be held accountable (with actions for change and an end to the excuses offered to justify) for preaching, programs, and practices that marginalize many, including women, children, the divorced, as well as members of the Gay/Lesbian/Bisexual/Transgendered communities. This subject, especially the last group, can be explored further in the essays by Chaplain Sue Jelinek and Dr. Inge Corless (Gilbert, 2001) as they explore the needs of people in these communities especially as they try to bring forth their spiritual needs and strengths during times of illness, trauma, and crisis.

Spirituality should always be about building up. There may be some tearing down, but it is the therapeutic surgery that nurtures, heals, and restores rather than marginalizes. Religious communities must continue to examine their rules, expectations, and judgments that tend to condemn rather than accept, that marginalize rather than welcome. Leo Booth, an Anglican priest, recovering alcoholic and a certified addictions therapist, has given much of his healing work and ministry to victims of religious oppression and spiritual abuse. Booth (2000) writes,

> Alongside this concept [of spiritual freedom] is the idea that human beings have been given the dignity to fight, if they choose for those things that ennoble the hearts of the peacemakers, sweat and work for integrity and justice in all areas of life, and die for those ideals and dreams they believe are important. Greatness must be earned!
>
> What kind of life would it be if God pulled every string to make us happy, protected us from all danger, and kept us safe from having to make decisions and take chances. That would be a life in hell. Think about it – no songs would be sung of the human adventure, no heroes or heroines would inspire future generations, the pain that feeds the soul of the poet would be quieted, and artists could paint only sunshine and joy. But what happened to the darkness and tears? Freedom allows for the shadow. Detachment. (p. 9)

Elsewhere Booth writes, "Spirituality is the healing balm for guilt and shame because it always beckons us to a new day, and new opportunities. It picks us up and dusts us off. And we need this" (p. 92). In talking about the system that marginalizes, and thus abuses, Booth captures our attention forcefully,

> "Unhealthy religion has played a significant role in keeping me sick." This may seem a strange thing to say, especially for a priest, but I remind you to notice the key word "unhealthy." I'm not talking about a healthy religion that allows for discussion, disagreements, inclusiveness, and tolerance. I'm talking about a dysfunctional system not a few of us associate with our families of origin. The child who grew up in a dysfunctional home heard·

- Don't talk.

- Don't trust.

- Don't feel.

In a similar way, the dysfunctional church creates the following:

- Don't think.

- Don't doubt.

- Don't question. (p. 58)

Br. Ron Francis knows firsthand the marginalization of the church. In order to be honest with himself he moved on to serving God in vocations outside the church. This became his "priestly role" because the church refused to see him, his gifts, his "call."

There are many who seek community beyond the traditional community. Occasionally there are people who are themselves destructive and seek a new playground to plant their poisonous words and actions (Rediger, 1997). Others reach out because they find themselves left hungry or unfulfilled by traditional preaching, ritual, worship, and community life. Others find themselves tumbling to the ground because the church, or some of her people, pulled the welcome mat out from under them and they are now among the marginalized. We distort the social justice issues addressed by Jesus when he discussed divorce, and now, in the name of protecting the "sanctity of marriage," condemn divorce. Even victims of horrendous violence and abuse in a marriage are encouraged by some (Miles, 2000) to be "better spouses" so that they won't give "cause" (i.e., justification) for abuse. Some are denied the sacraments. Some have been socially isolated or treated poorly in a confessional setting. Others are marginalized. We often affirm the sanctity of marriage, which is a noble and just cause, and fail to see that, in many congregations, the largest group is single adults. We stereotype and thus marginalize families defined in non-traditional ways who need our support and have much to offer those who fit into more traditional or stereotyped family structures.

Why would someone who is Gay, Lesbian, Bisexual, or Transgendered, or struggling with his or her sexual identity and values, stay with a community that calls them an "abomination"? How do you stay heathy and connect when the community denies them sexual health by demanding celibate lifestyles (often the "enforcers" are expected to follow the same rules, but may choose not to) because they follow a pathway that varies from the "game plan"?

The Mercy of God Community cannot fix all of the rules of the larger religious community. It also doesn't have to make excuses for it. It also can call for a justice that enables the marginalized to chose proactive pathways toward a community that welcomes, fosters spiritual growth and also talks about responsible membership and servanthood.

The Mercy of God Community is one of many communities growing within, and sometimes because of the larger religious community. Some studies suggest that the church of the next few decades will be a blending of small churches and the super churches, with many others choosing alternatives or complementary communities to better meet their spiritual needs and responsibilities. People who are marginalized will seek alternatives so that they can move beyond the margins and not be threatened with disenfranchisement.

CONCLUSION

Margins exist because of comfort levels, indifference, judgment, expedience, and fear, among other reasons. The congregation I belong to is facing a special congregational meeting because some people will not welcome change, whether it be in liturgical forms or worship schedules. Are they wrong? Fearful? Too comfortable? They want to rush through the established community their definitions and their ground rules. If allowed, and if they "win," the rest of us are at least disrupted for a time, and marginalized.

It is easy to condemn those who will not grow, move of center, or who seem to be conflicting with the way *we/I* believe things should be done. The risk is that we also become people who marginalize, because we see different rather than diversity, and because we are so guided by the win/lose mentality of this age.

The bereaved, generally, are marginalized by those who refuse (for whatever reason) to walk with them and stay comfortable with the journey and feelings of those who now must come to terms with the world that has thrust them into grief. When we seek forums for our mourning we run the risk of further marginalization when our beliefs, practices, professional needs and understanding, lifestyles and community values don't seem to fit the "norm" as defined by others. All of us as caregivers, and with a particular word of concern to clergy (however identified and defined), must ever be watchful for marginalization, especially the margins that we may produce, so that the bereaved may stay on track with their journey toward healing or wholeness.

Again from Tom Attig, "The paths we walk as we grieve will take us to terrain we have not seen before. No matter where they take us, there will always be a place of sadness in our hearts where we miss those who have died" (p. 14). "We can only bring order back into our lives by wrestling with, not ignoring, the chaos. . . . Grieving is not something more that happens to us after someone dies but rather what we do in response to it" (p. 17). As the bereaved offer response to the losses in their lives, may we do what we can to aid the process and not produce more detours.

REFERENCES

Attig, T. (2000). *The heart of grief: Death and the search for lasting love.* New York: Oxford University Press.

Booth, L. (2000). *The wisdom of letting go: The path of the wounded soul.* Long Beach, CA: SCP Ltd.

Corless, I. (2002). The HIV/AIDS patient. In R. Gilbert (Ed.)., *Healthcare & spirituality: Listening, assessing, caring.* Amityville, NY: Baywood.

Davies, B. (2000). Anticipatory mourning and the transition of fading away. In T. Rando (Ed.), *Clinical dimensions of anticipatory mourning: Theory and practice in working with the dying, their loved ones, and their caregivers* (pp. 135-153). Champaign: Research Press.

Dawn, M., & Peterson, E. (2000). *The unnecessary pastor: Rediscovering the call.* Grand Rapids: Eerdmans.

DeSpelder, L., & Strickland, A. (1999). *The last dance: Encountering death and dying.* Mountain View, CA: Mayfield.

Doka, K. (1983). *Disenfranchised grief: Recognizing hidden sorrow.* Lexington, MA: Lexington.

Doka, K. (2000). Re-creating meaning in the face of illness. In T. Rando (Ed.), *Clinical dimensions of anticipatory mourning: Theory and practice in working with the dying, their loved ones, and their caregivers* (pp. 103-114). Champaign: Research Press.

Egan, J. (1998). *A priest forever and no more.* Barnegat Light, NJ: Fragile Twilight.

Grollman, E., & Kosik, K. (1996). *When someone you love has Alzheimer's: The caregiver's journey.* Boston: Beacon.

Jelinek, S. (2002). The gay, lesbian, bisexual, transgendered patient. In R. Gilbert (Ed.), *Healthcare & spirituality: Listening, assessing, caring.* Amityville, NY: Baywood.

Langford, D. (1998). *The pastor's family: The challenges of family life and pastoral responsibilities.* Binghamton: Haworth.

Martin, T., & Doka, K. (2000). *Men don't cry . . . Women do: Transcending gender stereotypes of grief.* Philadelphia: Brunner/Mazel.

McBride, J. L. (1998). *Spiritual crisis: Surviving trauma to the soul.* Binghamton: Haworth.

Miles, A. (2000). *Domestic violence: What every pastor should know.* Minneapolis: Fortress.

Moe, T. (1997). *Pastoral care in pregnancy loss; A ministry long needed.* Binghamton: Haworth.

Rediger, G. L. (1997). *Clergy killers: Guidance for pastors and congregations under attack.* Louisville: Westminster John Knox Press.

Ritter, K., & O'Neill, C. (1996). *Righteous religion: Unmasking the illusions of fundamentalism and authoritarian catholicism.* Binghamton: Haworth.

Walmsley, R., & Lummis, A. (1997). *Healthy clergy wounded healers: Their families and their ministries.* New York: Church Publishing.

For Further Reading

Bowman, G., III. (1998). *Dying, grieving, faith, and family: A pastoral care approach.* Binghamton: Haworth.

Cox, G., & Fundis, R. (Eds.) (1991). *Spiritual, ethical and pastoral aspects of death and bereavement.* Amityville, NY: Baywood.

Doka, K., & Morgan, J. (1993). *Death and spirituality.* Amityville, NY: Baywood.

Gilbert, R. (1997). *Responding to grief: A complete resource guide.* Point Richmond: CA: Spirit of Health!

Gilbert, R. (1999). *Finding your way after your parent dies: Hope for adults.* Notre Dame: Ave Maria.

Oates, W. (1970). *When religion gets sick.* Philadelphia: Westminster.

Rando, T. (1993). *Treatment of complicated mourning.* Champaign: Research.

Roukema, R. (1997). *The soul in distress: What every pastoral counselor should know about emotional and mental illness.* Binghamton: Haworth.

Steere, D. (1997). *Spiritual presence in psychotherapy: A guide for caregivers.* Philadelphia: Brunner/Mazel.

Wilcock, P. (1997). *Spiritual care of dying and bereaved people.* Harrisburg: Morehouse.

Zurheide, J. (1997). *When faith is tested: Pastoral responses to suffering and death.* Minneapolis: Fortress.

SECTION V

Conclusion

CHAPTER 15
Spirituality in Nursing: Being in a Liminal Space

Cheryl Laskowski

This grounded theory research study explored the spiritual dimensions of nursing practice. Using grounded theory as a methodology and symbolic interaction as a sensitizing framework, 20 registered nurse participants were interviewed for this study. These participants, working in a wide variety of clinical settings, were asked to describe the spiritual dimensions of their nursing practice.

The vast majority of nurse participants highlighted their work with dying patients, the patients' family members, and sometimes nurse colleagues (Suffering Others) as being the experiences where their spirituality was most often manifested. The core category "Being in a Liminal Space" emerged from the data analysis.

Each nurse brings her/his personal history into spiritual encounters. Based on their personal history, most of the participants experienced positive dimensions of Openness and Vulnerability when being with Suffering Others. Nurse participants described the importance of both being and doing (labeled Comforting) with Suffering Others. Nursing occurs within a systems context; the findings from this study suggest that some settings (e.g., home, hospice) allow more room for nurturing the spiritual than do others (e.g., urban hospitals). This chapter addresses study findings and implications of these findings for nursing education and practice; systems changes that would create more room for "good deaths" are also identified.

BACKGROUND

The term spirituality is defined in numerous ways, including "not tangible or material," "concerned with or affecting the soul," and "pertaining to God" (Tormont Webster's Illustrated Dictionary, 1987, p. 1602). In their concept analysis of spirituality in nursing, Haase, Britt, Coward, Leidy, and Penn (1992) define spirituality as "an integrating creative energy based on belief in, and a feeling of connection with, a power greater than self" (p. 143). Stoll (1989), another early writer on the topic of spirituality in nursing, suggests that—given the multiple definitions of spirituality—an understanding of one's personal spiritual journey may be furthered by asking the question, "What is spirituality to me?"

Stoll (1989) further conceptualizes the spiritual as having both vertical and horizontal dimensions. The vertical dimensions are connected to an individual's relationship with a higher power, while the horizontal dimensions concern one's relationships with self, others, and nature. Barnum (1996) links spirituality with "a higher power" (p. 93). Watson (1999) incorporates the term spiritual in her description of the term transpersonal: ". . . a focus on the uniqueness of self and other coming together; moving from the fully embodied physical ego-self to deeper, more spiritual, transcendent even cosmic connections that tap into healing . . ." (p. 290). Reed (1992) called spirituality "a unique human capacity for self-transcendence that creates a fulfilling relatedness" (p. 349).

In actual day-to-day nursing practice, faced with multiple demands and declining resources, nurses are often left to make sense out of the inexplicable while they struggle to cope with the pain of illness, loss, and death. How do these front line health care providers maintain balance for themselves in the midst of turmoil? Some authors suggest that psychological mechanisms, in the form of stress management techniques, may not be enough. Arnold (1989), for example, notes that when faced with difficulties, nurses may journey beyond the psychological into the spiritual. Dossey, Keegan, Guzzetta, and Loklmeier (1995) differentiate the spiritual from the psychological by highlighting the transcendent nature of spirituality.

There is confusion in the medical literature (see, for example Koenig, 2000; Sloan et al., 2000) relating to the difference between the terms "spirituality" and "religion." For purposes of this study, I asked the nurse participants to describe the "spiritual" dimensions of their practice; although some participants did mention particular religious affiliations, most spoke about spirituality as being an experience separate from or in addition to organized religion. This study finding is consistent with distinctions made by O'Connor, Meakes, McCarroll-Butler, Gadowsky, and O'Neill (1997) who identified a distinction between spirituality and religiosity: "Religiosity is an expression of faith through the practices of a particular religion or denomination, while the predominant understanding of spirituality is meaning making" (p. 27).

STUDY

This qualitative research study explored the question: "How do nurses interpret the spiritual dimension of their practice?" Twenty registered nurse participants, having at least one year of practice experience, were interviewed for the study. Nineteen female participants and one male participant, ranging in age from 24 to 58, participated in semi-structured interviews designed to explore the participants' interpretations of the spiritual dimensions of their practice.

Symbolic interaction was used as the sensitizing framework for this qualitative study. Blumer (1969), considered by some to be the "father" of symbolic interaction, has written extensively about the interpretative process that guides individual action. Symbolic interaction also speaks to the social nature of interpretations. Human beings are recognized as responding to each other on the basis of this interpretative process, where meaning is generated, analyzed, and applied.

Grounded theory, a research method developed by Glaser and Strauss (1967), was used as the study methodology. Grounded theory provides a way of studying human interactions through a constant, comparative method. The methodology of grounded theory grew out of the theoretical framework of symbolic interaction, and is thus consistent with the tenets of symbolic interaction.

Snowball sampling was used to elicit participants working in a variety of clinical areas including: medical units, surgical units, intensive care units, cardiac care units, emergency rooms, parish nursing, hospice nursing, home care nursing, and obstetrical/neonatal settings. Human subjects permission was granted by the researcher's home institution. Each interview was audio-tape recorded and transcribed by the researcher. The researcher began coding the data using line-by-line analysis. Coding for categories and properties was next done, with the researcher comparing and contrasting data from all of the interviews.

A limited review of the literature was completed prior to the study; this preliminary literature review is represented in the background section above. After data collection and analysis, a secondary more thorough review of the literature was completed. The secondary review was incorporated throughout the study findings and discussion section of this chapter.

FINDINGS

Core Category

When asked to describe the spiritual dimension of their practice, the vast majority of the nurse participants emphasized their work with the dying and the bereaved. Working with dying patients (and their family members) led to the development of the core category, labeled "Being in a Liminal Space" (see Figure 1). Liminality, a term used by Van Gennep (1960) in reference to rites of passage, refers to the second stage of ritual transformation where one is separated from society and obtains new knowledge. More recent authors point to liminality as process rather than as stage (Murphy, Scheer, Murphy, & Mack, 1988). Liminality has been described elsewhere in the medical literature as a major category of the experience of cancer illness (Little, Jordens, Paul, Montgomery, & Philipson, 1998).

In the current study, the nurse participants described the strong personal impact of their work with dying clients. Working closely with dying individuals often forces nurses to experience their own vulnerability; concurrently, they have an opportunity to be more open to the experiences of others. This openness may lead to transformative moments that heighten the nurses' appreciation of life. Further, even as the nurses describe their immersion in the spiritual work of another's dying, the nurses also describe their need to "take care of other patients" and otherwise get on

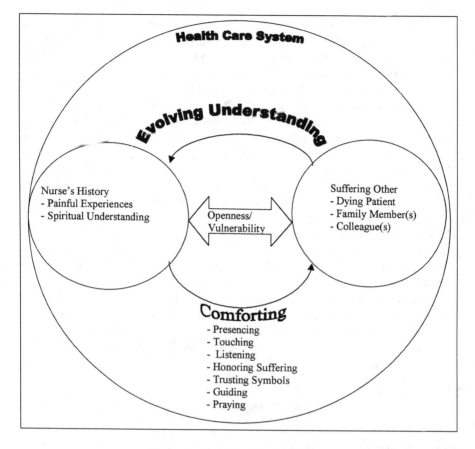

Figure 1. Being in a liminal space.

with the work of day-to-day life. The category of liminality captures this threshold, back and forth, dialectical experience described by the nurses in this study.

Another significant finding of this study was the active nature of nurses' spirituality. Nurses' understanding of the spiritual changes over time and in response to their experiences—both personal and professional. This Evolving Understanding occurs when the nurse is open to the other (be that patient, family member, or colleague). Increasing vulnerability and increasing openness co-existed for many of the nurses in this study. Vulnerability did not make most of the nurses in this study more withholding; rather it enhanced their practice, heightened their understanding of themselves, and expanded their appreciation of the world.

A surprising finding in this study was that many of the nurse participants did not share their spiritual beliefs or experiences with their colleagues; several participants expressed fears of being criticized or being otherwise labeled in a negative manner for their spiritual beliefs. This finding will be discussed further under "Discussion."

Nurses' History

Nurses' interpretations of spirituality involve the nurses' history, which is constantly in motion. Multiple understandings of the spiritual and personally painful experiences were part of the nurses' history. These understandings and experiences frequently motivated nurses to explore the spiritual dimensions of their lives and subsequently of their nursing practice.

Personally painful experiences were a call to choose between openness and distance; many of these participants expressed their ability to grow as a result of painful experiences. Two participants in this study, for example, spoke about their spiritual growth after the death of a child. Yet, one participant experienced some distress several years after the death of her mother and felt that this distress had caused her to distance herself from dying patients. Issues relating to health care provider's vulnerability are complex; these issues will be addressed further under "Discussion."

The finding that nurses' personal experiences influence their incorporation of the spiritual into practice has been addressed previously in the literature. Karns (1991) notes that, "the extent to which nurses can incorporate . . . spiritual care (into their practice) will be a direct reflection of their own ongoing spiritual work" (p. 12). In an earlier study, Benner (1984) remarks that "caring cannot be controlled or coerced . . . caring is embedded in personal and cultural meanings" (p. 170). The finding that spirituality involves each nurse's very personal history is, thus, consistent with the literature.

Nurses' Work with the Dying

By far, the most pronounced focus that emerged from this study was nurses' care for the dying, and those close to the dying. When asked to describe situations that exemplified the spiritual dimensions of their practice, the vast majority of participants spoke first and foremost about their experiences with dying patients, the families of dying patients, and at times—their colleagues (all categorized as "Suffering Others" in this research study). Nurses who work closely with dying patients and their families are often confronted with pain and suffering. They work to make sense of these feelings on both a psychological level and a spiritual level.

From the current study, being and doing were both recognized by the participants as important components of spiritual nursing care. The being/doing dialectic was evidenced throughout the participants' descriptions of spiritual nursing care. The intensity of this dialectic emerged throughout the nurses descriptions of their work with dying patients. The category of spiritual nursing care was labeled "Comforting" and was separated into the following properties: presencing, honoring suffering, listening, touching, trusting symbols, guiding, and praying.

Presencing was recognized by several participants as being an essential part of spiritual nursing care. Presence has been addressed elsewhere in the literature (Fredriksson, 1999) as involving "being with" and "being there." "Being there" speaks to the intersubjective and attentive component of presence (Osterman & Schwartz-Barcott, 1996); "being with" involves offering the gift of self (Pederson,

1993). For the purposes of this study, the "ing" ending was added to "presence," since the nurse participants often described this component of spiritual nursing care in a way that denoted movement and continuance over time. Presencing is exemplified by the following quote:

> How can you not be attached to a human being? Especially at the time of death. I mean, I've held peoples' hands when they have taken their last breath. . . . I've sat in the room and held their hand and told them "It's okay to die" and that "I'll make sure that your family knows that you weren't alone."

Presencing involved being with and being there, in the moment, and often in silence. The use of silent presence is especially important with dying patients who are experiencing a changing worldview, the physical limitations imposed by advanced disease, and the "lifetime of experience that we are only able to access in limited ways" (Aranda, 1998, p. 27).

Honoring Suffering was seen as another way of being with dying individuals and their family members. Honoring Suffering involved getting to know the illness story of the dying person and appreciating the pain that was associated with the story and with the anticipated and/or current loss. Honoring Suffering was described by one participant in the following manner:

> I worked in a Level One Trauma Center. There was an 18-year-old boy who had an argument with his girlfriend and she went to take off in a truck and he jumped onto the front of the truck and fell backwards and hit his head. And she took off and didn't know that he had been severely injured when he had hit the back of his head. . . . They did practically everything they could to save him. He ended up being brain dead. And it was one of my early experiences in nursing because I (had) never worked as a floor nurse. I went there right from graduation. . . . So, I had to ask the mother for an organ donation. And she ended up consenting and a couple of months later I got a card from her with little angels all over it. And she said, "God Bless You." And that she was really happy that I was there for her and I didn't really think that I had done anything for her, but obviously she felt that I did. I still keep the card.

In his hallmark book, *The Illness Narratives,* Kleinman (1988) speaks about "empathic witnessing . . . of the patient's and family's stories of the illness" (p. 10) as a central component of clinical work. Frank (1998) articulates the idea of honoring suffering when speaking about how health care providers can best work with the deeply ill. Frank (1998) tells us:

> To work with the deeply ill, I believe a clinician must be able to honor suffering. Honoring suffering shapes the spirit of helping. The helper who honors suffering can accept the "dark night of the soul" but also offers the immediate, practical help others need. Part of this help is recognizing that people are telling the story they need to tell, for a while, before they can move on. (p. 209)

Listening was addressed as another spiritual nursing intervention by several of the study participants. One nurse spoke of how she discovered the importance of listening:

> I don't remember how we (the dying patient and the nurse) started talking. I was there everyday and I was teaching an LPN how to do the flushes and the lines and so forth. And I think that it was just the spending time. You know . . . a lot of it was the listening . . . after I had listened for so long and she would feel comfort when I was there to listen and she was able to voice her thoughts and have somebody just to listen. Finally, I realized that this is a function, this is effective, this is helping her, this is helping me. I grew out of the experience.

The importance of Listening has also been addressed previously in the literature. Koshy (1989), an early writer in this area, spoke of listening as "a deliberate, active behavior; paying attention to the speaker; more than receiving sounds or words; it demands conscious effort; searching for meaning and understanding" (p. 28). True listening involves silence on the part of the listener (Eckes, 1996; Gibbons, 1993; Perry, 1996).

In addition to listening and communicating verbally, many of the study participants communicated their presence through the language of touch. Touching was generally described as physical, as in the following statement:

> I'll think nothing of walking into a patient's room and fluffing a pillow, you know? I mean, it takes all of two seconds. Sometimes, there's that little old lady who needs you to hold her hand for a second. You know, while you're assessing her, maybe listening to her lungs or her belly, what's to say you can't stand there or bend over her bed and hold her hand while you're doing it? It takes a few seconds.

Touching could also be non-physical, however, as for the following participant who describes her work using therapeutic touch (see Krieger, 1979) with individuals who are dying. This participant teaches interested family members how to do therapeutic touch for the dying person as well. This participant stated:

> We use our hands a lot, not just to describe what's going on as an adjunct to how we speak, but when we're talking to a patient, I don't think that we even realize how we are caressing them, their body space. Not necessarily even having to touch them, although sometimes we do.

Another nursing intervention, labeled "Trusting Symbols," emerged from the data analysis. The phrase "Trusting Symbols" was used to represent the belief identified by several study participants who understood certain occurrences and/or objects as having a meaning behind the obvious. There was a sense of transcendence in Trusting Symbols in that the symbols represented some experience that could not be quantified or explained. Trusting Symbols became a type of intervention when the symbolic meaning of an event or circumstance was shared with another. One nurse, for example, recounted a tale of unsuccessfully performing CPR on a critically ill man:

> And so, all through this code, we weren't paying any attention to what was going on with him (other than the CPR). Well, in his hand, after he died and we were doing his aftercare . . . it must have been near Easter because he had a napkin in his hand that said "He is risen." And it was just the weirdest feeling. All of us had it in the room. We should have just paid attention to that in the first place, you know?

In the above vignette, the same nurse later spoke more about her belief that the patient had predicted his own death. Dossey (1999, p. 133) uses the term "prophecy" from the Latin words meaning "to speak before" to describe this type of precognition.

Another study participant, who leads bereavement groups for parents of children who have died, spoke about the importance of encouraging others to Trust Symbols:

> When I talk to parents I say "If you ever question whether there is a message or whether your child is trying to give you a message, then it's probably real." That we, naturally question things that we don't see, feel, hear, that can't be scientifically tested. So, this one mom would pray for a dream. And she'd come back month after month saying that she was hoping for a dream and then one month she came back and said that she had a dream and her daughter had come to her and said, "It's important that you know I'm okay. It's really important. The accident, I didn't feel anything." (The daughter) had been driving in a car and there was a flat bed truck and it sheered off the top of her car and she died instantly. And the real horrible connotations of that. So, it was really important to (this mom) that her daughter was doing okay. And, it really has kept her. It was the gift that she got and she's been able to know that just from the dream. And even though I know that it can (sound) scary, I have not had a parent who has had contact with their child, somehow or other, who has been afraid. I've really not. So, it hasn't been something that by asking the question "does anyone think that they've been in contact with their child?," never in all the years that I have been doing this, have I had someone say "Oh, I wish you hadn't started talking to me about that."

Two participants recommended the book *Final Gifts* (Callanan & Kelley, 1992) to help family members interpret the language of their dying loved ones. These two study participants, and others who commonly dealt with dying patients (such as in hospice settings), had additional specific advice for families. This advice, labeled "Guiding" in the current study, is exemplified by the following quote:

> (I work at) getting the family to understand that this (death) is a normal occurrence. That they have given their love and support, and that it's hard to let go, but sometimes that the best gift we can give to this person is being able to say, "I give you my permission. I know that you are here and I don't want you to struggle any longer. And if you need to go right now, that's okay." And being able to turn to the patient who is in the bed and telling the family, "Now, I don't know you as a family, so I can't perceive how you have carried on in your daily life, but I encourage you to do whatever you need to do for this to be special and meaningful for you. Because this is your gift to him and this is his gift to you. And even though he won't be able to let you know that he hears, he will likely hear, so speak to him if you need, cry if you need, climb into bed and cuddle him if that's what you would normally do."

In his book *Dying Well*, Byock (1997) identifies "the five things of relationship completion—saying 'I forgive you'; 'forgive me'; 'thank you'; 'I love you' and 'goodbye.'" Guiding families in sharing relationship completion phrases was used as a spiritual intervention by three of the participants. The Five Wishes tool, available through Aging with Dignity, can also be used to facilitate relationship completion as well as end of life decision making (www.agingwithdignity.org).

Several participants also mentioned Praying as being important in working with dying individuals and their family members; some nurses would describe Praying quietly during a stressful event or before going to work. Some participants would also pray with individuals or encourage others to pray:

> One of the nurses recently, her mother was diagnosed with breast cancer and you could tell that one day at work she was at her wit's end and I said, "Why don't you pray about it? Say a prayer if all else fails," I said. "You may not get your answer right away, but praying helps people."

Dossey (1996) spoke of prayer as coming from the Latin "precarius," meaning to obtain by begging and "precari," meaning to beseech or implore. Theologian Ann Ulanov and Professor Barry Ulanov (1988) have described prayer as "primary speech" in that it is the most important, fundamental language that humans speak.

Systems Factors

Nursing care occurs within the context of a large health care system. Systems factors such as adequate staffing, time to spend with patients and their families, appropriate physical arrangements (e.g., a hospice room or minimally a single bed hospital room for dying patients), and the availability of system supports (e.g., pastoral care) were described by the nurse participants as facilitating the provision of spiritual nursing care. Table 1 describes specific Systems Factors that were described by the nurse participants as negatively impacting upon the spiritual dimension of nursing practice.

DISCUSSION

Implications For Nursing Practice

In an article on nurses caring for dying patients, Lev (1994) points to two main factors that promote nurses' psychological well-being on the job—satisfaction and system support. The majority of the nurse participants in this study clearly experienced satisfaction from interacting with dying patients and their family members, but recognized few system supports for this work. In part, the reluctance of these nurses to discuss the spiritual dimensions of their practice may have hindered potential support; however, and more likely, the systems limitations of time, rigidity, and excessive technology leave little room for nurturing the spiritual dimensions of nursing practice.

In a recent study, Maeve (1998) describes an initial study assumption that "nurses live with dying patients in ways that inform their lives, both personally and professionally" (p. 1136). Maeve goes on to speak to the inherent embodiment of nurses who are fully present in their work with the dying. These embodied nurses "recognize and associate, wholly, the experience of the other" (p. 1137). The findings from Maeve's (1998) naturalistic study speak to the point that "caring for these patients was an integral part of who (the nurses) were as whole human beings" (p. 1138). The metaphor of weaving a fabric of moral meaning emerged from Maeve's data analysis.

Table 1. Problematic Systems Factors

Time	"We are expected to do, not one on two care, but one on 20." "You don't have quality time to spend with patients." "There is not enough time." "Time is a big, big factor. And I think that it's going to get worse before it gets better."
Rigid settings	"In the hospital it seems more rigid and more sterile (than in the home-based setting). You don't have as many resources or supports in that way it seems." "Going to work in the hospital situation where I am working . . . it is a very constrained model. It's very physical, very concrete, and that is changing but—you know—it takes time." "For any kind of new concept in (health care)—it seems to take at least ten years to get things birthed."
Lack of knowledge (re: EOL care)	"I don't think that nursing school prepares you for dealing with death." "We don't talk about death in this society. We don't talk about how to act when someone is dying." "Well, we had Kübler-Ross and death and dying and that kind of thing (in school). But that was it, that was where you were supposed to stay within those stages, and not get into too much and that was it."
Lack of support	". . . You don't feel comfortable talking amongst your peers about it (the spiritual dimension of nursing practice)." "A lot of times, I think that we forget about . . .support(ing) one another."
Technology	"As we get into more technology, maybe we are moving away from that personal human touch, which is kind of scary."

In another recent study of spirituality in hospice and oncology nurses, the authors found that 96 percent of the nurse respondents (*n* = 813) noted that patients had influenced their spirituality; 67 percent of the respondents rated this influence as "substantial" (Highfield, Taylor, & Amenta, 2000, p. 57).

Although the current study did not specifically ask nurses to describe their work with dying patients, the data that emerged from this study supports the findings from Maeve (1998) and Highfield et al. (2000). Most of these nurse participants in the current study described personally painful life experiences that moved them to become more open and vulnerable in their interactions with dying patients and the patients' family members. The vast majority of participants in this study recognized their openness and vulnerability as positive parts of a fulfilling life. As in the studies by Maeve (1998) and Highfield et al. (2000), the nurses in the current study described their very selves as changing based on their nursing experiences with the dying.

In analyzing the concept of vulnerability, Daniel (1998, p. 191) spoke of vulnerability as "a vehicle for practicing authentic nursing." It should be noted, however, that vulnerability may not always be helpful for the nurse. Vulnerability has been recognized as a negative experience by some (Rogers, 1997). In this study, one nurse participant experienced her own vulnerability as detrimental. She described her mother's painful death from cancer seven years earlier, and her movement into nursing as a direct result of that loss. This nurse, who simultaneously worked with hospice patients and med-surg unit patients, described feeling overwhelmed by the emotional demands of her work and was considering leaving her work setting to find less emotionally taxing work. This participant highlights the problematic aspect of vulnerability, as vulnerability may lead to more openness or to more distance. Further research is needed to explore the paradoxical nature of vulnerability.

Implications for Systems

Not surprisingly, hospice was described by the nurses in this study as being the environment most conducive to spiritual work with the dying. In part, this may be due to the self-selection process regarding the nurses who choose to work at hospice; in addition, the multi-disciplinary team approach that is typical of hospice settings and the socialization of nurses (and other health care providers) to the hospice philosophy, create conditions ripe for a non-technological approach to dying (Rasmussen, Sandman, & Norberg, 1997).

In the current study, home care settings fared better than hospitals as spaces where there is room for spiritual nursing care to be delivered; however, there is evidence that time and personnel constraints may now be negatively impacting upon the practice of home care nurses. Community hospitals were seen as more receptive to spirituality than were urban hospitals. When exploring this difference with the nurse participants, I was told that in smaller community hospitals, people tend to know each other since they frequent the same schools, churches, and businesses. In urban settings, people are less likely to be known to each other.

Overall, the nurse participants in this study addressed the need to create more humanistic systems; these systems would literally and figuratively create a sacred space in which to care for the dying and their significant others. Participants highlighted the need for more system support in the form of collaborative, multi-disciplinary practice and adequate staffing. The need for more time to spend with patients/families was emphasized by many participants, as was the need for flexibility within systems (e.g., offering open "visiting" hours). Three participants also critiqued the paternalism of the health care system, and addressed the need for honesty with patients.

Implications for Education

In terms of educational systems, many of the participants identified the paucity of nursing education relating to end of life care as being problematic. Several participants recommended incorporating more information about end of life care into the nursing curriculum. It should be noted that there currently is a movement to incorporate more end of life information into undergraduate nursing programs.

There is also some discussion in the nursing literature about teaching spirituality. Since personal experience is such a large part of spiritual growth, one might ask about whether spirituality can even be taught in a classroom setting. In a paper describing barriers to teaching spirituality in a classroom setting, McSherry and Draper (1997) noted that the

> necessity for self-awareness will mean that individuals' attitudes and understandings of the concept need to be explored and often challenged, which can be a very daunting and threatening undertaking, in the sense that one's personal beliefs and ideologies can be brought into question. (p. 416)

As a faculty member teaching a course called "Spirituality in Health Care" (developed as a result of this research), I recognize and appreciate McSherry and Draper's (1997) concerns. It has been my experience, after co-facilitating two semesters of this course, that feelings (especially fear, sadness, and anxiety) and beliefs were aroused much more strongly in this course than in other nursing/health care courses that I have taught. Having a faculty colleague (Charles Sabatino, Professor of Philosophy) co-facilitate the course was invaluable both in assisting with in-class process issues, as well as in providing mutual feedback relating to the faculty members' personal issues/concerns. There are, of course, educational systems factors in place that discourage this type of team teaching.

The Good Death

As nurses who work with the dying, we may ask ourselves what is a "good death" from our own perspective and from the perspectives of our patients. As health care providers, we must remain cautious about projecting our own ideas about the good death onto others (McNamara, Waddell, & Colvin, 1994). Byock (1997) suggests that a good death is as personal and unique as a good life.

"Dying can push us from the superficial into the depths very quickly so that it is often only at death that we find out what we really mean" (English, 1998, p. 86). In a phenomenological study of nurses caring for dying patients (Rittman, Paige, Rivera, Sutphin, & Godwin, 1997), the nurse participants described themselves as "privileged" in having the opportunity to be involved "in one of life's most significant experiences." Experiencing the dying of others can take us to previously unexamined places, in our personal lives and in our clinical practice. Being in a liminal space is a call to live fully, to be mindfully present, and to become immersed in our spirituality—however we experience it.

REFERENCES

Aranda, S. (1998). Palliative care principles: Masking the complexity of practice. In J. Parker & S. Aranda (Eds.), *Palliative care: Explorations and challenges* (pp. 21-31). Sydney: Maclennan & Petty.

Arnold, E. (1989). Burnout as a spiritual issue: Rediscovering meaning in nursing practice. In V. Carson (Ed.), *Spiritual dimensions of nursing practice* (pp. 320-353). Philadelphia: W. B. Saunders Co.

Barnum, B. S. (1996). *Spirituality in nursing: From traditional to new age.* New York: Springer.

Benner, P. (1984). *From novice to expert.* Menlo Park, CA: Addison Wesley.

Blumer, H. (1969). *Symbolic interactionism: Perspective and method.* Englewood Cliffs, NJ: Prentice-Hall.

Byock, I. (1997). *Dying well: Peace and possibilities at the end of life.* New York: Riverhead Books.

Callanan, M., & Kelley, P. (1992). *Final gifts: Understanding the special awareness, needs, and communications of the dying.* New York: Bantam Books.

Daniel, L. (1998). Student scholarship: Vulnerability as a key to authenticity. *Image—Journal of Nursing Scholarship, 30*(2), 191-192.

Dossey, B., Keegan, L., Guzzetta, C., & Loklmeier, L. (1995). *Holistic nursing: A handbook for practice* (2nd ed.). Gaithersburg, MD: Aspen Publications.

Dossey, L. (1996). *Healing words: The power of prayer and the practice of medicine.* New York: HarperCollins.

Dossey, L. (1999). *Reinventing medicine: Beyond mind-body to a new era of healing.* San Francisco: Harper.

Eckes, L. M. (1996). Active listening. *Gastroenterology Nursing, 6,* 219-220.

English, G. (1998). This is it! An approach to spirituality. In J. Parker & S. Aranda (Eds.), *Palliative care: Explorations and challenges* (pp. 85-100). Sydney: Maclennan & Petty.

Frank, A. (1998). Just listening: Narrative and deep illness. *Families, Systems & Health, 16*(3), 197-212.

Fredriksson, L. (1999). Modes of relating in a caring conversation: A research synthesis on presence, touch, and listening. *Journal of Advanced Nursing, 30*(5), 1167-1176.

Gibbons, M. B. (1993). Listening to the lived experience of loss. *Pediatric Nursing, 6,* 597-599.

Glaser, B., & Strauss, A. (1967). *The discovery of grounded theory: Strategies for qualitative research.* New York: Aldine.

Haase, J., Britt, T., Coward, D., Leidy, N. K., & Penn, P. (1992). Simultaneous concept analysis of spiritual perspective, hope, acceptance and self-transcendence. *IMAGE: Journal of Nursing Scholarship, 24*(2), 141-147.

Karns, P. (1991). Building a foundation for spiritual care. *Journal of Christian Nursing, 8*(3), 10-13.

Highfield, M., Taylor, E., & Amenta, M. (2000). Preparation to care: The spiritual education of oncology and hospice nurses. *Journal of Hospice and Palliative Nursing, 2*(2), 53-63.

Kleinman, A. (1988). *The illness narratives: Suffering, healing, and the human condition.* New York: Basic Books.

Koenig, H. (2000). Religion, spirituality, and medicine: Application to clinical practice. *Journal of the American Medical Association, 284*(13), 1708.

Krieger, D. (1979). *The therapeutic touch: How to use your hands to help or to heal.* Englewood Cliffs, NJ: Prentice Hall.

Koshy, K. (1989). I only have ears for you . . . active listening. *Nursing Times, 85*(30), 26-29.

Lev, E. (1994). Issues for the nurse caring for dying patients. *Oncology Nursing, 1*(1), 1-10.

Little, M., Jordens, C., Paul, K., Montgomery, K., & Philipson, B. (1998). Liminality: A major category of the experience of cancer illness. *Social Science and Medicine, 47*(10), 1485-1494.

Maeve, K. (1998). Weaving a fabric of moral meaning: How nurses live with suffering and death. *Journal of Advanced Nursing, 27*(6), 1136-1142.

McNamara, B., Waddell, C., & Colvin, M. (1994). The institutionalization of the good death. *Social Science and Medicine, 39*(11), 1501-1508.

McSherry, W., & Draper, P. (1997). The spiritual dimension: Why the absence within nursing curricula? *Nurse Education Today, 17*(5), 413-417.

Murphy, R., Scheer, J., Murphy, Y., & Mack, R. (1988). Physical disability and social liminality: A study in the rituals of adversity. *Social Science & Medicine, 26*(2), 235-242.

O'Connor, T., Meakes, E., McCarroll-Butler, P., Gadowsky, S., & O'Neill, K. (1997). Making the most and making sense: Ethnographic research on spirituality in palliative care. *The Journal of Pastoral Care, 51*(1), 25-36.

Osterman, P., & Schwartz-Barcott, D. (1996). Presence: Four ways of being there. *Nursing Forum, 2*, 23-30.

Pederson, C. (1993). Presence as a nursing intervention with hospitalized children. *Maternal-Child Journal, 3*, 75-81.

Perry, B. (1996). Influence of nurse gender on the use of silence, touch and humour. *International Journal of Palliative Nursing, 2*, 7-14.

Rasmussen, B. (1997). Stories of being a hospice nurse: A journey towards finding one's footing. *Cancer Nursing, 20*(5), 330-341.

Rasmussen, B., Sandman, P., & Norberg, A. (1997). Stories of being a hospice nurse: A journey towards finding one's footing. *Cancer Nursing, 20*(5), 330-341.

Reed, P. (1992). An emerging paradigm for the investigation of spirituality in nursing. *Research in Nursing and Health, 15*, 349-357.

Rittman, M., Paige, P., Rivera, J., Sutphin, L., & Godwin, I. (1997). Phenomenological study of nurses caring for dying patients. *Cancer Nursing, 20*(2), 115-119.

Rogers, A. (1997). Vulnerability, health and health care. *Journal of Advanced Nursing, 26*, 65-72.

Sloan, R., Bagiella, E., VandeCreek, L., Hover, M., Casalone, C., Hirsch, T., Hasan, Y., Kreger, R., & Poulos, P. (2000). Should physicians prescribe religious activities? *New England Journal of Medicine, 342*(25), 1913-1916.

Stoll, R. (1989). The essence of spirituality. In V. Carson (Ed.), *Spiritual dimensions of nursing practice* (pp. 4-23). Philadelphia: W. B. Saunders.

Ulanov, A., & Ulanov, B. (1988). *Primary speech: A psychology of prayer.* Louisville, KY: John Knox Press.

Van Gennep, A. (1960). *The rites of passage.* Chicago: University of Chicago Press.

Watson, J. (1999). *Postmodern nursing.* New York: Churchill Livingstone.

CHAPTER 16

Spirituality and Loss

Gerry R. Cox

Spiritual growth is a journey. Most of us grow from our childhood view of the spiritual world to a more rational view that we call adult. Perhaps, the child's view is more comforting and satisfying. As adults, we can learn from children. What we can offer children is what we have learned in our own journey. For each of us, the journey is different. Our experiences cause our view of spirituality to be different.

All of us face losses. Adults can help children learn to manage those losses. Adults can help other adults to manage those losses. Children can help adults to mange their losses. One's spirituality can be an important component in that learning process.

The pattern of universe is such that to have life to continue, there will need to be loss and death. Losses are constant. No one lives in this world without loss and its hurt. Friends move away; people die; songs are forgotten; graduations occur; teachers change jobs, schools, or move away; toys get broken; and imaginary friends cease to exist. The world of each of us is filled with beauty and goodness. But we will only see the beauty and goodness if they have the eyes to behold the beauty and goodness that surrounds us. How can we learn to see ourselves or to teach others to see the beauty of an old, wrinkled face, the pains, or even the slums? Beauty is not just what Hollywood portrays as beauty. Beauty is what we see spiritually.

For most, unless the loss is a painful event or an ecstatic event, it is given little thought. Yet, loss may lead to growth. Loss and growth, death and life are as much a part of our lives as food and drink. Each person must learn that loss and growth are partners. One cannot experience growth without loss. In marriages, couples need some conflict to experience growth. As adult relationships may have pain that leads to growth, so too do those of children. The person who is grieving a loss may ask others questions that are painful and confronting when they are in pain. We need to listen to the pain of our loved ones without judging or lecturing on the rightness or wrongness of their reactions (McKissock, 1998, pp. 111-112). We may suffer dramatically over the loss of a favorite toy, a pet, or the loss our house to a fire or other disaster and show little emotion over the death of a loved one. Our public reaction to the loss does not necessarily reflect the magnitude of the loss. Our grief for the toy or pet or even our grief for a person who was distant from us may be an outlet for other losses that occurred long ago (Gilbert, 1999, p. 89).

Not all losses are of the same magnitude or kind, some losses are barely noticeable while others are overwhelming. One can observe the loss of limy greenness of aspen leaf as it makes way for the shimmering gold of a brilliant fall. A caterpillar goes into darkness and silence of the cocoon and ceases to be a caterpillar and becomes instead a brilliant butterfly that will offer beauty to others. Fields are plowed under to allow the growth of new crops. Our own bodies are constantly repairing and recreating themselves. Cuts and bruises repair themselves. New cells constantly replace dead cells. Even within our bodies, one can observe loss and growth, life and death. Our bodies also age. With that aging comes losses of shape, hair, youth, smoothness of skin, and much more.

We may or may not understand this process, but we need to try to understand the process of loss and growth to be able to aid grieving others and ourselves.

LOSS AND GROWTH AND THE SEASONS OF LIFE

James E. Miller, in *Wintergrief, Summer Grace: Returning to Life After a Loved One Dies* (1995), uses the seasons of life to describe the grief process. Loss and growth proceed each season of our lives. Our first loss may occur when we pass out of the protection of the womb into the world. Other losses occur when we venture into the tumult of school, when we leave the simplicity of the world of our family to doing lessons, performances, and getting along with people who were previously strangers to us. As we gain in experiences and learning, we leave childhood and enter into adolescence where people begin to expect us to act more grown up. Our bodies begin to change. Our child's body grows and changes. As the child is being lost, we vacillate between our childhood dependence and our demand for adult independence. We begin to expand our intellectual and emotional experience. This process continues throughout our life. As we get older, we develop a perspective on loss. As we lose objects, persons, dreams, positions, we learn that each experience is never the same as the previous loss. Each loss is unique. When we grieve, the loss of the object is not the same as what the object meant to us. Humans engage in meaning-making to make sense out of their lives and the events that occur in one's life. Janice Winchester Nadeau indicates that reality is always experienced through the meaning that we give it (1998, p. 3). For the individual, each loss is unique because as one connects with people, objects, ideas, wishes, values, images, and roles, the person will give them great power. One's identity is formed through these connections that are made. Objects, people, images, values, roles, ideas, and wishes are invested with meaning and symbolic importance. If one loses any of these connections, they lose not only the thing itself or person, but also what it represented to the person and the meaning that he or she invested in it. If a person loses a job, he or she may grieve profoundly over the loss of not just a job, but also the income, prestige, the reason to get up in the morning. Few realize how much they have invested in something until they lose it.

Why should children be any different? Mother will always be there. My life is great. It will stay this way, only it does not stay that way. Mothers leave. Mothers die.

Change always brings loss, even when change is welcomed. The child who goes to school for the first time may want to go to school. Going to school for first time may have been a greatly anticipated event for both the child and the parents. Yet both parent and child suffer loss when the event takes place. Few children dread graduation. Many cannot wait for graduation to occur; yet, when it happens, they experience loss whether it is from kindergarten, elementary school, high school, or college.

RESPONSE TO LOSS

Just as our losses are unique to each of us, so are our ways of coping with loss. As children, we often imitated our parent's ways of grieving. Over time, each of us learned a particular ways of coping. Each time we use a pattern of coping, it becomes more deeply ingrained in our pattern of responding to loss. Over time, we come to believe that we do not have choice in how we respond. Yet, we made choices that got us to where we are now. We need to learn to make choices that lead to healthy coping.

As we are humans, we are also imperfect people. Our parents, grandparents, siblings, teachers, also being imperfect, may have taught us and rewarded us for ways of behaving that later did not work well for us. Our adult task is to examine what we have learned, hold on to what is healthy, and discard what is not.

Many unhealthy ways of coping begin with such messages as, "Boys don't cry," "Don't be a sissy," "Be my little man." Some ways of coping seem to be fairly common. Consider how your coping styles play in your own life, and then consider how they would play in the lives of children. There are many patterns of coping that we may use. A few examples follow.

Denial or disbelief is a common reaction to loss. I have trouble accepting a death until I see the body. Perhaps seeing the body gives time to accept the reality of the loss and to adjust to the change. This is not necessarily all bad, but if one stays in denial or disbelief, it may not be such a good coping style.

Anger is also a common reaction when faced with our own inability to control forces in our life. Anger often happens when it seems that we need control for our own happiness and well-being. If something occurs which seems to threaten our happiness and well-being, we often react with anger. Typically, we blame others for our pain or misfortune. Blame is often attributed to someone who was not involved. A child may blame his or her mother for the father's death because she prepared the food that led to his cholesterol problem. Did she make him eat the food? Did she prepare foods that he wanted to eat? Perhaps he insisted she prepare the food. Anger as any emotion can be quite healthy for us. A little rage can make one feel a lot better more quickly than most coping techniques. Directed anger can be harmful. We can be angry at God, the physician, the person who died, or whoever. The person who is angry often takes his or her anger out on others. If the dying child throws his or her food at us, it is not us they are angry at, but they are angry at the pending loss of life. Children, like adults, need to use anger constructively. Many positive coping styles exist. Some, like former President Ronald Reagan, chop firewood. I run. Others hit a punching bag. Children play.

Guilt is another common method of coping. All of us, and especially children, are especially prone to guilt. Children have great imaginations. Adults also have excellent imaginations, but generally they suppress them. Magical thinking can easily make a child think they caused the illness or death. "I wanted her bedroom," "Mom said I would be the death of her yet." Even if you or another person was negligent and another person died, it is important to remember: 1) you did not intend for the death to occur; 2) you would have changed the situation if you could have done so; and 3) the person who died made decisions as well; you cannot control what others do.

Sadness is also a common style of coping. Whenever life takes away or asks us to let go of something that we have recognized as part of us, we can expect sadness.

Unfortunately, no magic formula or scientific scale can tell us how a person will react when something is lost from their life. There are many other reactions that may rage within us including fear, confusion, despair, loneliness.

We must be careful when judging the value of someone else's loss. We may grieve more for a pet than grandparent. We may grieve more for a person that we greatly admired than for a relative. A dear friend may be grieved more than a spouse. An ex-spouse may cause us to have grief that is surprising to others. We must also be careful when judging the techniques of coping used by another. Whatever method we use is not necessarily better than ones used by others. We also cannot see the heart of another. A loss that on surface should be devastating may not be, while a loss than seems trivial may devastate. Broken hearts cannot be see with a MRI.

Each of us needs to ask ourselves a number of questions.

1. How were you taught to cope with losses?
2. When you were a child, what did your parents or significant others tell you about showing your emotions?
3. What are the losses in your own life that you are having trouble releasing?
4. Are you willing to see the treasure of your own life and that your life is filled with opportunities for growth through the losses that you have experienced?

EACH LOSS IS AN OPPORTUNITY

Response to loss is a sign that life is happening through everything that we experience. Our own life history is filled with loss and opportunities for growth, for wholeness, and for holiness. Each life is filled with burdens and blessings. We cannot minimize the burdens and blessings that we experience. Losses are opportunities for us to grow. No one can control the losses in one's life, but each person can control how he or she reacts to them. The parable of wheat grain indicates that one must die to grow. One must experience loss to grow. Would you want to remain as you were in the womb? Would you want to remain a two-year-old child? Stay in elementary school until you retire?

HOW DO WE GROW THROUGH LOSSES?

In each of our experiences of loss, one can move toward life or death. Yet most of us do not see that we have choices. All of us need to be made aware of our choices. Most of us want to believe, at least secretly, that losses are unnecessary. We want to believe that our lives will never change; yet, change always occurs whether we want changes or not. We often focus our attention on the positive aspects of our life and thus avoid facing losses or perhaps we view the loss as an aberration. We hear of the losses of others and pretend that they will not happen to us, but they will. No one teaches us that the only way to new growth is through loss. No one tells us that loss is normal and natural. No one tells us that the only time change stops is after death. And no one shows us how to cope with loss in any organized, useful manner. Did anyone tell you about the trials and tribulations of dating and courtship before you began dating? Did anyone tell you the rules of using the car in your family before you got your license? Did anyone tell you about bullies and friendship and users and givers before you started making friends? Not being prepared for losses as children is common in most cultures. Preparing our children for loss is not that different than our failures to prepare our children for other of life's travails, but we can help prepare them. As adults or children, we all need to be aware of life's blessing and burdens.

As tragic, untimely, dreaded, and feared as loss and death may be, none of us will ever be able to avoid them. No matter how much we try to avoid loss and death, we cannot stop them from occurring. We can begin to acknowledge the losses in our own lives and to live and grow through them. Then we can better help others with their losses. By choosing to grow through small losses, we can then make better choices when big losses occur. All of us grow with the same process. Life is the continuous process of choice-making.

Every choice that one makes is another choice that one cannot make. If I buy a new car, the cost of the car is not the payment, but the trips, vacations, clothes, gifts, and so forth that I cannot purchase because I am making a car payment. Each choice that we make impacts future choices as well. If I choose to begin to smoke at thirteen, I may later experience shortness of breath or illnesses because of my earlier choice. We must all learn that choices have consequences. To truly make a choice, one must be aware of those consequences both good and bad. To begin to smoke without an awareness of consequences is not really a choice. Others model our behavior. We should know the consequences and help others make better choices by providing good role models.

WAYS TO HELP OTHERS DEVELOP STYLES
OF HEALTHY GRIEVING

1. Grieving begins when we openly acknowledge what has been lost.
2. Healthy grieving begins when we express whatever feelings and emotions that are called forth when we acknowledge the loss. No emotion is wrong. What we do with emotions is more important.

3. If we are healthy in our grieving, we need to choose to change the things we do that keep us tied to the lost person or object. We must finally choose to let go. Children who have experienced the death of a parent may want to go through the parent's belongings at some point. This can be the final farewell. Please remember that they may choose to keep some things that are seemingly of no value and to give away or sell things that clearly should be kept by them. A widow may give her children the house when she needs a place to live. What they choose to keep is part of their meaning and relationship with the deceased. As an adult, you can keep other items for them that they will appreciate later, but remember, also keep the items that they select.

THINGS TO DO WITH THOSE WHO EXPERIENCE LOSS

There are many things that we can do to aid those who experience loss.

1. Create a sacred place. This can be a memory room or spot in a room or hall. It can be a place to keep items of value to the child and to you in a visible, open place.

2. Journaling or story-telling is another technique to manage loss. Depending upon their age, try to get the person to write a journal of their journey through grief, or if they are young to chronicle through drawings or other art forms. Drawing or writing can be a process of discovery. If you draw or write for any length of time, you will probably state what is in your heart and your mind. You will unearth much that you may not recognize about your own grief for your losses.

3. Humor is an excellent coping mechanism. Laughter helps us find inner peace. Humorous stories, particularly about ourselves, are perhaps the easier form of humor to use to aid the grieving or the dying. Humor is not the absence of sadness. Humor allows us to view our situations with a different lens, to not take ourselves and our lives so seriously. Laughter helps us find inner peace. Humorous stories, particularly about ourselves, are perhaps the easier form of humor to use to aid the grieving or the dying. This is not laughing at other people, but laughing with other people.

4. Music, like other art forms, heals. The particular style of music to be used with a person depends upon that person. Your favorite music may not help them manage their loss, but it could help you manage yours. Each of us tends to find most satisfying the kind of music that we enjoyed while growing up. The heartbeat of the universe may be expressed with the beat of the music. It can speak to us in ways that can reach our inner existence. It can mirror our own heartbeat.

5. Art, drama, puppeteering, clay, drawing, painting, and other forms of expression like journaling may aid children who are attempting to cope with loss.

6. Friendship is a powerful form of coping. People may be the best source of help. Friends share their joys and their sorrows. Few of us have lives that we would want to trade with others.

7. Acceptance is also a coping tool. We must learn to accept each person as he or she is, trust his or her judgment while recognizing that each person, like us, will make mistakes. When your daughter or son chooses a spouse, do not second guess their

choice. It is their choice. If you show acceptance and trust, your relationship will be strong. If you question their choice, you will strain your relationship.

8. Balance may also help. Life is a series of blessings and burdens. One must find balance in one's own life. This can mean that one should find the place in life, the job, or vocation that one is called to serve. If one focuses upon making money, one may miss the career that would have offered joy and purpose to one's life. If one commits suicide because of youthful failures, one may miss the joy and purpose of one's life as a grandparent much later.

9. Love is another tool to help manage loss. People need each other. We cannot survive without one another. Family, friends, spiritual friends give life meaning and purpose. Knowing that friends and family will be there for you is a valuable lesson for children. Love is freely given in spite of mistakes. None of us is perfect. Children are loved in spite of their errors. Learning our heritage is part of this sharing of love. Stories about the great grandmother who died when you were an infant may show the love that she felt for you even though you no longer remember her. The quilt that she made or some other treasure may be a visible sign of her love.

10. Harmony and security can create a sense of harmony and security for the person experiencing loss. One needs to be secure in the home, school, work, play, and life.

11. Facing reality as it is can also help us to know what things that they can change, what things that they cannot. To accept what cannot be changed and to have the courage to change what can be changed as described in the Serenity Prayer of St. Francis.

12. Rituals can allow each person to express its spirituality. Family rituals may become a remembrance of the deceased family members and friends as they are offered on special days during the year. Such rituals may also include simply keeping family treasures because they belonged to deceased love ones. It can be making a basket, weaving a rug, a sand painting, or whatever. Rituals support belief and give purpose to faith.

13. For children, play is a major method of coping. For adults, work is a major method of coping. Play is a child's work. Just as our jobs can add meaning and purpose to our lives, so, too, can a child's play add meaning and purpose to his or her life. Children can experience unrestrained joy in play. Perhaps, we still feel that kind of joy in our work. Work and play are both spiritual and a source of spiritual growth. Play differs from sport in that it lacks rules. As adults, we impose rules on children and destroy their ability to play effectively.

14. Another useful tool is prayer. Life itself can be a prayer. One can pray for the animal or plant that gave its life to feed us, for the opportunity to have a job to support one's family, for one's family, for the earth that provides all that is needed for life, for the universe, for everything in life. Prayers can be ritualized, can take place in religious settings, be memorized, or simply lived. Pray may also involve rules, but children need to be able to "play" with their prayers.

15. People can also use forgiveness as a coping tool. Each of us has wronged others and been wronged by others. Our spiritual growth also includes moments of forgiving and being forgiven. Remember when you broke your mother's vase that

was a gift to her from her mother? You discovered that she actually cared more for you than the vase. The child must be taught that the pain or suffering that one caused is not necessarily forgotten, but that trust and growing together in spite of the betrayal allows us to go on with our lives. After scolding them for breaking the vase, you can give them a hug. Rivalries between siblings, friends, or others must be acknowledged openly and then trust and forgiveness can follow.

16. Each life must also have hope. Life is full of awe and wonder for the child and hopefully for adults as well, but it is also full of pain and suffering. As adults or parents, we try to protect our children from pain and suffering, but we cannot. From the cutting of the first tooth, to earaches, to death, life is full of pain and suffering. Hope does not come from sweetness and protecting children from poverty, racism, hate crimes, violence, death, and even the suffering of innocents. Hope comes from seeing the goodness in the hearts of people in spite of the suffering and pain that life offers. To sugarcoat life leads to cynicism and despair rather than hope. How could one face mobs in peace marches, Nazi's as Ann Frank, the poor as Mother Teresa, or any other act of courage without hope? Each of us has shortcomings, failings, and makes mistakes, yet life can still be full of hope, dreams, and fulfillment. Perhaps, you can save your soda cans and have your child give the bag to a homeless person. The joy in the face of the homeless person may allow your child to learn about hope.

17. We all need to be taught sharing and caring. As adults, we can experience joy when we share. So can children. The child who offers you a lick of their sucker or ice cream can feel real joy in watching you oblige their offer. Spirituality needs to include sharing and caring for others as well as the usual "me-first" ethic of the U.S. culture.

18. Those experiencing loss need to know that we are actually listening to them. Listening, both verbally and non-verbally, will help others cope. We must actually listen. Put down your paper, turn off the television, and give the person your true attention. True listening shows that you really care. Perhaps, you may remember being read stories as a child. It may be the last time that you had the undivided attention of your parents.

19. Spirituality itself is a coping tool. I am not sure if we can teach others about spirituality. Children may be the best teachers. It seems that they are better teachers for us. A Hopi child understood the conflict with the Navajo tribe better than most adults. She indicated that the battle was over the land. She said that the Navajo wanted to cut up the land, to farm it, which in her view of spirituality meant to harm the land. To divide the land was to hurt the land. The land deserved its freedom and chance to live. In her spiritual orientation she felt that the Hopi must protect the spirit and well-being of the land because the land can feel the difference. A Navajo child indicated that the white people who try to amass property and things have a problem. Their problem is that they have so much that they cannot choose what to love or need and are lost because they have no homeland, just houses and things. Another Navajo child facing the ultimate death of her grandmother saw no reason to pray for her to live. She saw that death is not bad. She saw that her grandmother was suffering in life. She prayed for her grandmother to have a peaceful death rather than to pray that she suffer by living longer.

20. Encouragement may also help others to cope. Offer encouragement rather than praising saying that the person is pretty or whatever. Encourage them by focusing upon the process rather than the outcome. Loss in athletics, school, or whatever is not failure. Failing to try is failure. Rather than allowing the other person to say that he or she cannot do something, encourage them to try. Real courage comes from the scars that come from trying to do the seemingly impossible. Have you ever clapped for a Special Olympics participant that you did not even know? Perhaps tears came to your eyes. Sharing is part of encouragement. As part of my training in an Outward Bound program, my feet were tied together, my hands tied behind my back, and I was tossed into the ocean for an hour. Being somewhat afraid of drowning, I was sure that I could not survive, but I did survive. In the process of training for the event, I received encouragement to try. I was told that I would be rescued if I needed to be. Life is a journey. We must all be encouraged to do the seemingly impossible. The struggle together adds much meaning and purpose to life.

21. We must also instill in others the desire to have freedom. They must become free to live until they die. The dying are not yet dead. They, too, must live life fully. Each day must be lived fully. In our culture we tend to live for the future. We must live for now rather than for someday that may not even happen.

22. We all need to be taught to try to live our dreams. We need to be aware of the power of dreams to help give meaning and purpose to life. Each day is a blessing. Each day should be better than yesterday and tomorrow better than today. Children do not have much of a past to live for, but we can foster pessimism, cynicism, and doom in children by living in the past rather than living in the present. We must try to live our dreams and strive to accomplish them. Everyone needs something to look forward to each day to have a reason to get up in the morning. Remember the excitement of your own childhood when an anticipated event kept you from sleeping the night before the event that so excited your sense of life?

23. We need to be taught the power of miracles. Saints tend to live ordinary lives and do ordinary things extraordinarily well. Instead of looking for great miracles in one's life, look for the little ones that make each day what it is. When you have no money for bills or whatever, a friend pays you what is owed or a painting is sold or whatever. When you are tired and nearly falling asleep while driving something occurs to cause you to awaken fully. The beauty of the face of a homeless woman or the singing voice of a developmentally disabled child. The miracle of birth or even death. The first word that your child speaks, the cry when the light shocks them as they leave the womb. What are your life's miracles? They need not be what makes the fodder for books or movies, and yet maybe they are. Perhaps the greatest miracle is our life. That every human and animal has something to offer and that every life is precious. Are your children a miracle? Are they not precious and special?

CONCLUSIONS

Spirituality can aid the grieving of children by allowing them to be open to the power of grieving. As adults, we can offer a model of grieving that can allow them to grow through their grief. We need to open ourselves to the power of grieving. Let the spirit awaken within you. Live each day for today and tomorrow will follow with flourish!

Spiritual journeys have paths that each must develop and follow as we go through our lives. Each journey is special and different. We must accept both the blessings and burdens that life has to offer. Each journey is unique. We cannot make the journey for others. We can at best be spiritual guides. Let the journey begin!

REFERENCES

Gilbert, R. (1999). *Finding your way after your parent dies.* Notre Dame, IN: Ave Maria Press.

McKissock, D. (1998). *The grief of our children.* Sydney, Australia: Australian Broadcasting Company.

Miller, J. E. (1995). *Winter grief, summer grace: Returning to life after a loved one dies.* Minneapolis: Augsburg Press.

Nadeau, J. W. (1998). *Families making sense of death.* Thousand Oaks: Sage.

Contributors

DAVID W. ADAMS is Professor Emeritus, Department of Psychiatry and Behavioural Neurosciences, Faculty of Health Sciences, McMaster University, Hamilton, Ontario, Canada. He is a certified death educator and grief therapist in private practice. He is internationally recognized for his lectures and writing concerning seriously ill, traumatized, dying, and bereaved people and is especially concerned about the spiritual needs of care providers and their clientele.

LISA BYERS has her MSW from Washington University, St. Louis, Missouri. She is currently completing her Ph.D. in social work at Washington University with an emphasis in Native American Mental Health.

STEVEN R. BYERS, Ph.D., is an assistant professor at the University of Colorado at Denver. He teaches courses in Abnormal Psychology and Multicultural Psychology. He received his doctorate from the University of Colorado at Boulder and his MA from the University of Michigan, Ann Arbor. Dr. Byers' areas of interest are mental health, grief and loss and education as these topics pertain to improving the quality of life of indigenous communities.

GERRY R. COX is a Professor of Sociology at University of Wisconsin-La Crosse. He received his B.A. (1965), M.A. (1966), and Ph.D. (1975) from Ball State University. His teaching focuses upon Theory/Theory Construction, Deviance and Criminology, Death and Dying, Social Psychology, and Minority Peoples. He has been publishing materials since 1973 in sociology and teaching-oriented professional journals. He is a member of the International Work Group on Dying, Death, and Bereavement, the Midwest Sociological Society, the American Sociological Association, The International Sociological Association, Phi Kappa Phi, and Great Plains Sociological Society, and the Association of Death Education and Counseling.

RICK CSIERNIK, M.S.W., Ph.D., R.S.W. is an associate professor at the School of Social Work, King's College, University of Western Ontario, London, Ontario, Canada. He serves on the editorial board of *Canadian Social Work and Employee Assistance Quarterly.*

RUTH DEAN, R.N., M.S., Ph.D.(c) teaches palliative care nursing in the Faculty of Nursing at the University of Manitoba. She is a doctoral candidate in Interdisciplinary Studies at the University of Manitoba, where she holds a fellowship from the

Social Sciences and Humanities Research Council of Canada. She is presently conducting an ethnographic study of humor and laughter in care of the dying.

LARRY W. EASTERLING is Vice President of Mission and Spiritual Care at Advocate Christ Medical Center in Oak Lawn, Illinois. He is an ordained United Methodist pastor with over 20 years experience in chaplaincy and clinical pastoral education. He is a Marriage and Family Therapist and a Fellow in the American Association of Pastoral Counselors.

THERESA T. ERDKAMP is an MSW graduate student at the School of Social Work at Colorado State University. She has a certificate in Women's Studies. After graduation she will continue her work in the mental health field and pursue research in her main area of interest: domestic violence.

LOUIS A. GAMINO is a Diplomate in Clinical Psychology with the Scott & White Clinic in Temple, Texas and an Associate Professor of Psychiatry and Behavioral Sciences, Texas A & M University Health Science Center College of Medicine. In addition to a clinical practice specializing in bereavement-related problems, Dr. Gamino is the Principal Investigator of the Scott & White Grief Study.

REV. RICHARD B. GILBERT, BCC, D.Min., is Director of Chaplaincy Services for Sherman Hospital, Elgin and Executive Director, The World Pastoral Care Center. He has presented throughout the United States and internationally on bereavement, pastoral care, spirituality, and health care. An Anglican priest, he is extensively published, including as editor of *Healthcare & Spirituality: Listening, Assessing, Caring* (Baywood). His current research, for his dissertation, is on clergy health and well-being.

HERMANN GRUENWALD is a professor at the Michael F. Price College of Business, Management Information Systems Division at the University of Oklahoma. He holds an engineering degree from Germany, a Master of Architecture in computer applications from the University of Houston, an MBA from Southern Methodist University in Dallas, a master of Education from the University of Oklahoma, and a Ph.D. from OU, Norman, Oklahoma. He has conducted research in Medicine, Theology, and Law. Prior to joining academia, Dr. Gruenwald worked in industry positions ranging from Application Engineer, Manager of R&D, to Vice President. His administrative positions at the university level include Director of Development and Director of Research. His research interests focus on e-business applications in the health care and death care industries. He is also the director of the MIPT (Memorial Institute for the Prevention of Terrorism) Terrorism Database project which has been funded by NIJ (National Institute of Justice). This Web-enabled database includes Incident and Indictment information as well as information related to counter terrorism technology. He is a reviewer for numerous books and journals, and has presented guest lectures on e-commerce at universities in North and South America, Asia, and Europe. He has been teaching a variety of MIS courses including C, C++, Java, Database, Web-Enabled Databases, and E-Commerce Architecture as well as Cyber Marketing and Cyber Terrorism courses.

LE GRUENWALD is a Samuel Roberts Noble Foundation Presidential Professor and an Associate Professor in the School of Computer Science at University of

Oklahoma. She received her Ph.D. in Computer Science from Southern Methodist University in 1990. She was a Software Engineer at White River Technologies, a Lecturer in the Computer Science and Engineering Department at Southern Methodist University, and a Member of Technical Staff in the Database Management Group at the Advanced Switching Laboratory of NEC, America. Her major research interests include Web-Enabled Databases, Mobile Databases, Real-Time Main Memory Databases, Multimedia Databases, Data Warehouse, and Data Mining. She is a member of ACM, SIGMOD, and IEEE Computer Society.

KENT KOPPELMAN teaches about human diversity at the University of Wisconsin-La Crosse. He has written numerous essays and two books including *The Fall of a Sparrow: Of Death and Dreams and Healing* concerning the death of his son.

ARTHUR O. LEDOUX, with Philosophy degrees from Tufts University (B.A.) and the University of Notre Dame (Ph.D.), has taught since 1975 at Merrimack College, North Andover, Massachusetts. A former Fulbright Fellow to Sri Lanka, he teaches such courses as Asian Philosophy. His wife, Nancy, is a hospice chaplain.

CHERYL LASKOWSKI is a doctorally prepared nurse educator who teaches in the Advanced Practice Palliative Care Nursing Program at Daemen College in Amherst, New York. She also maintains a private practice as a nurse psychotherapist, working with women around issues of loss and grief.

RAYMOND L. M. LEE is an Associate Professor of Sociology at the University of Malaya in Kuala Lumpur, Malaysia. His current research is on death awareness and lucid dreaming. He published *The Tao of Representation: Postmodernity, Asia and the West* in 1999. His latest work is *The Challenge of Religion After Modernity: Beyond Disenchantment* (2002).

DIANE MIDLAND, B.S.W., M.S., is a certified Independent Social Worker and is Bereavement Educator for Gundersen Lutheran Medical Foundation in La Crosse, Wisconsin. In addition to assisting with staff development programs at Gundersen Lutheran Medical Center, she also teaches the *RTS* perinatal loss course and the *Compassionate Bereavement Care* course nationally. She was instrumental in the development of a general bereavement program at Gundersen Lutheran and works with physicians in compassionate death notification training. Prior to her current position, Diane was a social worker in the Trauma and Emergency Center for approximately 15 years. She remains active in local and state Critical Incident Management programs.

JOHN D. MORGAN is a pioneer in the death awareness movement. Dr. Morgan brings to the podium a wide range of topics in the field of death and bereavement, drawn from his work as educator, author, lecturer, and program organizer. In 1997 he received an award from the Association for Death Education and Counseling for his work in Death Education. He has spoken extensively throughout the world, has edited 18 books, and is Series Editor for the Death, Value, and Meaning Series (Baywood), which now has over 40 volumes. Dr. Morgan's most recent project (with Dr. Pittu Laungani) is a five volume *Death and Bereavement Around the World* (Baywood).

KEVIN ANN OLTJENBRUNS is a Professor of Human Development and Family Studies at Colorado State University and is co-author of a textbook entitled *Dying and Grieving: Lifespan and Family Perspectives*, now in its second edition. She is a member of the International Work Group for Grief and Loss.

RABBI DANIEL A. ROBERTS, D.D., D.Min., has lectured several times at the King's College International Conference on Death and Bereavement in London, Ontario, and is an acknowledged expert on spirituality, dying, and teenage suicide. Rabbi Roberts has also written chapters in published books, including "Ask Your Ancestors and They Will Tell You" in *Ethical Issues in the Care of the Dying and Bereaved* (edited by John D. Morgan, Amityville, NY: Baywood Publishing Co.); "It's Not Over When It's Over—The Aftermath of Suicide," in *Personal Care in an Impersonal World: A Multidimensional Look at Bereavement* (edited by John D. Morgan, Amityville, NY: Baywood Publishing Co., 1993); "Jewish Religious Education as an Aid in Crisis Intervention," in *What Shall We Do? Preparing the School Community to Cope With Crises* (edited by Robert Stevenson, 1994 and soon to be republished). He has produced a multimedia presentation on teenage suicide prevention, *Inside, I Ache,* which is used in schools all over the country. Rabbi Roberts holds a D.Min. from Pittsburgh Theological Seminary and wrote his thesis on comforting the mourner. He has been the spiritual leader of Temple Emanu El since 1972.

FRAN RYBARIK, R.N., M.P.H., serves as director of Bereavement Services at Gundersen Lutheran Medical Foundation in La Crosse, Wisconsin, focusing on perinatal loss and hospital-based bereavement programs. In addition to teaching RTS perinatal bereavement courses and Compassionate Bereavement Care courses nationally, Fran has been a speaker at national conferences for the Association of Death Education and Counseling (ADEC) and National Perinatal Bereavement Conferences. She is a member of ADEC, and has published bereavement articles in the *Lifelines, AWHONN Voice, Advance for Nurse Practitioners, Journal of Pastoral Care,* and *Midwifery Today.*

KENNETH W. SEWELL is Professor of Psychology and Director of Clinical Training, Department of Psychology, University of North Texas, Denton, Texas. His areas of professional emphasis include constructivism, traumatic stress, grief, and forensic assessment.

SUSAN J. ZONNEBELT-SMEENGE, R.N., Ed.D., is a registered nurse and a licensed clinical psychologist employed by Pine Rest Christian Mental Health Services in Grand Rapids, Michigan. She deals with a variety of issues associated with older adolescents and adults, including eating disorders, marital concerns, depression and anxiety, and death, grief, and loss issues.

ROBERT C. DEVRIES, D.Min., Ph.D., is an ordained minister and a Professor of Church Education at Calvin Theological Seminary, Grand Rapids, Michigan. He teaches courses at the seminary and conducts workshops in churches on teaching methods, youth ministry, adult ministry, and spiritual development.

Susan and Robert have both experienced the death of their previous spouses. As a result of their grieving process, they have collaborated on writing *Getting to the Other Side of Grief: Overcoming the Loss of a Spouse* (Grand Rapids, MI: Baker

Book House Company, 1998). Their next book, entitled *The Empty Chair: Handling Grief on Holidays and Special Occasions* (also published by Baker Books), was published in August, 2001. Both books deal sensitively with the mental health and the spiritual issues associated with grief. In addition to maintaining their own professions, they consult and speak frequently on grief and loss issues for local and regional groups as well as national and international conferences.

ROBERT STEVENSON has been an educator for over 35 years. He currently works in a residential alcohol/drug rehabilitation program and teaches graduate counseling courses at Mercy College in New York. He has published over 60 articles on loss and grief in professional journals and texts and has edited four books of his own. He is an active member of the International Work Group On Death, Dying, and Bereavement (I.W.G.) and the Association for Death Education and Counseling (A.D.E.C.). He is a graduate of the College of the Holy Cross (B.A.) and holds master's degrees from Fairleigh Dickinson University (M.A.T.), Montclair State University (M.A.), and a doctorate from Fairleigh Dickinson (Ed.D.). He is nationally certified by the Association for Death Education and Counseling as a death educator and grief counselor, has served on their board of directors and as chairman of their Education Institute and on their board of certification review. Dr. Stevenson has written curricula for social studies, health, and death education and has been honored for his work as an educator and counselor by: The New Jersey Professional Counselors' Association, the New Jersey Governor's Office, the Best Practice Awards of the NJ Department of Education, NJ School Boards' Association, United States Chess Federation, and the National Council for the Social Studies. He is listed in Who's Who Among America's Teachers, Who's Who Among Human Service Professionals, and Who's Who Among International Authors.

SUZANNE TOCHTERMAN is an assistant professor in the School of Education at Colorado State University. Research interests include teacher preparation, school violence, multicultural education, educational reform, and special needs education. Before joining the faculty at Colorado State in 1998, she taught troubled students in the Washington D.C. area.

Index

Aboriginal cultures in Australia, 148
Abraham (Bible, the), 132
Acceptance as a coping tool/mechanism,
    226–227
Accompaniers, a taste of heaven for the,
    63–64
Adjourning stage of team development and
    meeting spiritual needs in health care
    settings, 168
*After Heaven: Spirituality in American
    Since 1950* (Wuthnow), 56
Afterlife, the, 22, 37, 39, 64
Alaska Natives, 137–138
    See also Native Americans
Alcohol abuse and Native Americans, 141
Alone in the cosmos, evil rooted in anxiety
    over feeling, 134
Altered states of consciousness, 92–93
Alzheimer's disease, 195
Ambiguity as fate of humans, 129
American Beauty, 97
American Psychological Association
    (APA), 30
*Anatomy of an Illness: As Perceived by the
    Patient* (Cousins), 80
Anger at God, 24–25, 40, 223
Anticipatory grief support and meeting
    spiritual needs in health care settings,
    166
Anxiety, with consciousness comes, 132,
    134
Aristotle, 131
Art/drama as a coping tool/mechanism, 226
Aspiration, Buddhism and right, 104, 106
Assimilation policies/programs and Native
    Americans, 139–141, 143–144, 147

Assisted suicide, 88
Attachment and Buddhism, 103–104
Attig, Tom, 192
Auschwitz monument to commemorate
    victims, 2
Australia, aboriginal cultures in, 148
Awareness of death, living with the terrible,
    129–130

Balance as a coping tool/mechanism,
    finding, 227
Baudrillard, Jean, 90–91, 97
Becker, Ernest, 129, 133, 134
Behavioral sciences relationship with
    Native Americans, 138
Benet, Stephen V., 71
Bereaved Families of Ontario, 135
Bereavement: Guidelines for Care, 164
Bereavement adaptation, role of spiritual/
    religious factors in
    afterlife, the, 22
    church attendance *vs.* spiritual
        experience, 18–22
    concepts and history, 13–16
    emotion relocation, 23
    growth, personal, 20–23
    intrinsic *vs.* extrinsic spirituality, 13–14,
        16–17, 163
    political economy of individual
        salvation, 91
    priorities, personal growth and altered,
        22–23
    reachable moment, 24–25
    Scott & White Grief Study, 17–23
    summary/conclusions, 25

[Bereavement adaptation, role of spiritual/
religious factors in]

theoretical applications of Scott & White
Grief Study, 21–23
See also Child, death of a; Health care
settings, meeting spiritual needs in;
Loss and spirituality; Marginalization;
Spouse, death of a; individual subject
headings
Bereavement Conference at King's College
(1999), 152, 191
See also Columbine tragedy: opportunity
for transformation
Bible, the
accompaniers, a taste of heaven for the,
62–63
child, death of a, 50–51
creation story, 42
lament, encouragement to, 40
marginalization, 199
silence/solitude, nearness to God in times
of, 32
where are you in life, 59
Black humor, 76–77
Blame as a coping tool/mechanism, 223
Body-self dualism, guilt stemming from, 88
Booth, Leo, 199
Breath of life, spirituality as the, 56–57
Buddhism
aspiration, right, 104, 106
concentration, right, 104, 108
conduct, right, 104, 106–107
cross religious shopping, 4
desire, dealing with, 48
effort, right, 104, 107–108
Eightfold Path, 104, 106–109
history of the Buddha, 101–102
knowledge, right, 104, 106
livelihood, right, 104, 107
mindfulness, right, 104, 108
nirvana, 109
speech, right, 104, 106
teachings, the Buddha's, 102–105
Bureau of Indian Affairs (BIA), 145
Byers, Steven R., 152

Calvinism, 90
Candlelighters, 135

Caregiver-client relations, humor and,
74–75
See also Clergy/health care
professionals, spirituality among;
Health care settings, meeting spiritual
needs in
Cartoons as black humor, 77
Cemetery, visiting the, 45–47
See also Cyber cemeteries
Change always brings loss, 223
Child, death of a
Bible, the, 50–51
cemetery, visiting the, 45–47
Compassionate Friends, 16
desire, dealing with, 48
dreams, 48–52
faith and unbelief, struggling with, 51–52
funerals, 46–47
groups, grief, 49–50
habit, living life out of a sense of, 47–48
Christian practice
afterlife, the, 37
anxiety, with consciousness comes, 132
confessional prayers, 60
cross religious shopping, 4
lament, encouragement to, 40
marriage, emphasizing the permanency
of, 42
self-knowledge, 42–43
spouse, death of a, 37
See also Bible, the
Christopher, Peter, 193
Church attendance vs. spiritual experience,
18–22
See also Bereavement adaptation, role of
spiritual/religious factors in
Clergy/health care professionals,
spirituality among
assisting clients' efforts to meet their
spiritual needs, 185–188
broader context of spirituality, 174–175
comfort with spirituality, personal,
178–180
consequences of not meeting one's
spiritual needs, 181–182, 184
differences between clergy and other
professionals, predictable, 186–187
differences between clergy and other
professionals, surprising, 187
health care industry, changes in the, 173

[Clergy/health care professionals, spirituality among]

helping professionals *vs.* the clergy, 174
how spiritual needs of professionals are met, 179–181
impediments to meeting one's spiritual needs, 181, 183
importance of spirituality in personal and work life, 178, 179
marginalization, 195–198
meaning of spirituality, 176, 178
methodology, study, 175
results, study, 176–186
strengthening and changing spirituality, 180, 183
summary/conclusions, 186–189
work, impact of spirituality on, 185
Collaborative approach and meeting spiritual needs in health care settings, 169–171
Colorado State University (CSU), 151
Columbine tragedy: opportunity for transformation
meaning in the loss, finding, 159
overview, 151–152
pain, experiencing the, 155–156
relationship healing and making connections, 158
spiritual change, crisis and, 152–154
suffering, understanding/transforming, 157
summary/conclusions, 160
Community/connection, spirituality/religion and no realization of, 133
Compassion and religion in the face of death, 4
Compassionate Friends, 16, 135
Concentration, Buddhism and right, 104, 108
Conduct, Buddhism and right, 104, 106–107
Confessional prayers, 60, 63
Connection, the soul and a yearning for a deep, 31–32
Consciousness, postmodern self and the fate of, 91–93, 97–98
Corless, Inge, 199
Cousins, Norman, 60

Cox, Gerry, 133
Creation story, 42
Creative drive, the soul as seat of, 32
Cruzan, Nancy, 87
Culture identification/character and Native Americans, 144
Cyber cemeteries
accessibility, 116–117
communication and community, 118
defining terms, 113–114
features and costs, 123–124
how to find on-line memorials, 114–115
limitations and control, 120–121
obituaries to monuments, 120
present and future of on-line memorials, 125
private-public space, 118–119
religion and culture, 121–123
remembrance and commemoration, 119
sample sites, 124
special losses and the bereaved with special needs, 117–118
who offers on-line memorials, 115
why on-line memorials, 115–116

Davies, Betty, 191
Dawn, Marva, 197
Deaf community and marginalization, 193, 198
"Dear God why me? Why us?" (Grollman & Kosik), 195
Deathbeds as powerful places for spiritual/emotional healing, 60
Death-consciousness, postmodern self and, 93, 94, 97–98
Delight/joy, the soul and a hunger for, 32
Denial as a coping tool/mechanism, 129, 223
Depression, effects of religious belief/activity on, 14–15
See also Bereavement adaptation, role of spiritual/religious factors in
Descartes, René, 131
Desensitization period and realizing the finality of death, 39
Desire, dealing with, 48, 103–104
Despair, helping dying overcome, 57–59
DeVries, Robert C., 29–30
Dignity, death with, 60

Disenfranchised grief, 139–140, 191–192
See also Marginalization; Native
Americans
Doctor-patient interactions, humor and, 75
See also Clergy/health care
professionals, spirituality among
Does the Soul Survive? (Spitzoffer), 64
Doka, Kenneth, 59, 191
Domestic violence and marginalization,
192
Dreams and death of a child, 48–52
Dropout rates, Native Americans and high
school/college, 140
Drug abuse and Native Americans, 141
Durable power of attorney for health care,
87
Dying Well (Byock), 214

Economic conditions for Native Americans,
140–141, 143
Education, nursing, 218
Effort, Buddhism and right, 104, 107–108
Ego boundaries becoming permeable,
132
Eightfold Path and Buddhism, 104,
106–109
Elkins, David, 55
Emotions, experiencing/expressing, 23,
40–41, 61–62
Empathic witnessing, 212
*Empty Chair, The: Handling Grief on the
Holidays and Other Special Occasions*
(Zonnebelt-Smeenge & DeVries),
30
Encouragement as a coping
tool/mechanism, 229
Environmental conditions for Native
Americans, 141
Episcopal Church, 196, 199
"Ethical Principles of Psychologists and
Code of Conduct," 30
Ethical will, 62–63
Euphemisms and realizing the finality of
death, 39
Euthanasia, 88
Euthanasia Educational Council, 87
Evil, the corollary of good and, 36–37
Evil rooted in anxiety over feeling alone in
the cosmos, 134

Faith and unbelief, struggling with, 51–52
Faith as commitment to the object of one's
spirituality, 31
Family relationships, 61–63
See also Child, death of a; Spouse, death
of a
Fear of death, 93
Feelings, experiencing/expressing, 23,
40–41, 61–62
Fields, W. C., 78
Final Gifts (Callanan & Kelley), 214
Finality of death, realizing the, 38–39
Follow-up and meeting spiritual needs in
health care settings, 167
Forgiveness as a coping tool/mechanism,
227–228
Forming stage of team development and
meeting spiritual needs in health care
settings, 168
Fragmentation of the self, 85
See also Postmodern self, death and the
Francis, Ronald, 199, 200
Frankl, Victor, 57
Frazer, James, 89
Freud, Sigmund, 38, 76
Funerals, 46–47

Gallows humor, 76–77
Gates of Repentance, 70
Gautama, Siddartha, 101
Gender and marginalization, 192
Genesis, book of, 59, 63–64
Genocidal relations between Europeans and
Native Americans, 138–139
*Getting to the Other Side of Grief:
Overcoming the Loss of a Spouse*
(Zonnebelt-Smeenge & DeVries), 30
God
creation of a human being, 56
lament and wail in presence of, freedom
to, 41
the soul and intimacy with, 34–35
spouse, God's role in death of a, 35–36
Good death, the, 218
Good Death, The (Webb), 60
Green, Alan S., 67
Grief. *See* Bereavement adaptation, role of
spiritual/religious factors in
Grief Experience Inventory (GEI), 17

Grief Observed, A (Lewis), 38
Grounded theory research, 207, 209
Groups, grief, 49–50
Growth, spiritual experience and personal, 20–23, 61, 221–222, 225
Guilt, feelings of, 4, 88, 224
Gundersen Lutheran Medical Center, 163
  See also Health care settings, meeting spiritual needs in

Habit, living life out of a sense of, 47–48
Harper, Jeanne, 59
Health care settings, meeting spiritual needs in
  case study, 171
  collaborative approach, 169–171
  guidelines for care, 166–167
  interdisciplinary approach, 169, 170
  overview, 163–164
  roles, primary team, 165–169
  summary/conclusions, 171
  team approach/development, 164–165, 168
Health professionals/caregivers and spirituality. *See* Clergy/health care professionals, spirituality among; Health care settings, meeting spiritual needs in; Nursing
Health/wellness, Native Americans and, 140–141
Healthy grieving, helping others develop styles of, 225–226
Hebrew Ethical Wills (Abraham), 63
Hero response to the awareness of death, 129–130
Heschel, Abraham J., 56
Hobbes, Thomas, 131
Hogan Grief Reaction Checklist (HGRC), 17
  See also Bereavement adaptation, role of spiritual/religious factors in
Holistic approach to one's physical/emotional/social/spiritual aspects, 30
Holocaust, 2, 57
Homosexuals, violence against, 133
Homosexuals and marginalization, 192, 199, 200
Hope as a coping tool/mechanism, 228

Hospice/pallative care, 75–76
Hospitals. *See* Health care settings, meeting spiritual needs in
Humanistic systems, nurses' belief in need for, 217
Humanness, accompaniers helping the dying by accepting their, 60–61
Humor
  black humor, 76–77
  client-caregiver relationships, 74–75
  as a coping tool/mechanism, 76–78, 226
  guidelines for introducing, 80–81
  hospice/palliative care, 75–76
  nursing, 74, 81
  overview, 74
  as release, 77–78
  and spirituality, 78–80
  summary/conclusions, 82
  as therapy, 80

Identity
  connections used to form an, 222
  integrate various identities, spirituality as ability to, 131
  irony becoming a metaphor for transformation, the puncturing of, 97–98
  Native Americans, 144
  postmodern self and multiple identities, 95–96
  spirituality, identity of the person related to, 6
Illness Narratives, The (Kleinman), 212
Immediacy, spirituality and the ability of the mind to transcend, 130–131
Incarceration rates and Native Americans, 141
Incest and Native Americans, 141
Index of Core Spiritual Experiences (INSPIRIT), 15–16
  See also Bereavement adaptation, role of spiritual/religious factors in
Indian Health Services, 145
Individual, misuse of the term, 127
Individualism and technology, conflict between, 86
  See also Postmodern self, death and the
Individualistic culture and no realization of community, 133

Initiation, the soul and the need for, 32–33
Interdisciplinary approach and meeting
    spiritual needs in health care settings,
    169, 170
Internet, the. *See* Cyber cemeteries
*In the Aftermath of the Columbine
    Shootings-Reactions of Grief
    Professionals,* 152
Intimacy with others, the soul and, 34
"Invitation, The" (Oriah Mountain
    Dreamer), 70–71
Irony of death, postmodern self and the,
    96–98

Jelinek, Sue, 199
Jesus of Nazareth, 130
Jewish faith
    confessional prayers, 60, 63
    cyber cemeteries, 121–122
    God/woman/man as partners in the
        creation of a human being, 56
    lament, encouragement to, 40–41
    meaning out of life, making, 56–57
    where are you in life, 59
    will to live, 57
Journaling as a coping tool/mechanism, 226
Joy/delight, the soul and a hunger for, 32

Kass, Jared, 15
Kass, Leon, 60
Kervokian, Jack, 88
Kessler, Rachael, 31
King's College, 152, 191
Klein, Allen, 78
Knowledge, Buddhism and right, 104, 106
Kübler-Ross, Elisabeth, 38, 88, 93

Lament, religion and encouragement to,
    40–41
Langford, Daniel, 198
Language of dying, nursing and the, 214
Last rites in Catholicism, 60
Laughter. *See* Humor
Legislation
    Patient Self-Determination Act of 1991,
        87
License to Kill Homosexuals, 133

Life after death, 22, 37, 39, 64
"Life After Death" (Gilpin), 69
Life Lessons (Kessler & Kübler-Ross), 65
"Life's Journey" (Fine), 70
Liminality and nursing, 209–210
Listening skills, 185, 212–213, 228
Livelihood, Buddhism and right, 104, 107
Living last days rather than simply existing,
    58–59, 229
Living will, 87
Loneliness of being a person, 132–133
Loss and spirituality
    change always brings loss, 223
    coping tools/mechanisms, 223–224,
        226–229
    growth, loss leading to, 221–222, 225
    healthy grieving, helping others develop
        styles of, 225–226
    identity formed through connections, 222
    opportunity, each loss is an, 224
    response to loss, 223–224
    seasons of life used to describe grief
        process, 222
    summary/conclusions, 229–230
Love as a coping tool/mechanism, 227

Making Loss Matter (Wolpe), 59–60
Man's Search for Meaning (Frankl), 57
Many Lives, Many Masters (Weiss), 64
Marginalization
    disenfranchisement compared to, 192
    homosexuals, 192, 199, 200
    nature of the relationship, 192–193
    open community, those marginalized in
        search for an, 198–201
    overview, 193–194
    professionally marginalized, 195–198
    spiritual and religious parameters,
        194–195
    subcultures, 193
    summary/conclusions, 201
Marriage. *See* Spouse, death of a
Meaning out of life, making
    accompaniers helping those in face of
        death, 59–61
    Columbine tragedy, 159
    Jewish faith, 56–57
    personal make-up, search of your, 2–3
    prayer, 60, 61, 63

[Meaning out of life, making]
  priorities, personal growth and altered,
    23
  reality experienced through meaning we
    give it, 222
  soul, the, 32
  spirituality as the formulation of meaning
    systems, 131–132
  suffering minus meaning means despair,
    57
  void, confrontation with a, 3
  will to live, 57–59
  See also Sense of death, making
Medicaid/Medicare, 87
Memories, death of a spouse and finding a
    place for, 41
Mercy of God Community, 199, 201
Michelangelo, 128
Mindfulness, Buddhism and right, 104,
    108
Miracles, the power of, 229
Modernity, death and, 85
  See also Postmodern self, death and the
Monuments, virtual, 120
Morgan, Jack, 152
Morgan, John, 59
Moses, 60–61
Mother Knight (Vonnegut), 47–48
Mothers Against Drunk Driving, 135
Mother Teresa, 129–130
Mumford, Louis, 134
Muscle tension release, humor and, 78
Music, 62, 226

Nadeau, Janice W., 222
Native Americans
  assimilation policies/programs, 139–141,
    143–144, 147
  awareness of disenfranchised grief,
    144–145
  counseling work with, 146, 149
  cyber cemeteries, 123
  disenfranchised grief focused on when
    dealing with, 137, 146–149
  distrust felt by, 145–148
  dreams, 49–50
  economic conditions, 140–141, 143

[Native Americans]
  environmental conditions, 141
  genocidal relations between Europeans
    and, 138–139
  health and wellness, 140–141
  historical context, 138–140
  reconceptualizations needed when
    working with, 148–149
  social justice orientation needed when
    working with, 148
  summary of loss/grief dynamic: formal
    case for disenfranchised grief,
    146–149
  variations in trauma and loss histories,
    144
  Yellow Horse Brave Heart study,
    142–143, 147
Neo-modern death, 93–94
Netherlands, 2, 3
Neurotic response to the awareness of
    death, 129
Nigeria, 1
Nihilism, 85–86
Nirvana, 109
Non-attachment and Buddhism, 103–104
Norming stage of team development and
    meeting spiritual needs in health care
    settings, 168
Nursing
  education, 218
  good death, the, 218
  grounded theory research, 207, 209
  history, nurses' personal, 211
  humanistic systems, need for, 217
  humor, 74, 81
  language of dying, 214
  liminality, 209–210
  listening, 212–213
  nursing practice, implications for,
    215–217
  other, recognizing/assisting wholly the
    experience of the, 215–217
  prayer, 215
  presencing, 211–212
  spirituality, defining, 207–208
  suffering, honoring, 212
  symbolic interaction as a sensitizing
    framework, 207, 208–209
  systems factors, 215–218

[Nursing]
tasks for meeting spiritual needs in health care settings, 165
touching, 213
trust symbols, 213–214
vulnerability, 217
See also Clergy/health care professionals, spirituality among

Obituaries, virtual, 120
Objects activating human powers, 128
Old Testament, 32, 40, 59, 63–64
Oltjenbruns, Kevin A., 152
On-line memorials. See Cyber cemeteries
Ortega y Gasset, Jose, 131
Oswold, Roy, 198

Pain, Native Americans and balance/release of, 143
Pain dedicated to hope of alleviating other's pain, 61–63
Palliative/hospice care, humor and, 75–76
Pastoral vs. spiritual care, 4–5, 167–168
See also Clergy/health care professionals, spirituality among
Paternalism in the health care system, 217
Patient Self-Determination Act of 1991, 87
Paul (Apostle), 43
Performing stage of team development and meeting spiritual needs in health care settings, 168
Personal art to dying, 1
Person as subject having powers, 127–128
Peterson, Eugene, 197
Philosophy, modern Western, 85–86
Physicians' tasks for meeting spiritual needs in health care settings, 165
See also Clergy/health care professionals, spirituality among
Physiological release, humor and, 77–78
Pieta, The (Michelangelo), 128
Plato, 130, 131
Play as a coping tool/mechanism, 227
Political economy and death, 90–91
Postmodern self, death and the
consciousness, the fate of, 91–93, 97–98
conundrum, the postmodern, 93–96

[Postmodern self, death and the]
identities, multiple, 95–96
individualism in death, 86–88
irony of death, 96–98
Neo-modern death, 93–94
overview, 85–86
philosophy, modern Western, 85–86
religion, the alienation of, 88–91
restructuring thinking on meaning of the self, 85
saturated self, 95
subjectivity in death, 94–96
summary/conclusions, 98
Powerlessness in the face of mystery of the universe, 134
Powers as capacities to do, human, 127–128
Prayer
clergy/health care professionals, spirituality among, 185, 186
confessional, 60, 63
as a coping tool/mechanism, 227
meaning-making in the face of death, 60, 61, 63
nursing, 215
samples/examples, 69–71
Precognition, 213–214
Presencing and nursing, 211–212
Priorities, personal growth and altered, 22–23
Professional caregivers and spirituality.
See Clergy/health care professionals, spirituality among; Health care settings, meeting spiritual needs in; Nursing
Protestant ethic, 90
Psalm (23rd), 64
Psychology and religion moving toward each other, 30, 33
Puritans, 90

Quinlan, Karen A., 87

Reachable moment, 24–25
Reagan, Ronald, 224
Reality experienced through meaning we give it, 222

"Re-Creating Meaning in the Face of Illness," 194
Reflexivity empowering renewal in modern consciousness, 92, 94–95
Reincarnation, 64
Reinvesting in life, death of a spouse and, 43–44
Relatedness and modern spirituality, 6
Relationship completion, 214
Religion
community/connection, no realization of, 133
cyber cemeteries, 121–123
depression, 14–15
external/extrinsic religious activities/orientation, 13, 14
finality of death, realizing the, 39
marginalization, 194–195, 199–201
postmodern self, death and the, 88–91
psychology and religion moving towards each other, 30, 33
self-creation, reinforcing, 132
sense of death, making, 3–5, 7
soul, the, 4, 31–35, 59
spirituality contrasted with, 55, 208
See also Bible, the; Buddhism; Christian practice; Clergy/health care professionals, spirituality among; God; Jewish faith; Prayer; Spirituality, dimensions of; individual subject headings
Religious Orientation Inventory (ROI), 14
See also Bereavement adaptation, role of spiritual/religious factors in
Renewal in modern consciousness empowered by reflexivity, 92, 94–95
Repentance from God or from another, 60
Right to die, 87
Rites of death/resurrection critical to maintaining social order, 89–90
Rituals as a coping tool/mechanism, 227
Roberts, Daniel A., 68, 69
Rousseau, Jean-Jacques, 131

Sadness as a coping tool/mechanism, 224
Sadness over death, why the, 2
Sangha, 108
Satipatthana Sutra, 106
Saturated self, 95

Saunders, Cicely, 108
Scott & White Grief Study, 17–23
Seasons of life used to describe grief process, 222
Self, the soul and intimacy with, 33–34
See also Postmodern self, death and the
Self-creation, religion reinforcing, 132
Self-knowledge, death of a spouse and, 39–40, 42–43
Sense of death, making
future, challenges for the, 6–7
many dying at same time, 1–2
meaning out of life, making, 2–3
pastoral vs. spiritual care, 4–5
religion, 3–5, 7
sadness, why the, 2
spirituality, secularized, 5–6
suffering as confrontation with a void, 3
See also Meaning out of life, making
September 11 attacks, 1
Sexual abuse and Native Americans, 141
Silence, the soul and a longing for, 32
Sioux tribes, 142–143
Social cohesion, religious function of death in maintaining, 89–90
Social justice orientation when working with Native Americans, 148
Social services and meeting spiritual needs in health care settings, 167
Solitude, the soul and a longing for, 32
So That Your Values Live On: Ethical Wills and How to Prepare Them (Reimer), 63
Soul, the, 4, 31–35, 59
See also Spouse, death of a
Spain, 1
Speech, Buddhism and right, 104, 106
Spirituality, dimensions of
accompaniers, a taste of heaven for the, 63–64
breath of life, spirituality as the, 56–57
Columbine tragedy, 152–154
community/connection, no realization of, 133
as a coping tool/mechanism, 228
defining terms, 31, 55–56, 207–208
despair, helping dying overcome, 58–59
humor, 78–80
immediacy, the ability of the mind to transcend, 130–131

[Spirituality, dimensions of]
  intrinsic *vs.* extrinsic, 13–14, 16–17
  marginalization, 194–195
  meaning-making in face of death, 59–61
  meaning systems, the formulation of,
    131–132
  new beginnings and being remembered,
    61–63
  pastoral *vs.* spiritual care, 4–5
  prayers, 69–71
  religion contrasted with spirituality, 55,
    208
  secularized spirituality, 5–6
  sense of death, making, 5–7
  soul as center of spirituality, 31–35
  summary/conclusions, 66
  survivors, helping the, 65–66
  "To My Boys" (Brenner), 66–67
  vagueness of concept, 55–56
  will to live, 57–59
  See also Bereavement adaptation, role
    of spiritual/religious factors in;
    Clergy/health care professionals,
    spirituality among; Loss and
    spirituality; *individual subject
    headings*
Spouse, death of a
  afterlife, the, 37
  bereaved's role in death, 36
  evil, the reality of, 36–37
  feelings, experiencing/expressing,
    40–41
  finality of death, realizing the, 38–39
  God's role in death, 35–36
  memories, finding a place for, 41
  moving on with life, 41–42
  overview, 29–30
  psychology and religion: moving toward
    each other, 30, 33
  reinvesting in life, 43–44
  self-knowledge, 39–40, 42–43
  soul as center of spirituality, 31–35
  spirituality, defining, 31
  summary/conclusions, 44
  tasks of grief, 38–44
Stages of dying (Kübler-Ross), 38, 93
Storming stage of team development and
    meeting spiritual needs in health care
    settings, 168

Story-telling as a coping tool/mechanism,
    226
Subcultures and marginalization, 193
Subjectivity, human uniqueness and
    moment of, 128
Subjectivity in death, postmodern self and,
    94–96
Subjects and objects, connection between,
    128
Suffering
  and Buddhism, 102–103
  Columbine tragedy, 157
  as confrontation with a void, 3
  minus meaning means despair, 57
  nursing and honoring, 212
Suicide, assisted, 88
Support groups, grief, 49–50
Survivors, helping the, 65–66
Symbolic interaction as a sensitizing
    framework, 207, 208–209
Systems factors, nursing and, 215–218

Tabula rasa, the dogma of, 94
Team approach/development and meeting
    spiritual needs in health care settings,
    164–165, 168
Technology and individualism, conflict
    between, 86
  See also Postmodern self, death and the
Themes in one life and quest for
    spirituality, 6
Tibetan Book of Living and Dying, 60, 61
Tochterman, Suzanne, 152
"To My Boys" (Brenner), 66–67
Touching and nursing, 213
Transcendent, the soul and the urge for the,
    32, 39
Transformation, identity punctured by irony
    becoming a metaphor for, 97–98
Transition, death a mere, 4
Transitory experience, Buddhism and, 102
Treblinka (concentration camp), 57
Trust symbols and nursing, 213–214

Ulanov, Barry, 215
Unfinished business, listening to grief of,
    60, 65

Uniqueness, industrialization/technology making it hard to believe in our, 133

Values and spirituality/violence, personal choice of, 133–134
Viddui prayer in Judaism, 60, 63
Violence, 133–135, 142
    See also Columbine tragedy: opportunity for transformation
Virtual memorials, 113
    See also Cyber cemeteries
Void, suffering as confrontation with a, 3
Vulnerability and nursing, 217

Weber, Max, 90
Western philosophy, modern, 85–86
"Where Heaven and Earth Touch" (Taubman), 66

Widowed people. *See* Spouse, death of a
Will, ethical, 62–63
Will, living, 87
Will to live, 57–59
Wintergrief, Summer Grace: Returning to Life After a Loved One Dies (Miller), 222
Wolkovits, Paul, 195
Words uttered at death, Netherlands and, 3
World Trade Center, September 11 attacks on, 1

Yellow Horse Brave Heart study of Native Americans, 142–143, 147

Zonnebelt-Smeenge, Susan J., 29–30